GOLDEN
EAGLE YEARS

GOLDEN EAGLE YEARS

New Revised Edition

Mike Tomkies

JONATHAN CAPE
LONDON

First published 1982 © Mike Tomkies 1982
This revised edition, with some new photographs,
published in 1994
Revised text and photographs © Mike Tomkies 1994

1 3 5 7 9 10 8 6 4 2

Mike Tomkies has asserted his right
under the Copyright, Designs and Patents Act, 1988
to be identified as the author of this work

First published in the United Kingdom in 1994 by
Jonathan Cape
Random House, 20 Vauxhall Bridge Road, London SW1V 2SA

Random House Australia (Pty) Limited
20 Alfred Street, Milsons Point, Sydney,
New South Wales 2061, Australia

Random House New Zealand Limited
18 Poland Road, Glenfield,
Auckland 10, New Zealand

Random House South Africa (Pty) Limited
PO Box 337, Bergvlei, South Africa

Random House UK Limited Reg. No. 954009

A CIP catalogue record for this book
is available from the British Library

ISBN 0–224–03682–3

Typeset by Deltatype Limited, Ellesmere Port

Printed in Great Britain by
Mackays of Chatham plc, Chatham, Kent

Contents

Preface

Both egg and chick thieves have been known in the past to use non-fiction books about rare birds to locate nests – poring over the books in winter with large scale maps to hand, planning their spring time tactics like a military campaign. For this reason, much as I would have liked to pay tribute to them in print, I have been forced to fictionalise the names of my helpers, and disguise directions and whereabouts of eyries. I have also refrained from quoting old anecdotes, incredible or otherwise, from the golden eagle literature of the past. All the incidents in this book are set down exactly as they happened.

Mike Tomkies

Introduction

In recent years I have nursed one last great ambition concerning golden eagles. The idea came to me after I had finally left my lochside home, Wildernesse, in the western Highlands, where this present story began. I went to live in Spain for five years and at first felt wonderfully free from the burden of a difficult lifestyle in a harsh environment, where the incursions of fish farmers and the increase in summer tourists were contributing to the declining welfare of wildlife in the region. Eagles, in particular, had suffered a disastrous breeding season. I took a break from the arduous pursuit of Spain's rare wildlife (including bear, wolf and lynx) in the spring of 1989 when Scottish Television persuaded me to revisit Wildernesse briefly to make a film about my previous life there. 'Wild Cathedral' was well received and went out on the ITV network before being repeated several times on local Scottish TV channels.

It was while making the film that all the good memories of my thirteen years at Wildernesse came flooding back and I decided, come what may, to return and spend my 65th birthday, on May 25 1993, watching one of my favourite golden eagles back on Eagle Rock Mountain above my old home loch.

On the day beforehand, the project seemed doomed. The friend who was to be my helper fell ill at the last moment, and I was left to cope alone. The only boat I could find for hire to go down the river and across the loch was a big, heavy old wooden sea-going tub that I could only *just* wrestle into the water. I attached my ancient 4hp engine, which I had tested before leaving my new home near the

Scottish border, and pulled the cord. I pulled it again, many times. The motor refused to start. I spent the next twenty minutes frenziedly fending off with an oar from one bank or the other until the river swept boat and me downstream and deposited us on the loch itself.

From the river's entrance it was only a mile to the shore below Eagle Rock Mountain. I decided to forget the engine and started to row. I was only a quarter of the way across the loch when the left rowlock burst out of the decayed wood of the gunwale and refused to be wedged back. The only way I could use the oar was to make an anchor rope sling for it and tie it to the empty seat in front. I never had a more awkward row and it took nearly an hour to reach the mountain.

Almost knackered already, I bundled all the movie equipment and hide into some bog myrtle bushes and slogged around the mountain without a pack. At last I located the eagle I called Juno on a high sheer cliff in a small eyrie which I had never known her to use before. I had reached a heathery ridge on the other side of the valley, about two hundred yards away, when she came sailing along and flapped leisurely into the nest, landing beside a white chick almost a month old. I now knew exactly where to pitch my hide for my birthday vigil the following day.

Stiffly I clambered back down to the boat. It was fortunate that I got the engine working for the return trip, or I would never have got back up the river.

I was up at 4 a.m. next day, telling myself this really *was* to be the last time. Soon I was slogging and perspiring up through steep larch and spruce woods to 1,700 feet. Well hidden in the heather, I spent a marvellous five hours watching Juno feed her chick, groom it, squat by it and just look about her mountain domain. Not once did she leave the nest. The magic of it all returned and I was back in my old eagle paradise! My long-held last ambition realised, tired but happy, I staggered with everything back down to my van which I had left three miles away in an old sandpit. I would not trust the boat again on the vital day.

Over the next two days I went on to film a pair of eagles on a 500-foot inland cliff 200 miles to the east, and then joined one of my West Highland readers who had been watching a pair of eagles which inhabited a vast, dramatic, south-facing sea cliff. He turned out to be the keenest, most talented young man I had ever met in the wildlife field. With him, I filmed both male and female flying and

10

diving, being mobbed by ravens, and both birds spiralling from a great height down the dramatic cliff before levelling out and soaring into their eyrie. It was one of my best days ever with eagles, and we achieved it all unseen by the birds.

It was then that I overstepped the mark and went to the mountain top one time too many.

On my next visit to the sea cliff, I was climbing down with 50lbs of gear between steep jagged boulders when I lost my footing and fell. I bounced, rolling over two great rocks, desperately trying to protect my head, unable to see where I was going – a horrible, helpless feeling – before I crashed into a small cavern. My left leg came whipping over last and was hit by the heavy tripod. Both smashed up against sharp rock, and instantly the blood spurted. I bled so fast that had my new young friend not been with me, and with a first aid kit in his pack, I might not be writing this now. As it was, we managed to staunch the flow, and with him carrying all my gear as well as his own, I limped weakly the two miles back up to the van. A nurse in the nearby village cleaned and dressed the five-inch gash, and my friend's father drove us twenty miles to a doctor who stitched up the wound.

Only a fool could ignore such a sign that I was now past it, past carrying 50 to 60lbs of gear up or down precipitous and murderous rocky slopes. I sold all my heavy movie gear to my young friend for a knock-down price, and then drove back to Eagle Rock Mountain. There, within sight of Juno's nest, I gave thanks for my miraculous eagle years, and for being able to campaign for them and write three books about these great birds, Scotland's veritable symbols of wildness. Later, back at my new remote outpost in the Borders, I hung up my eagle boots.

★

That was how my eagle years came to an end; how it all started at Wildernesse is told in *Golden Eagle Years*, which has been out of print for a decade or so. In the meantime I have received literally hundreds of letters asking for the book to be made available again. Finally my present publisher agreed, provided that I revised the text, brought all the facts and figures up to date and allowed it to be redesigned in the current series style. Now we have the complete Wildernesse saga in print.

I have changed nothing in this story, only here and there the manner of telling it. The short factual history of eagles in Britain,

11

which I wrote originally as a context for the events I witnessed, now introduces in its updated form the account I hope you are about to enjoy.

★

Eagles have fascinated men for thousands of years. They were painted on cave walls by early man, and have been the national emblems of Russia, Germany, Austria, France, Poland and Mexico. In 1792 the bald eagle became the national symbol of the United States of America. In Indian headdress, eagles' flight feathers proclaimed their owners' powers as both hunter and warrior, and the great Thunderbird, direct emissary of the Great Spirit, was an eagle. Kirghiz Tartars flew golden eagles at antelopes, and in Siberia they were flown at wolves. During the height of falconry in medieval Europe only kings were allowed to fly the golden eagle. To the ancient Greeks the eagle was the messenger of Zeus, ruler of the Universe, who sometimes assumed the eagle's form himself. To the Romans the eagle was the bird of their highest god, Jupiter, and each Legion had as its standard a silver, bronze or golden eagle with its wings extended. To the Israelites the bird (which nested on Mount Sinai) symbolised the Lord's protection, bearing them away from Egyptian bondage on its figurative wings. Eagles were among the highest deities of Babylonia, Egypt and Assyria and were referred to in the Talmud as the 'King of birds'. When Napoleon became Emperor of the French in 1804, he chose the eagle as his emblem, following the example of Saladin, Sultan of Egypt and Syria, and Charlemagne, master of the German Empire. He kept live eagles in his entourage and even declared that his only son was to be called 'L'Aiglon' (The Eaglet). Napoleon decreed that the eagle should be the battle standard of each regiment of his grand army, and the capture of these by British regiments during the Wars was always an important event. The eagle device from such capturings at Waterloo was incorporated into badges and is still used today by such regiments as the Royal Dragoons and the Royal Scots Greys. Many Highland chieftains wore eagle flight feathers in their headdress as a mark of rank, and the eagle motif appears on eighteen of the historic Arms of the Scottish Clan chiefs.

Despite such esteem, the golden eagle has faced, and still faces, many problems in Britain. Little more than a century and a half ago eagles were not uncommon in many of the upland areas of England and Wales as well as Scotland, but as human populations increased

12

and agriculture intensified, direct persecution, including egg collecting, also increased, and the bird was driven further north to the remote fastnesses of Scotland. Here too great changes had been taking place. The crushing of the 1745 Jacobite uprising, the ending of clan warfare and the introduction of the potato as a basic food led to a population increase in the Highlands, and as more and more land was sold off to sheep graziers from the south, the notorious Highland Clearances were perpetrated where the human natives from large areas were dispossessed to make way for the sheep. Slowly the old clan system was replaced by a kind of feudal ownership as great tracts were also sold to the industrial rich of the nineteenth century, now able to go north on the new railways.

The fashionable sports of deer, grouse and hare shooting became strongly established and the new estates, grouse moors especially, employed thousands of gamekeepers who regarded all predators as vermin. Eagles and many other birds of prey, as well as wildcats, pine martens and foxes, were trapped, shot and poisoned in large numbers. Persecution also came from shepherds for alleged depredations on lambs in the days when virtually no-one questioned how many lambs had been found already dead. Added to this, as is all too clear in the works of 'sportsmen naturalists', eminent in their day, such as Charles St John, John Colquhoun and Osgood Mackenzie, the eagle was regarded as a choice sporting target too. High prices were also paid for the carcasses for stuffing purposes, and with the hobby of egg collecting at its height the persecution of the golden eagle, white tailed sea eagle and osprey was compounded. Indeed, the last two were extinct as breeding species shortly after the turn of the century, largely because of this persecution. The golden eagle, capable of surviving on the remotest highest ground by preying on 'high tops' species like ptarmigan, were far less persecuted in the new deer forests (3,000,000 acres by 1915) where they scavenged efficiently for carrion and managed to cling on.

While exact figures are not available, it is clear from contemporary accounts that eagle numbers by the early 1900s were probably only a quarter of the 420 or so breeding pairs surviving in Scotland today, plus the two pairs now nesting with varying success in England, the first of which began as late as 1970. Some naturalists were then predicting it would become extinct as a breeding bird. As with other rare predatory species, eagles enjoyed accidental amnesties during World Wars I and II when 'keepers and shepherds were away after targets of a different kind. Increased carrion from the growing sheep flocks and expanding rabbit populations undoubtedly helped the eagles to recover at this time, aided by the strengthened bird protection act of 1954 and more enlightened land owners who wanted to see eagles on their land. But when myxomatosis came to the Highlands in 1954–55, the breeding success of pairs that preyed heavily on rabbits was affected.

The current population of some 420 breeding pairs, plus about eighty immatures and unmated adults, in the Scottish Highlands represents almost a quarter of these birds' total numbers in all western Europe; they are therefore an important population. Although enjoying special protection in law, as Schedule 1 species, eagles today still suffer from four main causes of deprivation:

1. *Direct Persecution*

On the sporting grouse moors some die-hard 'keepers still shoot and trap eagles and also set out illegal poisoned carcasses and baits, ostensibly to kill foxes, crows and gulls – as do a few shepherds on north western sheep runs. But such poisons are unselective and kill many eagles. The report, '*Silent Death*', published by the Royal Society for the Protection of Birds in 1980, revealed *proved* cases of nine golden eagles killed in Scotland by these poisons between 1973 and 1979, plus four more suspected cases. Since then 30 more poisoned eagles have been found in Scotland. These are merely the known instances – on large private estates the chances of poisoned eagles being reported are remote, so many more cases probably occurred. Such over-kill of alleged predators on grouse is founded on faulty thinking. A Nature Conservancy study proved that grouse shooting never exploits the annual production of birds to the full, and surplus grouse were still driven out to marginal areas where, being less nourished, carrying more parasites, they were the weaker slower birds most subject to predation. Healthy breeding stock was little affected. The effect of one rare predator like the eagle is minimal. The complaint that eagles scare grouse and scatter them about, so ruining a shoot, is ridiculous. So does a summer storm, another natural phenomenon. And no-one complains when his neighbour's grouse are perhaps driven on to *his* estate.

A few shepherds destroy eyries, eggs or chicks, or else keep eagles off their eggs by a prolonged lunch by an eyrie, or even 'accidentally' destroy nests by fire when burning long heather in spring – still believing the birds to be significant predators on lambs. This despite several scientific studies (*see* Bibliography), proving that such

14

predation is infinitesimal and far less than natural losses. Scotland's first great eagle expert, the late Seton Gordon CBE, wrote that in over thirty years of study he knew of only three cases of eagles actually *killing* lambs. In the mountain fastnesses lambs suffer high mortality – a 14-year study up to 1958 showed lamb mortality in Argyll to be 13 per cent, indicating it might be higher on the harsher sheep runs in the north and west. In recent years the Animal Breeding Research Organization in Edinburgh has estimated that 17 per cent of all lambs on Scottish hills are either dead at birth or die within twenty-four hours, due mainly to poor ewe nutrition in the winter months. And this is a conservative figure. In the more severe regions such lamb loss is as high as 40 per cent. Most lambs taken by eagles (great carrion feeders) are already dead.

There are more than a dozen egg and chick stealing gangs operating in the Highlands each spring and with illicit egg collectors willing to pay £300 for an egg, fanciers and falconers up to £3,000 for an eaglet, their depradations continue at a steady level, despite the maximum penalty now standing at a fine of £5,000 and/or a term in jail.

2. *Disturbance*

Increasing numbers of tourists, climbers, hikers and campers often innocently disturb nesting eagles which lay their eggs from mid-March to mid-April, and need to incubate them from thirty-eight to forty-four days before hatching.

I regard it as a crime to put a sitting eagle off its eggs and in recent years have never gone near an occupied nest until early May, at which time any chick or chicks are well hatched, and only then in warm, fine weather when the parents can be away for some hours at a time. We have more than enough information on eagle breeding and we don't have to check things like how many eggs were laid, when they were laid, and so on. It is possible to observe most nests from a distance, and once the smaller male is seen to be incubating we know eggs have been laid. I am also concerned – when the big national surveys are made – at just how many 'official' visits are made by helpers hired for the summer. One eagle worker I know was annoyed at having to take out five different 'wardens' to one nest, and even more so to find some later took their pals or their lady friends to 'see the eagles'.

3. *Pesticides*

In the early 1960s the use of pesticides (especially dieldrin used in sheep dips, which tainted carrion) was found to be causing sterility in eagles and also the laying of contaminated and thin-shelled eggs which broke easily in the nest. When dieldrin was banned voluntarily from dips and sprays in 1966, along with a decreased use of DDE and DDT, the proportion of eagles successfully rearing young in west Scotland rose from 31 per cent in 1963–65 to 69 per cent in 1966–68. (*See* Lockie, Ratcliffe and Balharry, in Bibliography.) A few farmers still used the pesticides they had stockpiled. Dieldrin was banned legally in 1974. Since then the problem has virtually disappeared as far as eagles are concerned.

4. *Loss of Habitat and Prey*

More and more land is being forested in the Highlands, so reducing the eagle's hunting area after 10 to 15 years when the canopy closes. (Though the *young* plantations can encourage grouse, hares, rabbits and voles for this relatively brief period.) When the plantations take over former hill sheep areas, amounts of sheep carrion in winter are significantly reduced. There has also been a decline in hill sheep farming over the last quarter century. Periodic outbreaks of myxomatosis still decimate rabbit populations in some areas. In the past both these factors have probably been more than offset by the great increase in deer carrion. After the mid-1960s, red deer numbers rose rapidly from 180,000 to some 300,000 by 1990 (15,000 deer were estimated to have died on the more over-stocked parts of their range in the harsh winter of 1978–9 alone.) However, alarm was felt at the deterioration of the range, overgrazing and damage to woodlands, and the Red Deer Commission urged a cull of 50,000 hinds, which were outnumbering stags by two to one by 1990. And this over and above the normal annual cull of 25,000 of both sexes. Such a dramatically increased cull would see a big fall in the amount of deer carrion – not good news for eagles in winter.

*

Eagle Mountain Year – a new 125-minute VHS video tape – is the result of my years of filming the eagles I studied. It tells the story of a magical Highland mountain through all four seasons and has many unique sequences – golden eagles at the nest and their glorious courtship 'air dances', an eaglet swallowing a complete stoat, a female eagle hauling a deer uphill on her own. Rare black-throated divers are seen diving, courting, and at their nest. Pine martens are shown hunting, at their den, even coming through my study window to take food from my hands. Hunting and nesting peregrine falcons are shown in detail, as is all the comic, and tragic, sibling rivalry at buzzard nests. There are courting red-breasted mergansers, ospreys, ravens at a carcass, foxes, and even a hunting wildcat. A host of other species are woven into the mountain's fascinating year, and through it all I show the lives of the red deer herds, including dramatic stag fights in the autumn rut. While limited stocks last, a copy of the videotape will be sent to anyone writing to me c/o The Post Office, Hawick, Roxburghshire TD9 7NQ and enclosing £25, which includes first class return post. Please allow one month for delivery of the tape (closing date, 30th September 1995).

1 · *The Coming of Atalanta*

She came gliding towards me from the east like some extra-terrestrial being, dark, massive and silent as a ghost, with an aura of the primeval about her. With her great wings angled back like thick fangs, she moved against the south-westerly March gales without the need of a single wing beat but with consummate ease, as if owning a secret of aerial mastery no other bird possessed. She was a mere hundred feet up, and as she came nearer I saw the huge yellow talons bunched up into her breast like the undercarriage of a plane, and the wide wedge-shaped reptilian head with its powerful steely blue hooked beak and piercing orange eyes that glared at the ground.

I ducked behind the cottage wall, hoping she had not seen me. She banked suddenly and twice circled the topmost spire of the tall spruce tree that dominates the woods around my remote home as if trying to land on it. I heard her give two clear but oddly weak high-pitched calls '*keeya keeya*', I saw her make three powerful but easy beats to steady herself on course again then once more she angled her wings, which spanned at least seven feet, and just seemed to glide sideways against the winds, travelling in an incredibly fast glide towards the west. As she passed above my far wood, one flight feather fluttered loose.

Transfixed with awe as in seconds the golden eagle vanished from my sight, I watched the feather spiral slowly down, a lifeless relic of its owner who was now nearly a mile away, and settle in the grasses at the edge of the wood. I looked down at Moobli, the huge four-month-old Alsatian pup I was training to help me scent and track wildlife in the western Highlands of Scotland. He was still looking in the direction the great bird had taken, as if unable to believe his eyes. He had neither barked nor shown fear, but he too had glimpsed the prehistoric wonder whose ancestors had been soaring and hunting the Highland hills long before the first human inhabitants. Together we hurried over to retrieve the feather, which almost seemed to have been dropped as a gift. Once indoors, I found it was longer than any swan's, measuring twenty-three inches.

'My god,' I thought. 'Wouldn't it be something if she nested in the nearby hills.'

In fact it was a full seven years before that huge dark female and her smaller mate used an eyrie relatively close to my cottage. By then, after covering more than 1,500 steep mountain miles on foot, many more by boat and Land Rover, I had, alone and through friends, located a total of twenty-eight golden eagle eyries over 300 square miles of the western Highlands in the intervening years. I had enjoyed a series of extraordinary adventures with five pairs of these magnificent rare birds of prey, and had made discoveries which I hope, through this book, will add to our knowledge of the eagle.

I confess that, at the age of forty-six when I began, I had perhaps left it a little late to start slogging over the mountains with hefty hides and packs of cameras and equipment. In each season I had shivered through long cold nights on cliff ledges, been drenched in constant rains and semi-frozen in late snows, baked by the sun on long treks, knocked off my feet by raging burns, beleaguered by camera failures, scared of falling from the heights, and even slightly injured in short falls. I swore I would never 'work eagles' again. But each autumn and winter I would witness new aspects of eagle life, realise that there were still many things I wanted to know, and would succumb once again to the fascination that began that mid-March day when the big female flew so close over my home. None of these activities did I foresee on that day, however.

After measuring the huge eagle flight pinion I held it in my hand and flapped it steadily up and down, trying to simulate the beat of the bird herself. To my surprise, that single feather generated a wind so strong behind it that it lifted several sheets of paper from my desk and wafted them away – yet in front of the moving feather there was no draught at all. The natural forward thrust from its sheer design was considerable. What a masterpiece of evolution, I thought, just as is the golden eagle itself, the most widespread of all eagles, unchanged in form for at least two million years. Indeed, it was flying in the warmer countries thousands of years before modern man evolved, and in northern Europe and America, after the retreat of the Ice Age, it has existed for some 9,000 years.

At the time, I thought I knew something about eagles, having read books and papers about them, and from some personal experiences. I recall it was an eagle which had prompted my own initial desire for a life in the wilds. In February 1965 a golden eagle called Goldie escaped from London Zoo and for thirteen days he was free in the trees around Regent's Park. He attracted more headlines and radio and television coverage than any single event in Britain that year. Thousands flocked to see him from all over the capital and from abroad, sent meat parcels, suggested trapping ideas; advertisers, cartoonists and comedians starred him in their work. At the time I was a jaded former Fleet Street journalist who had worked in many of the big cities of Europe and America, and I longed to live a more natural life. My flat was near the Park, and twice I joined the crowds to see the great bird perched in the trees, all of us unconsciously paying homage to the proud solitary 'King of Birds' whose desire for freedom reflected our own. I had become bogged down in a city rut, a sort of jail of my own making, and I felt I had much in common with that great eagle. Within months I had sold up, packed and flown away to a wild sea coast in British Columbia where bears and cougar still roamed in the wild and eagles soared in the skies.

In Canada, after jobs as logger, blaster and boat deck hand, I regained my youthful love of nature which had begun in boyhood years with a fine old Sussex gamekeeper. I studied a pair of bald eagles which nested near my little log cabin. To see these great birds, the national symbols of America, tumbling over each other in mid-air with talons locked in their courtship display, and then to see one stoop at a salmon on the sea's surface, be dragged underneath temporarily by the big fish, and then *swim* ashore with its prey by hunching its wings, had been two of the most incredible wildlife experiences I had known. Observing their nesting behaviour from a precarious tree hide had really been the start of my adult years of wildlife watching.

On returning to Britain, I spent three-and-a-half years in an old wooden croft on the Atlantic end of Eilean Shona, a small sea island off Scotland's west coast. There, after a bit of a struggle, I managed to break away from my former kind of journalism and start making a meagre living by writing of the wildlife round me.

I had been there nearly a year before catching sight of a golden eagle. Then one misty dark January morning, while trekking past a small ridge on the high slopes above the forest on the east side of the island, I was startled to see an immense bird, looking gunmetal grey-brown in the poor light, spread great wings, flap heavily a few times, and soar away. On descending, I found a decaying carcass of a winter-dead red deer hind. A large hole had been torn behind her ribs, exposing remains of the lungs and heart on which the bird had been feeding. I only caught two more distant glimpses of eagles on Shona after that, both times flying straight over the island. When I told the local people of these sightings I was surprised to hear some say, 'You're lucky. I've lived here all my life and *never* seen an eagle!'

Feeling the need to study a greater range of wildlife over a far larger area of higher hills and bigger woodlands, I then moved halfway up a long freshwater loch to the home I call Wildernesse.

It is a truly remote place, perhaps one of the wildest in all Britain. My nearest neighbour lived six miles away. No road led to Wildernesse, and my only access was to make the journey by boat, having left my Land Rover in a pine wood. I could walk to it, but there was no path, only a few barely discernible deer and sheep trails, and the circuitous route crossed bogs, acres of ankle-wrenching tussocks, high rocky ledges and fallen trees – impractical for one man carrying heavy supplies. There was no electricity, gas, telephone, television, and my only 'mod con' was a plastic pipe for water from a pool in the burn fifty yards up the hill. The old stone cottage stood forty yards above the lochshore, while behind it the land rose steeply in a series of rocky crests and led by heather and tussock-covered undulations into a maze of wild glens, rivers and mountains whose peaks rose to just under 3,000 feet. Here lay sixty square miles of the wildest, roadless and least inhabited land in Britain. Across the loch to the south lay an area just as wild but three times the size. Here too for many miles the only signs of man were deer fences round forestry compartments, scattered sheep and a few cattle in the lower reaches of the more accessible glens. One of the reasons I had leased Wildernesse was the presence of golden eagles. On the winter day I boated down to view it for the first time, I had seen a pair of golden eagles wafting along the high ridges above the cottage. They were the first pair I had ever seen together in the wild, and at the time it had seemed a good omen. Nevertheless it was six months after the day I had moved in that the first really close encounter with the big female eagle occurred.

Before that, there had been only the occasional glimpse. On

December 5 I was skirting the edge of the little west wood, eyeing the trees above because in the south-west gales a few dead branches were crashing down, when I saw an eagle floating over the cottage. I raised my telephoto lens – and jumped involuntarily as I pressed the button. She suddenly looked so big and dark it was as if she had dropped in an air pocket. I felt as might a mountain hare, rabbit or grouse on first catching sight of her – here was the veritable shadow, the dark angel of death. I rewound, lost her behind a tree and by the time my lens was on to her again she was too far away. I realised then that the apparent slow speed of the gliding eagle is deceptive, her sheer size making her appear to be moving slower than she was – even in a casual prospecting glide she must have been travelling at forty miles an hour. But at least I had my first clear photo of an eagle after nearly four years in the Highlands!

Three days later I was a mile along the shore and had just completed a stalk to within fifty yards of red deer hinds and calves, which were scraping snow from grassy tufts so that they could graze, when I stood up. Immediately there was a woofing of great wings above. It was a smaller eagle and it had probably not recognised the bunched up camouflaged form between the tussocks as human. As it turned I saw that the normal golden mantle feathers over its neck were almost grey. It seemed to be an old male but my thought that it might be the mate of the big female seemed wrong when, instead of turning north-west as she had done, it sailed right across the loch to a high broad mountain and vanished over its eastern ridges.

A few times in that first winter I came to doubt my sanity in coming to live in so wild and remote a spot. Gales made supply trips by boat very dangerous, with spray spewing over the bows for the entire outward journey, and deep watery troughs threatening to engulf the boat while coming home. I often had the utmost difficulty winching the boat out of the water with my icy hands before the waves filled it up. And many long treks in far harsher hills than those on Shona often proved fruitless but for a few distant glimpses of red deer or an occasional buzzard. I began to feel that I had made a terrible mistake. Even the eagles seemed to have disappeared. I wondered if they had migrated further south to the gentler, less snowy hills of west Argyll.

In mid-January, perhaps to counter increasing loneliness as much as to have a good scenting dog to help me track wildlife, I bought Moobli, a three-month-old Alsatian pup. Training and coping with this boisterous playful little monster, who was at first not old enough for hill treks, along with gathering and handsawing firewood logs and a busy writing schedule, kept me occupied. On February 6 I was boating home in fading light when the male eagle with the grey-looking mantle flew above, again heading for the big mountain to the south. I little knew then that I would one day trace that eagle to its home territory, nor that it would take me four years.

It was on March 21, four days after the close encounter with the female circling my spruce tree, that I had a further insight into the bird's extraordinary flight powers. I was at my desk when I faintly heard the spirited '*krruk krruk*' of a calling raven, Scotland's earliest nesting bird. Thinking it might be mobbing a buzzard, I dashed out – only to see the great form of the female eagle sailing serenely along. She was moving like some ethereal goddess of the aerial chase, and in that brief moment I thought of a good name for her – Atalanta, after the fleet mythical Greek goddess of the Calydonian Hunt who (as is also true in the eagle world) could outdistance and more than had the measure of any male of her species! Then I also saw the cause of the noise. From the high north-east ridges a raven had taken umbrage at the sight of her. Beating as hard as a woodpigeon to make up the quarter mile between them, it gained on the eagle and with even higher pitched '*krruks*' it rolled and dived to try and drive her from its aerial territory. Twice it came close enough to annoy the eagle, which pulled in her left wing, turned on her side and made raking slashes at the swooping raven with her talons. Each time the raven sheered off and then renewed the attack by coming in from above or behind. Soon irritated with this, Atalanta just changed the angle of her glide and, as if powered by an invisible motor, began to move half against the north-west wind at great speed. She covered the whole arch of the sky in less than half a minute, leaving the raven, normally a great aerobat and master of flight in its own right, limping uselessly behind. However, it must have felt it had won the encounter for it flew back to the high ridges '*krock*'ing with triumph, like some impudent glorified crow. Once again I wondered just how an eagle achieved these fast glides. Just what speed could it attain in them?

As yet I would find no answer to such questions for I was writing ten hours a day for survival. I made a dash to Canada to trek after grizzly bears and mountain lions for the photos to help *prove* the book I was writing about those years. When I got back I started a wildcat breeding project, which took up almost all the rest of my time. Despite several hill treks with Moobli, I saw no more golden eagles until May the following year. Once again they seemed to have gone away for the winter.

In Scotland eagles feed through the year mainly on mountain hares, rabbits, red grouse, ptarmigan and carrion from dead red deer and sheep. This carrion is both more plentiful and more important to eagles in winter and spring in the western Highlands where there is far less live prey than in the east. But eagles prefer live prey, such as rabbits, if they can find them. I had noticed that while there were no rabbits on the rough ground round Wildernesse, nor within a good five miles, they were reasonably common on the lower hills, the fertile sheep runs and the river meadows and coastal land of the peninsulas to the west. With the various summer ducks and waders (on which eagles also prey) wintering further south, I felt the great birds of prey must have migrated to the more prey-filled areas.

This theory did not, however, coincide with the studies published in the 1960s by two eminent eagle men, Leslie Brown and Adam Watson. After studying eagles in the four main areas of the Highlands – the eastern deer forests, south-west hills of Argyll, the western region of Torridon in Wester Ross, and north-west Sutherland – they came to some fascinating conclusions. They deduced that an adult eagle eats 84 kg of meat a year, that over-all (when free of human persecution and nesting failures) Scotland's eagles rear 0.8 young per pair per year★ and that on average an eagle family needs 249 kg of meat annually from its home range. This consists of some 50 kg carrion, 127 kg mammals, and 72 kg birds. Taking into account the wastage from inedible portions of live prey, this meant the eagle family would eat annually, for instance: 2 dead sheep, 70 mountain hares, and 140 red grouse. (Or one dead stag, 110 rabbits and 160 ptarmigan.)

While these figures apply to the eagles in the Highlands as a whole, Brown and Watson found that the differences in the diets of eagles in the western Highlands to those in the east were considerable. They deduced that in the eastern deer forests the mountain tops contain one-and-a-half to four-and-a-half times as much live prey as the three western areas, the eastern moors four-and-a-half to 130 times as much, and the eastern glen bottoms nine to nineteen times as much. But they proved the carrion supply in the western areas, where the eagles largely depended on it, to be far greater than in the

★ A five-year study by the Royal Society for the Protection of Birds (1964–68) revealed that out of 315 known breeding results, 37 per cent (118) failed, due largely to human interference. This brings the figure down to 0.56 young per pair per year.

east. They found that deer and sheep carrion combined – while only
27 kg per 100 acres per year in the east (where few sheep are kept) –
was as high as 203 kg in the south-west area of Argyll, 86 kg in the
Torridon area of Wester Ross, and 106 kg per year in north-west
Sutherland. Thus, taking both live prey and carrion into account,
if eagle numbers were directly related to total food supply, their density would be highest in the south-western area. In fact, they were
less dense there than in the other three areas. On the other hand, if
the amount of *live* prey was directly related to eagle numbers, density should be many times higher in the east. Brown and Watson
discovered that the size of eagles' home ranges did not differ all that
much. They averaged 11,400 acres in the live prey rich area of the
east, 17,884 acres in the south-west Argyll area, 15,079 acres in
the Torridon area of Wester Ross, and 13,015 acres in north-west
Sutherland. Even the largest difference – between the eastern area
and south-west Argyll – would be minimised if all the low lying
ground in the latter area, over which eagles only occasionally hunted,
was excluded.

Brown and Watson concluded that Scotland's golden eagles exist
in a fairly definite and nearly constant spatial relationship to each
other, largely for territorial reasons. Further, that their average food
potential in *all* areas was greatly in excess of food requirements, in
spite of annual and seasonal fluctuations in supply, and the eagles
fixed their home ranges so high that a critical food level is probably
very rarely reached. This immensely valuable study★ also first
indicated to me that in my area – north Argyll and south-west
Inverness-shire – the home range of a pair of eagles could average as
high as 16,000 acres or more. If this were so, and Atalanta's range
was elliptical rather than roughly circular, then it could probably
include some of the rabbit areas further west if winter carrion was
ever in short supply.

I was also beginning to feel that while eagles may hold a home
range more rigidly in the breeding season, especially around the
particular glen of any eyrie they were using, in winter the boundaries
would possibly become far more elastic. With their young reared,
perhaps outer boundaries loosen, depending on where were situated
the greater concentrations of prey or carrion in the harsher time of
year. It was some years before I could throw any light on these
mysteries.

★ *The Golden Eagle In Relation To Its Food Supply*. L. H. Brown and A. Watson. (*Ibis*
106. Pp. 78–100.)

On May 11 I was boating along half a mile east of my Land Rover when again I saw an eagle heading towards the big mountain to the south. This time it had no greyish mantle and though I knew by now that one cannot identify eagles definitely by plumage alone from year to year – after the summer moult the arrangement of fawns, browns and golds on the generally dark brown feathers can alter – it was certainly smaller than Atalanta, and I wondered if it could be her mate. A week later I was out in the garden working on a short BBC television film when Atalanta herself came soaring above the north-west ridges – this time chased by two ravens *and* two crows which had a nest in the nearby woods. Again she turned over momentarily to slash at her tormentors with her talons but failed to make contact. The mouths of the film crew dropped open at the sheer size and majesty of her. It always amused me to see that the reactions of others at their first close sight of a wild golden eagle were much as mine had been. By now I had located the ravens' nest, high on a woodland cliff to the east. It surprised me that both birds would leave their young and chase the eagle a full mile or more every time she passed. What if her mate was following on behind? Would he be averse to seizing a juicy fat young raven from its nest? I realised then that in the year-and-a-half I had been glimpsing Atalanta, I had never seen a smaller eagle with her or near her. Maybe she had not bred this year, or was temporarily mateless, and that being intelligent birds, and doubtless having seen her more often than I, the ravens knew this.

All summer, despite hill treks, rearing wildcat kittens and working with kestrels and owls so that I was outside a good deal, I saw no more eagles. But on October 22, when I was wallowing in the troughs of a strong easterly on a supply trip, I saw a large ruddy brown bird sailing over the lochshore woods towards my home. It saw the boat, lowered the rear edges of its wings, looped up and landed in a tree. Then it lifted its tail feathers high and ejected a mute – a sure sign it was not a large female buzzard whose excreta falls straight to the ground. I saw through my fieldglass the grey-looking mantle behind the head. It was the male eagle I had occasionally seen flying towards the big southern mountain, and apparently that part of its plumage had not changed at all.

The eagle spread its wings again and, with no jump-off, just drifted into the air. Spiralling effortlessly, gaining height each time it turned into the wind, without a single wing beat, it was soon over a thousand feet high, whereupon it again glided south. I made a mental note of the ridge over which it vanished.

Now things began to speed up. In the next two days I twice saw Atalanta soaring over the north-east crests but now she did head more to the south west, and each time the two crows gave futile chase. On October 27, while taking a break from planting oaks and sweet chestnuts to replace some fallen conifers in my woods, I was halfway up the loch in the boat when I saw what looked like a plane flying in total silence high above. Through the glass, as it headed southwards, I saw it was a gliding eagle, almost certainly Atalanta by its size.

She was so high that she kept vanishing and reappearing between the misty clouds, her whole body and wings burnished by the sun that shone clearly above them. Again she was going at great speed with no apparent effort, wreathed then unwreathed in mist, like a jetliner with engines closed down. How could she see when in cloud? Where was she going? Was she just having fun up there? What would it sound like to be perched on her mighty back, to hear the wind rushing and singing through all those great feathers? I felt then the stirrings of a relentless fascination, for surely, here in the wild Highlands, no more intriguing bird could exist.

Through November more tantalising glimpses of eagles occurred. On the ninth I was trekking up in the hills to photograph stags when Moobli began to prance head high, scenting something ahead. Keeping him back, I stalked to a small rocky ridge and, with telephoto lens at the ready, peered over. Instantly a large eagle, keener sighted than any deer, took off with powerful wing beats towards dark higher ridges ahead. *Click* – but all I got was a picture of two long wavy lines, which were its wings, while its body came out as a round smudge between them! It had been feeding from a gralloch – the stomach and guts of a red deer hind that the estate stalkers had left after shooting the beast and dragging it down to their boat.

Winter was approaching, and it was interesting that an eagle would be at a gralloch. Hitherto I had only associated crows and ravens with such remains. Indeed, ravens occasionally flew close, riding the air like black hawks, croaking musically to each other, when Moobli and I were on treks, for these clever birds have long associated men on the Hill at this time of year with the shooting of deer and the leaving of grallochs. Six days later we were out tracking the movements of my wildcats, which were now running free, when a male eagle, a good six inches smaller than Atalanta, appeared from behind and soared in a circle over our heads. At first I thought it was the large female buzzard which often flew over the cottage but his greater size was soon obvious, as was his more protruding head and neck, darker plumage and greater length of wings. The spread out 'fingers' of his wing tip feathers, commonly believed to be an identification clue of the flying eagle, told me little. Both eagle and buzzard spread out their 'fingers' in this way when soaring in light winds or just before landing; so do ravens and even rooks.

This was surely not the grey-mantled male I had seen before. I felt that at last I probably *was* looking at Atalanta's mate. As he circled once more, as if having another good look at us, then soared away to the north west, I gave him a name. What else, I thought, but Meleager, for in the Greek myths it was Meleager who had led the Calydonian Hunt with Atalanta, who loved her and once saved her life from a ferocious giant wild boar! Yes, Meleager would be an apt name, if indeed this eagle *was* her mate.

Oddly, as if to confirm my hunch was correct, it was between hail and sleet showers on December 1 that I next saw Atalanta, cruising low over the long wood a mile to the west. And there, floating lazily behind her, was a smaller eagle which again, through the glass, was not the grey-mantled male. I was sure it was Meleager. I realised then also, that they might actually be looking for grallochs. Why, if I wanted to see and photograph them at close quarters, did I not put out some bait for them? Now the differences from the buzzards were becoming even more obvious – the eagles' wings were not only longer but far broader, great supple, almost rectangular 'sails', and they flapped them far less often and with less effort, mere casual strokings of the air. They were also much more stable – whereas a buzzard can be wafted up or down by sudden powerful gusts and makes rapid wing beats to get back on course, the eagles merely pulled in or tilted a wing tip occasionally. Their aerial circles too were far wider. Two days later when I boated out for supplies I also cadged some huge meaty cattle bones from Euan, my butcher in the village at the foot of the loch.

'Ye'll be needing a big pot if you're making soup out of them!' he joked, wrapping them in paper. When I told him they were for eagles he smiled even more. 'Big as they are, ye'll be needing to tie them down!' I knew by the size of the salmon that bald eagles could lift in Canada that he was right.

I did not set the bones out in the next few days because driving drizzle made photography impossible but then the rain gave way to snow showers. During the sunny intervals I again had to postpone putting out the bones because two part time estate stalkers boated down the loch to shoot a few of the hinds that sheltered in my woods, and I didn't want to risk the eagles being scared by the shots. On December 18, with the north winds changed to the south west, poor for deer stalking from the shore line, I saw both the eagles heading over from the east, Meleager over land while Atalanta flew over the loch waters. Suddenly Meleager banked and glided fast to the north-west ridges. He had clearly spied a gralloch and as he landed a small group of ravens and crows scattered from it. Ravens have been known to mob an eagle from carrion but I was sure this was only when the eagle had eaten enough itself. Certainly they showed no wish to tangle with this hungry eagle. When Atalanta glided down to join him they all dispersed to ridges at a respectful distance, the crows '*karr*'ing morosely. I tried to stalk up out of sight to an adjacent ridge for photos but whether they were given the alarm by a single crow that flew over us and gave out a loud '*karr*' or had felt the vibration of my boots crunching the snow, I didn't know. But when I peered through the old grasses at the top they had gone, and so had most of the gralloch. Eagles, I was finding again, are far more wary than deer.

An hour later I took the huge bones from my calor gas fridge and carried them up the hill. Selecting a heathery shelf at about 200 feet which I could overlook from my bedroom, I pegged the bones down with thick green nylon fishing line and covered up line and pegs with dead brown bracken that was also growing there. 'Na!' I said to Moobli, using the command that meant the bones were forbidden. 'Don't touch. Na!' Then with him casting longing glances at the bones, we descended the hill. I opened the window and set the 640 mm lens and camera on a tripod so that it gave a clear view of the spot where I had left the bones.

Two hours later I realised the cottage was unusually silent. I shot outside. There on the hill, lying low so as not to be seen and casually gnawing at the bones, was Moobli! I yelled his name and immediately he shot to the east, vanishing behind the ridges. Several minutes later I heard heavy panting behind me. The cunning young dog had sneaked all the way out of sight down the gorge of the burn to the loch shore and had come running up from the rear as if he'd been down there all the time. There was an affable expression of total innocence on his face.

'Badog!' I said, whacking his rump. 'No touch bones. Na!' And off he crept, guiltily, into the house. I kept sporadic watch but realised I had never seen the eagles go back once they had passed over my area on any single day. Maybe they did work their range on a roughly oblong route.

Nothing went near the meat bones next day but on December 20 I sneaked into the bedroom, almost as icy as the outside with the open window, and kept watch from dawn. Suddenly huge Atalanta appeared, high in the sky, heading west. She turned her head as she passed above the white and red tangle, then carried on. As if following her came a raven and two hooded crows. They too just flew on, and I felt they all suspected the artificial sight – or because the weather had again turned mild and drizzly, they were finding enough normal prey.

Not till the fourth day, when I slid into the room before dawn, dressed in three sweaters for a long watch, did my ruse succeed. As I looked through the lens into the near-dark scene it appeared as if something black had been laid across the bones which showed up as thin whitish slivers. As my eyes became more accustomed, I saw it was moving up and down like an irregularly pumping oil derrick. Then I made out the form of one of the eagles. The nearest yellow foot with its long black talons overlapped the broad blade of the cow's leg bone and with its beak it was making long downward scrapes, tearing off slivers of meat and jerking its head back to gulp them down. In the gloom it looked more like a gorgon than a bird. Even at a full second the camera's meter needle didn't quiver. After a few minutes the eagle crouched, spread its great wings, jumped into the still air and vanished. What surprised me most was that an eagle would be out hunting in light better suited to an owl.

I waited until light but no eagle returned. When a hoody that had been waiting in the trees that lined the burn gorge flew down to peck at the meat, I hiked up. I didn't want it taking food for 'my' eagles. It was interesting to find the eagle's beak marks, almost three inches long, where it had scraped off the slivers. And when I measured the blade bone where the eagle's foot had gripped, it was clear that the distance between the end of its rear talon to its longest front talon must span at least seven inches.

Nothing went near the bones in photographable daylight, but when I hiked up on December 24 I saw more beak marks on them. A fox had also been chewing off meat. It left its grey-black dropping on a nearby tuft and, judging from Moobli's scenting behaviour, it urinated over the bones too. Typical smart fox trick, to mark it against other foxes and put off other scavengers. The remaining slivers would be finished off by the fox the next night and there would be nothing left for the eagles.

If I had failed to organise anything for myself over Christmas I had at least saved up a little treat for the eagles. On my last supply trip I had found a fresh traffic-killed rabbit. On Christmas Day I stumped up to a small ledge at 300 feet through cold sleet showers and set it so that its white belly would be visible through the grasses from below.

When I returned to the cottage I switched on the radio. Among the usual jingly Christmas programmes someone was singing 'When You Walk Through A Storm Hold Your Head Up High.' Well, a quicker way to freeze to death, I thought as I switched it off again. Try it in a blizzard! I sipped morosely at sherry and took out a box of photos of my life halfway across the world, ready for my usual Christmas Day wallow in nostalgia. This was my tenth Christmas alone in wild places, my sixth in Scotland. Like many folk, I suppose, what I had feared most of my life was loneliness. I had felt from the start that if I could beat that, learn to use isolation as the spur from which to study wild nature and write, I had life partly by the tail. But as I flicked through the photos of old loves and pals I realised I wasn't feeling lonely. I had subconsciously sentenced myself to ten years solitary in the wilds, to try and complete some good work, and had fallen in love with the jail itself! This Christmas I was no longer alone anyway. Outside I had three wildcats, enjoying their festive lunch in the pens, and chaffinches, tits and robins were making the bird table a riot of colour as they competed for scraps. And, as he thrust his great bear-like muzzle under my arm to be patted, had not Moobli become one of the gentlest and best companions I'd ever had?

What was more, had not the two eagles, for the first time in my three Christmases at Wildernesse, decided to spend the winter around the cottage? At the thought I went into the bedroom to peer through the lens. I was just in time to see Meleager flying off to the west, a great brownish lump hanging beneath him – my rabbit clutched in his talons! My self anger, however, was mitigated by the thought, and hope, that he was bearing it off to share with Atalanta for they should soon be visiting their various eyrie sites and beginning to rebuild one of them with twigs and small branches.

But where were these eyries?

On New Year's Eve, after five days of south-west gales and driving rain, the loch had risen several feet, waves had filled the stern of the boat and it was see-sawing up and down on its trolley at the end of the winch wire. As I wound the handle to haul it higher up its wooden runway the wire sang in the wind under the great strain of the half-filled boat's weight. Suddenly there was a tearing sound, something whizzed past my head, clipping my left ear as it went, then shot twenty yards to the shore and landed with a splash in the raging waters. It was the entire winch. Two more inches to the right and it would have taken some of my skull with it, and I'd have been killed. As I held the bleeding edge of my ear I saw a movement overhead. Atalanta was making a tight circle merely thirty yards above my head, as if fascinated by what had been going on. Then away she sailed again, riding the winds easily to the west. It took three hours to rescue the boat, now submerged and banging against the bank.

That night, despite the storms, I camped out below a huge oak in the woodlands, a yearly ritual of renewing close contact with nature that made more sense than jigging about alone to the festive music on the radio. Behind some rocks, to the light of four guttering candles, I cooked my and Moobli's suppers over a smoky campfire that hissed as wet drops plapped down from the foliage above. I switched on the radio to play softly and was just in time to hear a superbly emotional and melancholy rendering of one of my favourite songs, 'The Rowan Tree', by the singer Danny Street, where he made the lines
Now a' are gane!
We meet nae mair, aneath the rowan tree
almost unbearably affecting. The jigging music had just started up again when the radio suddenly went dead. A splash of water from the oak branches had doused the terminals. Now in the icy wet cold I could hear only the songs of the wild wind, the stirring of leaves and the falling of the rain. The lines came back to my memory and I thought of the stunted rowan trees alone up there on the high harsh slopes, often clinging in precarious isolation to fissures in the rock faces where they had escaped the hungry sheep and deer, enduring the blasts of wind and hail. I thought of all the wild creatures in the woods and hills around us, fighting to survive in winter's icy grasp but particularly I thought of the great eagles.

If I was finding it hard to make a simple human meal out in such weather, how did they survive hundreds of much worse nights without respite every winter of their long lives? It was then I made one New Year resolution – to find out more about golden eagles, and to photograph and study them closely. I did not have, it seemed,

33

as I had in Canada with the bald eagles, a pair that happened to be nesting near my home. Could I, in these wild open mountains, starting from nowhere, get on close terms with such magnificent creatures? And, more important, could I do it without disturbing their lives?

2 · *Search Under Licence*

In mid-January, battling through a snow blizzard just before it closed Glencoe, I drove south with Moobli to do some biological research, discuss wildlife writings with editors and deliver some rare butterflies and moths to the British Museum of Natural History in London. There I met an unusual man – Geoffrey Kinns – who worked as an artist but spent all his spare time photographing wildlife, despite the handicap of losing his left leg below the knee in World War II.

I was astonished to see above his desk fine pictures of golden eagles. How had he taken them while working in London? Over lunch, he told me. Several years before, wanting to cover such creatures as wildcats and eagles in their own Highland domain, he had written to Richard Balharry, then head warden of the Ben Eighe reserve in Wester Ross, who later became head warden of the Cairngorm Reserve and after that Chief Warden of the North East Highlands for the Nature Conservancy Council. Balharry, a leading authority on the golden eagle, invited him to pay a visit, and found him prepared to be let down a cliff on a rope, to endure long cold stints in hides, and, while slow on the Hill, to plod doggedly upwards with a 45lb pack. And Geoffrey got his eagle pictures that year, and over the years since. Once he photographed an eagle carrying a 9lb fox into its eyrie. I was impressed by his courageous determination, glad of his friendship, and felt inspired to make greater efforts myself when I got home.

Next day I went to Her Majesty's Stationery Office in High Holborn and bought some relevant wildlife protection acts. There, in the Protection of Birds Act 1967, section 4, was the clause applying to eagles... 'If any person wilfully disturbs any wild bird included in Schedule 1 to the principal Act (wild birds protected by special penalties) while it is on or near a nest containing eggs or unflown young of any such bird he shall be guilty of an offence against that Act and liable to a special penalty under that Act.' At least, unlike the jargon of some wildlife legislation at the time, the clause was clear.*

We arrived back at the small pinewood to hear on the radio that unusual Force Eleven gales were expected in the area, a Force Eight was already blowing. The loch level had risen so high that my upside down dinghy was banging about on its pine roots berth. But as soon as I loaded up and set off for home the wind subsided to total calm, and only began to rage again when the boat was safely up. I felt as if I was being protected by a benign power. On the trip I was delighted to see Atalanta. She was quartering the high ridges so closely she looked like a moving shadow. It seemed that as she sheered up, often just clearing large rocks, she was hoping to drop unsuspected on any prey she might find on their far sides, an interesting hunting technique. There was a dead hind in the woods, with many warble fly larvae in her coat. After taking her rear haunches for Moobli and the wildcats, I hauled the rest up to a high ridge as food for the eagles.

Between January 21 and mid-March we found sixteen dead or dying deer, old hinds and young calves, some of whose mothers had been shot, in a half-mile radius of Wildernesse where they had come for last shelter in the woods. It was an exceptionally wet winter – worse for deer than a colder but dry one as they lose heat through constant evaporation – and with thousands of acres recently fenced off for forestry in the area and growing populations after several mild winters, the mortality rate was unusually high.

Now I realised why the eagles had been reluctant to come down to the previous baits, only doing so in dawn twilight – because they had been too near the cottage. I began hauling up split open hinds and calves to the 400 and 500 foot levels, even though I could not photograph them from my rear window. The important thing seemed to be to feed them, in the hope that they would use an eyrie close to the cottage – if there was one. Dragging deer carcasses, as

* This Act was superseded by the Wildlife and Countryside Act 1981, where the clause was strengthened, making it a special offence to disturb any Schedule 1 bird 'while it is building a nest or is in, on or near a nest containing eggs or young'; or disturb 'dependent young of such a bird'.

any stalker knows who has to haul them mainly downhill, is hard work. But hauling them *up* steep slopes, frequently getting stuck between rocks or tussocks, pounds the heart, aches your knees, back and arms and soon has perspiration pouring, even in winter. I hoped it would all be worth it. To clear other carcasses from being a health hazard, I towed them by boat along the wooded loch shore for other predators to eliminate.

Before the end of January, I had applied to the Nature Conservancy Council for the necessary photographic licence. On January 31, my primitive water system froze up. I carried buckets to the loch, glanced up in the bright sunlight, and was just in time to see Meleager raise his long wings and lazily flap away from one of my carcasses. Way beyond to the north, hanging in the sky, was Atalanta. In the sun they both seemed to be made of burnished gold. Well, it was good to know they were still patrolling the hills near me. But where were their eyries?

Eagles, I knew, usually have several eyries, varying from as few as two to as many as seven, and sometimes more. While they are used from year to year in a rough rotation, one site is usually more favoured. The nests, built of an untidy mass of small dead branches up to an inch and a half thick and heather sprigs, have a shallow re-cess occasionally lined with great wood-rush, tufts of grass or leafy sprays. They are situated usually on high inaccessible ledges on crags and rock faces, but sometimes (one third, estimated Leslie Brown) they are accessible to an agile unequipped climber. Heights of eyries in the west vary usually from 800 to 1,800 feet, though on sea cliffs they can be as low as 50 feet. (One, in Wester Ross, was found actually on the ground.) In the eastern Highlands eyries are generally higher and Brown discovered a few near the 3,000 feet mark. Eagles do not nest in the highest crags available for it would mean they constantly had to fly upwards with heavy prey. At medium heights they can often soar down from the high tops with food. Tree sites are occasionally used, usually in large old Scots pines, far rarer now than they were a century ago due to felling, and rarer in the north and western Highlands than in the east.

Nests have also been recorded in oaks, birches, rowans and, more rarely, in larch. While rock ledge nests seldom measure more than two to three feet deep and six feet across, tree nests have been known to reach huge dimensions. Brown recorded one seventeen feet deep and Seton Gordon one that was so heavy it undoubtedly contributed to the tree's falling in a severe gale. Ledge nests are often built under the shelter of an overhanging rock and the commonly held belief was that eagles generally choose through a 160 degree arc, sites with a northerly aspect so that eggs and eaglets, which are in the nest some two-and-a-half months before flying, are thus shielded from the sun at its height by the rocks and cliff face above them.

Eagles lay one to three eggs, usually two, creamy white with faint red-brown markings (the first egg usually paler than the second) between mid-March and mid-April depending on several factors such as food supply and the severity of the season. The female does most of the incubation but the cock bird does also share this duty. Sometimes the male brings food to the sitting female, or to near the nest which she may leave briefly to take it. In mild weather she will leave the eggs to hunt for herself for a short while. The eggs hatch in thirty-eight to forty-four days.

Bearing this in mind, I set off with Moobli next day on a ten-mile triangular trek, heading north west to west then back south east in the hope of finding one of my pair's eyries. Right from the start – although they would not yet be laying, I knew they could be rebuilding an eyrie – I planned to cause no disturbance. I would scan every rock face with binoculars from at least 150 yards and just note the location of any eyrie. I would not attempt photography from a hide until after any eggs had hatched for, like many birds, eagles would be less likely to desert if they had live chicks.

It was a hard day, plugging upwards, winding our way between small rocky ridges, over undulating bogs, beds of crunchy snow, to above a long glen at nearly 1,500 feet. Down again, skirting black peaty hollows and past a hill lochan with green ice trying to reflect the bitter blue of the sky. It was so thick one could have driven a bulldozer across it, and at one end wind-whipped water now clung in glassy icicle chunks to blackened rushes. Up again to the ridge of Guardian Mountain, a white expanse of snow everywhere as we were then well over 2,000 feet. The snow was frozen so hard on the surface that I could barely stamp each foot through to make footholds on the steeper parts. But at least it covered tussocks in the dells so that I no longer had them to negotiate. Moobli loved it all, his rough four-inch pads enabling him to drift, wolf-like, without a slip, and he gulped up loose snow with his lower teeth whenever he felt thirsty.

As we passed over the ridge I could see for many miles, deep glens with ranges of sharp peaks and narrow ridges of volcanic rock – no sign of human habitation in sight – and it was like looking down on original creation beyond mere man. We covered a mile in the blinding light reflected from the snow, then cut down a steep hill again to the south west, making hairy crossings of frozen burns, where every rock had a covering of slippery ice lying across its top like molten glass. Down to the snowless bottom of the glen, barely higher than sea level, then upward again, thrusting to over 1,600 feet before turning back over the bogs, ravines, frosty rock outcrops and the last tussocky slopes, where a few hinds and calves shivered, to Wildernesse. Ten miles we covered, up and down over 8,000 feet, and although I had scanned more than fifty rock faces, not an eyrie did we find. Neither had I seen a single eagle!

On February 7 we made a nine-mile trek along the lochside ridges westward, to no avail, then next day another nine miles fruitless climb-walk, to search the eastern ridges and a tramp back over the tops, criss-crossing from rockface to rockface but still no eyries or eagles seen. Three days later I was watching a small late-born red deer calf, so weak it could hardly follow the others up the slopes, when Atalanta came over the cottage, circled over the west wood, then turned and made a fast glide over us again to the west. I wondered why, as she was so low, she had ignored the new calf carcass I had hauled up to the 400 feet level that morning. But when I went up to look, I saw that she *had* been at it, a great white excreta splash over the limp faded grasses, and a hole six inches across had been torn between its ribs, with some of the lungs and heart eaten. She had been low because she had just come from it!

Years later I was to recognise this hole, between or just behind the rear ribs, as the typical work of an eagle.

With sun beaming on the landscape on February 15, we were tramping east through the lochside woods, ready to search an entire two-and-a-half mile glen for eyries, when I saw two eagles high in the sky. They appeared to be hunting together above an 1,800 foot peak, but these were not 'my' eagles – both had whitish patches under their wings denoting immature birds. I watched the smaller one, which also had a white band in his tail, ride higher and higher in tight circles, then dive on the soaring female. As he passed she turned briefly on her side with talons out, but they didn't touch and nothing was exchanged. He wheeled above her, then zoomed down again. Because of their size they appeared to be moving slowly, but it was almost impossible to follow his flight with the long lens. So I held it steady on the female and pressed the button the moment the male appeared in frame, hoping to get the dive in action.

Then he flew beside her, matching his speed to hers for a few beats, but quite suddenly, as if they had decided it together, he turned abruptly and headed south across the loch, while she made a fast glide to the east, leaning sideways on the wind. Again I had the impression of a silent jet.

I looked at my watch as she headed for a high conical peak, knowing I could find it on the map and that from the inlet where I stood it was probably two and a half miles away. When she vanished over the peak I checked the time again – two minutes and ten seconds.

As we tramped through the river valley and I paused to scan many high rugged grey faces, time and again I thought I had found an eyrie, but each time it proved to be a tangle of old grasses, some old woodrush on a shelf, discoloured striations of rock, or just shadows. Wearily we retraced our steps. Another abortive eight miler day. But when I checked the map I found it was three miles between the far peak and the inlet. That eagle had covered the distance at about 86 mph! Both of them were immatures – who will form a pair and take over a vacant range – and the female was probably no more than three years old, a year too young to breed. The male would not be more than two. I realised that I was probably unfortunately situated on the periphery of the adult pair's home range, so it was unlikely I would find an eyrie near my home. But it was fascinating that a younger pair had moved in to the land east of theirs and were experimenting with their first courtship displays.

A few days later huge Atalanta passed over westwards, again vainly pursued by the two '*krock*'ing ravens but this time she sailed on as if they were beneath contempt before heading south over the loch. I made a quick six-mile trek up and down the steep wooded slopes of the loch to see if she had a tree site – to no avail. After a wash down, I read all the diary evidence I had so far – it was clear that the eagles often flew across the loch to the big mountain to the south, so the loch was not a natural boundary to them.

In early March, I boated to the mountain's shore, tramped over the tussocky bogs with Moobli, wended my way up between the north-east ridges to the 2,000 foot level, then trekked right round the entire mountain, west, south, east and north, descending often to a thousand feet and up again, trying to scan every rockface for likely ledges. They seemed innumerable as we plodded past high black lochans, great jagged granite escarpments that dwarfed us, over countless folds in the terrain, rockfalls still covered in ice and smooth faces that gleamed metallically with mica flicks in the occasional sunlight. Crossing some of the old rocky beds over which burns tinkled was treacherous because of ice in the clefts and the only way to pass over small stretches of frozen snow on slopes of one in two was to slide down them.

As we moved on to the far south slopes, so high now that I could see my loch stretching out like a silver ribbon to the right, matched on the south by the snaky winding of a broad blue sea loch, it felt as if we were on the roof of the world. A heady sight but commonplace to an eagle. I saw two men heading up towards the peak to the east. They carried long sticks but, without collies, were probably not shepherds. Were they egg collectors, I wondered, for about a dozen gangs of egg thieves operate in the Highlands. I dropped low and 'stalked' them, for if they were they might know of a particular eyrie, could lead me to it, and I could photograph them in the act. But when an eagle came drifting from the south and glided over the peak without stopping and the men gave it not a glance, I decided they were not. Scanning one rockface, I found a perfect eyrie site, a few sticks on a ledge below an overhanging rock with two white splashes below. There were no added twigs of rowan, conifer or other trees that denote an eyrie about to be used. Maybe an immature attempt at a nest.

Just before we topped a dark heathery ridge Moobli walked stiff-legged and nose high – something ahead. I peered round a rock – to see three plump ptarmigan, still in white winter plumage, feet as furry as owls', and managed a few close photos before they whirred off with wheezy grunts. When we began the long steep ascent back north east, as if with deliberate malevolence the clouds rolled away and the sun burned as fiercely as on a clear summer's day. I was soon drenched from my own exertions.

As I wearily came out on to the north-east ridges and began the steep winding descent, my knees beginning to hurt after the ten hard miles already covered, I looked to where Wildernesse lay tucked below the far hills, a tiny white dot amid a patch of grey fur of leafless trees, still so far away. Then I saw them through the binoculars – Meleager and Atalanta circling close to the ridge where that morning I'd hauled up a new calf carcass! Naturally, when we arrived home they were nowhere to be seen.

After the next supply trip we bounced back in Force Eight southerly gales, spray everywhere, banging so hard in the troughs that the boat's seat snapped beneath me. But I didn't mind for in my pack was the reply marked OHMS from the Nature Conservancy Council. Indoors, I confidently opened the envelope – and received a shock. They had turned my application down. Although I had sent photos of wild grizzly bears, mountain lions, stags with hinds, a wildcat in the wild and many others, they felt I had not enough nest photography experience to tackle eagles – although I could photograph any such rare bird AWAY from the nest.

At first I felt outrage and drafted a protest letter... I had lived for nearly ten years in primitive conditions in wild places, in Canada and in the Scottish Highlands, purely to study and later to photograph wild nature through the seasons. I had trekked many miles in some of the world's wildest places, had successfully watched bald eagles at the nest from a tree hide. I had trained as a gamekeeper, and my first wildlife book, for which I had received full co-operation from the United States and Canadian governments, was shortly to be published. I was halfway through another book about the rare Scottish wildcats I had bred and was releasing back to the wild, and had written fourteen wildlife articles for *Reader's Digest* – who had the pick of writers – in just three years. I had been taking wildlife photos seriously every week for four years and was not a dilettante who did so on his annual holiday in the fair weather season... and so on.

After dashing this out in hasty shorthand I simmered down. Really, the Nature Conservancy Council was right. I had produced no evidence of nest photography, purely because I had been reluctant to commit my best pictures, which I was saving for my own books, to the post. They didn't care about my harsh life style, or my intentions, nor did successful stalking of wild grizzlies, cougars or stags bear much relation to golden eagle eyries. Instead I wrote a courteous letter of appeal, pointing out the facts, that most of my photos were taken without creatures ever knowing I was there, and offering to bring my best photos, including birds at the nest, to their offices so that I could present my case more fully.

When I boated out to post the letter it seemed ironic that both eagles should be soaring above the carcasses I had so laboriously hauled up for them. I felt almost that by this alone I had earned the right to work with them at the nest! But that seemed to be that for the year.

On March 14 Moobli and I were walking along the 1,500 foot ridges a mile north west of the cottage on a red deer trek when both eagles passed overhead. As I took my camera from the pack Atalanta circled as if taking a second look at us, but by the time I had screwed on the long lens they were both heading over a ridge to the south east. Then Meleager made a steep dive towards where the newest deer calf carcass was lying in a tussocky dell, and both birds vanished. I hastened over, belly-crawled a soggy fifty yards, but when I peered round a rock so as not to show my head on the skyline, the carcass was alone. It had, however, been well torn about by foxes.

As I looked round I noticed a natural recess between some rocks thirty yards to the west, and I had an idea. As I had been refused legality to photograph eagles at an eyrie, why didn't I put up a hide here, overlooking the carcass? I hastened home, cut hazel wands, lashed them at intervals to stout plastic garden fencing, and with wooden pegs, cord and some sacking, carried the contraption up to the recess. In an hour I had fashioned a hide, covered with long heather interlocked in the netting. From only three yards it looked like the overgrown rocks on each side of it, totally invisible, I hoped, to eagles.

Next morning I heaved a new hind carcass halfway up to the dell, then completed the haul in near darkness so as not to be seen by any birds. I hurled the old carcass, now a stinking ragbag of loose bones hanging together by cartilage and skin, to below the trees lining the burn, then cut open the new one on gut and rear haunch to expose flesh, so making it more tempting.

Before dawn I crept up and into the hide, spread plastic over the wet tussocks and with camera set up on tripod, settled down to wait. It was not only hideously uncomfortable – wherever I set my back against the rear rock some small projection seemed to be trying to thrust through to my ribs – but the north-easterly breeze blew stronger and brought with it cold drizzle. Within half an hour my feet were so icy I could hardly feel them and I began to shiver. Although I heard ravens' *'prruk prruk'* calls from high above, observing first as they always do from the air whereas a crow will perch on a rock or in a tree, nothing came down and after three hours I was so cold I had to give up. I would let the carcass 'settle' for a few days and then return. Once foxes started on it at night, the birds should follow in the day. I had almost reached home when I saw Atalanta fly up with ponderous wing beats from below a ridge. I hiked over – she had been feeding from an almost demolished carcass of another deer calf that had died sheltering under a rock. Luckily fox droppings indicated that if these nocturnal prowlers visited it once more, there would be nothing left – hence I had hopes that Atalanta or her mate would be driven over to my bait, if they did not find yet another elsewhere. The trouble was that her heavy flight told me she was full of meat – an eagle can consume 3lbs at one meal – and she wouldn't need to eat again for at least two days.

On my next supply trip a local farmer and my butcher, who had lived all their lives in the area, told me they had heard of an old eyrie near a place called Creag Iolaihre (Eagle Rock) on a certain mountain south of the loch. Neither had ever seen it but believed it was not high up. After boating back in hail showers I searched my maps but no Creag Iolaihre could I find.

On March 18, leaving Moobli morose in the house after exercising him hard with thrown sticks, I hiked up to the hide at dusk. Nothing had been at the new carcass. I meant to sit in the hide all night to have a good chance around dawn and this time I had a sleeping bag, cushion for my backside and a thin one for my back against the rock. No sooner had I wormed into the bag than the zip broke, baring one side completely. It was a bitter cold, neck and back-aching night for I could only doze in snatches, clutching the broken bag together with my hands. The cold crept from my feet to my thighs and then to my numb backside. I felt weak in the stomach and, after one brief doze, felt panic that I might suffer from exposure because there was nothing between me and the wintery elements but the hide's thin vegetation covering.

Several times I thought I saw through the lens shadows moving near the carcass which might have been foxes. Slowly the light began to improve – and I saw with surprise it had been snowing! I was just telling myself I was mad when I spotted something in the sky through the heather above the camera lens. A large bird was circling. There was a pause as I tried to control even my breathing movements, then it looked as if someone had thrown up a huge brown sack from below as it landed on a rock to the left and upwards of the carcass. I peered through a larger gap – it was an eagle, almost certainly Atalanta!

As she clung to the rock, motionless, like some gorgon from a bygone age, I realised that her gnarled yellow feet and dark talons were probably bigger than my own fingers. I daren't try to take a picture for the long lens was trained purely on the carcass and the slightest movement would have been detected by her blood-orange eyes that seemed to glare at the world from beneath imperious jutting eyebrows, and she would be away. Shivering from excite-

44

ment as much as from cold, I peered through the viewer. The sightless upper eye, already opaque, of the dead hind seemed to reflect the dark greyness of the winter sky and her lips drawn back from her teeth in the lower jaw seemed frozen in a permanent smile. I waited several minutes but, when I looked through the vegetation again for the eagle, she had gone. In total silence she had floated away like a ghost. Nor, in the further hour I waited with gritted teeth, did she return. When I left the hide, moving as creakily as a bear from winter hibernation, I found the carcass still untouched. I had seen no foxes in the night either, merely the tricks tiredness plays on the retina of the eyes. When I got home Moobli banged out of the half open door, whining and prancing with delight – unusual for him.

Over the next few days I saw only one of the eagles above the highest north-western ridges and though I frequently scanned the far mountain where the old eyrie was said to be, I saw no sign of any of the birds. When we boated out again on March 26 I found among my mail another OHMS envelope from the Nature Conservancy. I knew what it would say '...we regret we cannot change our decision, etc...' For some hours I left it unopened on my desk while I peeled supper vegetables. Finally, to hell with it, I tore it open.

My whoop of joy woke Moobli on the floor as I read with delight '...after further consideration I am pleased to tell you the Council is prepared to grant you the approval you seek...' and the precious licence was enclosed! My triumphant dance on the grass outside, however, was short lived when I realised what lay ahead. After all the treks I had not yet found a single eyrie. Now not only was it essential to do so, but I also had to find one that I could work from a hide without disturbing the birds. A form was enclosed on which I had to make a full report on their breeding success. Suddenly, the responsibility of the task seemed enormous.

I began to search systematically, marking off on maps the areas I had covered. On one ten-mile trek I found a short sheer cliff with a dark recess behind a leafless dwarf rowan. It looked an ideal eyrie site for my pair. I climbed up to a narrow ledge and was edging along it when the strong east wind blew off my bush hat, then rolled my camera pack towards the edge. As I grabbed for it I was surprised to feel a sudden attack of vertigo. The thirty-foot drop below, on to extremely steep ground, looked terrifying and I froze, fingers clutching the tufts of grass on the ledge as hard as an eagle's clutching its prey. I had suffered vertigo, a dizzying fear of heights, for some years after falling from a clifftop in Canada, where only a shale-covered ledge six feet down had saved my life. But I had thought myself long over it. Now, just as I was to tackle eagles seriously, it was clear that I was not.

I forced myself on until I could look into the recess – no nest – then found I daren't turn round on the ledge. I had to back up on all fours until I could make a shivering descent.

I took a different route home and was carefully scanning a small rounded buttress when I saw something move. A broad eagle tail feather had caught up in a clump of wood-rush on a short ledge and was twisting in the wind. There were also white downy feathers fluttering in the herbage, the sort shed by an eagle preening at a roost site. I looked to the left and there, obscured by heather, was a huge nest of dead twigs as dark as the wet granite of the rockface above it, so even at close quarters it was hard to see. Here was my first eagle eyrie, doubtless one belonging to Atalanta and Meleager.

Without a rope and a companion there was no way I could climb the bulging cliff but by climbing up a hill some forty yards away I could see down into the nest. It was an ideal place for a hide too, among the bracken that would be growing fast again in April. But the nest was empty – no eggs or even leafy sprays which eagles use to decorate and refurbish their eyries. Well, an eagle had certainly been there recently. I decided to leave that whole area alone and to check it again in mid-May when, if eggs were laid late, the chicks would be hatched.

3 · Hide and Seek

As if by some perverse occult communication, Atalanta and Meleager, whom I had been helping to feed so assiduously through the winter, seemed to disappear from the vicinity. Feeling they must have chosen a site at the other end of their range, possibly in the hills across the loch, I boated over on March 21 to try to locate the rumoured eyrie near the Eagle Rock. I zig-zagged along the 1,200-foot level from north to south, then back again at the 800-foot level. Heavy rain made the rocks slippery, but I found an ideal site, a perfect rock recess which was dry and protected on three sides and above by huge rock slabs. Apart from a few sticks on the ground, which could have been blown from an old nest, it was not in use.

Below, silhouetted against the loch, I saw a huge square rock squatting as if set down by a giant hand on a ridge at some 750 feet. I was sure that this was the Creag Iolaihre, that I had found the eyrie, long disused. I continued to search. Suddenly I was looking at a ledge under a huge old birch that had fallen sideways over a rock-face. It was covered with wood-rush and there was a grey mass behind it. I climbed up slippery steep turf, using my fingers for extra support, but to see more of the dark ledge I had to climb an almost sheer rock covered with thick moss. With rain still pouring down I reached its top and found the grey mass to be merely old heather.

As I turned to climb down, a chunk of moss broke off, and I slithered down the rock in a half-sitting position, trying to keep the camera pack from damage and using the elbow pads of my camouflage jacket as impromptu brakes. When I hit the wet steep

47

slope I had to perform some fast knee-jarring jumps to prevent a headlong descent. Moobli pranced down beside me with a big grin, as if I'd been fooling about on purpose.

Not once did I see an eagle and we returned home soaked. Even inside the pack the camera and lenses were wet and had to be carefully dried.

On our next trek, along a wide river valley dwarfed by towering cliffs, my only reward was a few shots of red deer stags, two of which looked lop-sided each having dropped one antler. Another trek to examine more lochside ridges also failed. I had always prided myself that all my wildlife experiences – except one of the grizzly treks in Canada – had been achieved alone; now it was clear that to find the eyries of eagles which covered such a vast terrain I would have to stop being a hermit and work with others who might know of some. The lack of rabbits in my region indicated that I would have to range far afield as they are a favourite prey of breeding eagles in the west. It was also essential to have helpers to walk me into and away from any hide. The eagle, like most birds except the cunning raven which can count to at least four, relaxes and behaves normally once it has seen someone walking away from a nest site.

Right from the start I decided to look for helpers who were also keen on wildlife and who already knew of eyries. Thus I would not have to disclose an eyrie to someone who did not know it, and could also try to channel the finder's interest into legally creative work.

I went first to a local Forestry Commission office and found that the two leading foresters, Norman Mackenzie and David Jamieson, were both keen ornithologists. They gave me permission to work over their 50,000 acres, which included Eagle Rock Mountain and extended some eighteen miles. Three years earlier David had seen an immature eagle with white in its tail dive upon a red deer calf in June. 'As it circled for another go, the calf made a tremendous bleating and its mother dashed over to protect it,' he told me. 'She actually charged at the eagle and reared up, lashing out with her forefeet until it gave up and flew away.'

Two days later I boated out and drove thirty miles to see a retired gamekeeper who, once satisfied that I was not an egg thief, was happy to talk. He had spent his life in the local hills and he too had seen eagles meet in the air, fly along together, then go off fast in different directions, as if having agreed on different errands. Once he had seen an eagle drop behind a rock and emerge with a lamb in its talons. The lamb did not struggle. Then seven ravens chased the eagle, harassing it enough to make it drop its prey, whereupon the gamekeeper picked up the lamb, saw the talon marks but found no blood. He felt the lamb had been dead before the eagle picked it up. He marked on my map an old eyrie situated in an unusual position lower than the surrounding land in a deep river gorge, although he no longer knew if it was used.

In his village I also met by chance the forestry keeper Allan Peters, a young man with a passionate love for the Highlands and who thought out his answers carefully before replying to my questions in a quiet voice.

'I don't want any eagles disturbed right now,' he said frankly. 'When they have eggs they are more liable to desert than when the young are hatched.'

Here was a keeper who *protected* eagles! Once I had explained that I had no wish to set up a hide until mid or late May, when any chicks would be a week or two old, he agreed to help. He knew several likely sites over his huge domain.

Next day, after driving over some high passes on a rough single track road, Allan and I set off up a steep green ride that cut a firebreak through a dark spruce forest. It was steep after the first quarter mile and as we cut into the gloom below the trees we had to cling to trunks or roots to haul our way up over the carpet of brown needles and rocky outcrops. I kept well back from Allan's agile form as the swish back of the sitka spruce branches with their thick sharp needles were dangerous to the face, never mind the eyes. After much hard progress we were almost out of the forest and there ahead, rising almost sheer, was an area of huge rockfalls topped by beetling cliffs. Allan scanned the faces with binoculars.

'Found it by accident two years back,' he said. 'My Labrador bitch smelt the carrion on the nest. When I went to look, I saw just the end of the eagle's tail sticking out. She was probably brooding chicks. It was a cold day, so I left her alone. Haven't been back since. Aye, there it is.'

Halfway up the steep face, in a cleft on a long crag, sat the stick-pile of an eyrie, a good five feet across.

We climbed higher over rocky ridges covered with wet slippery heather above short but sheer drops and reached some broad boulders twenty yards abreast of the eyrie. On these grew really long heather which disguised the dangerous gaps between. From here we examined what I came to call Eyrie 2 with our glasses. There were no signs of occupation, no fresh greenery or feathers, and we'd had no glimpse of an eagle in the sky. As we sat talking in the heather I glanced out over the way we had come. We were over 1,000 feet high and wraiths of mist kept drifting across the dark spruce forest below. It reminded me of the great British Columbian forests. Some of the older trees had fallen and birch, ash and rowan had sprouted in the gaps. I almost expected to see a grizzly emerge in a clearing. Suddenly I felt dizzy and my head reeled with an attack of vertigo, a sense of unreality and a desire to jump off. I shook my head and coughed a few times, which helped me gain some self possession. It would be a hard place in which to spend days in a hide, I thought. I would have to master the vertigo if I was to work eagles in such high places.

Allan, perched imperturbably over a sheer drop, explained that he only became a keeper because of his love of the outdoors. He actually *disliked* killing, and took out only nuisance animals, deer which had broken into young forestry compartments where they topped and strip-barked trees, or the older, sick and runty beasts on annual culls. He was as disappointed as I that Eyrie 2 was not in use. Last year he had found the beginnings of an eyrie, a few sticks on a high ledge near an old nest up a long green glen some miles away, and we agreed to check it in mid-May. We headed back, Allan leaping down small rockfaces with the agility of a chamois. I had a task keeping up with him.

On April 11 Moobli and I made another abortive six-miler, and three days later I drove to see Allan again. He told me he had seen a pair of eagles just the day before, flying near a sheer rockface on the north slopes of Eagle Rock Mountain.

Next morning Moobli and I were climbing it again. After banging my way up a sheer three-sided chimney – feet stuck either side and nowhere to go but down – I emerged on a higher ridge at the 1,200-foot level where Moobli, having taken a longer route, panted up to join me. We clambered over two more bulging outcrops, not sheer but if you fell you'd not be able to stop and jagged rocks would rip out chunks as you went down, and found ourselves overlooking a steep cliff of blackened granite. I scanned it, working upwards over the numerous shelves where heather and wood-rush shivered in the wind, and in a narrow recess saw some thick grey sticks projecting from the edge. Here was Eyrie 3, but again it had not been built up and there were no white splashes or decorative greenery.

I was just thinking there was nowhere to put a hide anyway when a golden eagle sailed over from behind, landed on a boulder below the eyrie and folded its great wings, flicking them as if with irritation to settle them above its thick tail. It was not as big as Atalanta but, merely thirty yards away, the tips of fawn and gold on its dark brown feathers and mantle were burnished to copper in the sunlight. What a sight! It looked steadily at us, then calmly floated off as I woke from my trance, grabbed the camera from my pack and managed two shots as it glided in circles higher and higher overhead. Perhaps in the warm air this eagle had taken a break from incubating eggs. I would check again in May.

When I returned in early May from a brief business trip, a farmer friend who lived twenty miles away told me his teenage daughter Lauren had accidentally found an eyrie with two eggs while hiking in the hills. I rang Lauren who agreed to show me the eyrie on Saturday. Then I arranged to hike out with Allan to the eyries in the long green glen on the Sunday.

Despite the mist and drizzle showers when I reached Lauren's farmhouse, she was ready to go. Chestnut haired, a riding instructress, she said 'I'm not very good on the Hill,' and promptly set off at a fast clip in a pair of aged wellies that gave the lie to her last remark. Here the land was more open than mine, broad folding hills with views of the sea and only an occasional crag in the distance. After a mile I asked her where exactly the eyrie was.

'Oh, we can't see it yet. It's away over the next range!'

As we ploughed through bogs decorated with white plumes of cotton grass, and leaped to the firmer spurs of peat hags, the drizzle was replaced by relentless heavy rain, but having got so far we decided to keep going. Over the ridge Lauren pointed to a long cliff just below a mountain peak two miles ahead. Even at that distance I could make out the V-shaped fissure and the eyrie ledge near the top, a good 1,300 feet high.

We plugged upwards. To avoid putting the sitting eagle off the nest, we struck off to the right to climb through loose boulders out of her sight. After clambering up steep ledges to the top of the cliff, we gingerly worked our way along until we estimated we were above the eyrie fissure. Quaking with fear, I edged towards the eighty-foot drop. With one foot braced well back, slowly I poked my bush-hatted head over.

There, a mere twenty feet down on a seven-foot broad ledge covered in wood-rush with almost no sticks to form a nest, sat the mother eagle. She looked as dark and vast as Atalanta, though younger, the thick rounded 'shoulders' of her wings held slightly out as if to shelter much of the ledge from rain, and occasionally she shook the raindrops from her beak. As I watched, knee trembling, my vertigo almost forgotten at such a sight, she stood up and thrust her beak between her legs. I saw her hook one of her eggs into a different position.

I withdrew slowly. As we tiptoed away we saw another eagle, the smaller male, soaring high above. He had something in his talons. Sure that he was bringing food to his mate, we saw as we reached the side of the cliff the female winging out over the void. She wheeled to the left, must have seen us but gave no sign, and disappeared round a ridge, followed by the male in a long downwards glide. Despite the rain, it wasn't cold, and it seemed as if she had gone to meet him, perhaps to take the food from him. Certainly we had not dislodged her. The clifftop heather was too short to disguise a hide, and when I tried a quick scramble up a steep heathered gully to look for a suitable ledge, the miniature waterfalls caused by the rain poured inside my rain trousers as I stretched for handholds. I gave up then, knowing I'd have to return on a sunny day when the chicks were hatched. It was clearly another tough place to work. As we hurried away we saw the mother sail back to the eyrie, landing on it delicately after an easy upwards swoop.

I was wearing new rubber boots and after my trip found to my chagrin that the skin on my heels had softened and was blistering. We were both soaked to the skin, rain suits ineffective against such a deluge, long before we reached the farmhouse. That night I camped out in a wood halfway to Allan's, cursing myself for not bringing spare dry clothing, having believed the weather would improve.

Next morning, May 16, I put on the damp clothes again, gave Moobli a run, then drove to Allan's. The downpour had not ceased all night and was now even worse. He was putting on freshly oiled boots that had an odd curve to them when I arrived. Was I game? Yes, I said, never feeling less game in my life. Right then. I shoved some paper over my heel blisters and we drove a long way to the long green glen. Allan pointed to some huge forbidding cliffs where the eyries were, away in the distance. We plunged down through steep spruce forest, over fences and burns, zig-zagging low by a raging river so as to keep out of sight of any sitting eagle. Despite Allan's bouncy deer-like pace, we kept an eye on the sky all the time, and not once in the long walk did we see an eagle.

When we reached a ridge half a mile from the cliffs, we scanned them with our glasses. The eyrie ledge, over 1,500 feet up, was a good twenty feet long and deeply cut into the rock. One nest sat on the right while the other, looking like a mere blackened tangle of old vegetation, was set at the base of a rowan tree at the other end of the ledge. Neither of us could make out the form of a sitting eagle.

We stumped steadily upwards, my raw blisters giving me hell in the wet new boots, climbed some slippery outcrops which I would not have tackled alone, then began the almost sheer ascent of little turfed ridges to the side of the dark cliffs. Allan went higher to the last grassy spur where I joined him, quaking inwardly. One wrong step here and one would be away to a bouncing, scraping death.

There were two eggs in the far nest, looking through our glasses from where we stood forty yards away almost as white as giant billiard balls. But the whole place had a deserted air, and we had still not seen an eagle. Allan went nearer, carefully placing one boot after another along a three-inch wide ledge above a 200-foot sheer drop on to boulders. I could not follow him. When he came back he said there were a few small white feathers in the other nest. Probably roosting feathers of the male, I said.

'I don't like it at all,' said Allan.

'Nor do I,' I said. 'The eggs should be hatched by now. Maybe they've deserted already for some reason. If not, we'd better get out of here, let her come back. She may just be up there in the low clouds.'

'Aye,' said Allan. 'You could be right.' I looked around – the only place for a hide would be on a small ledge with heather and stunted rowans, a dangerous place to spend any time.

I turned round to an extraordinary sight. Never had I seen a man go down so steep a slope so fast before. Allan sort of trundled down with short rapid steps as if his feet had suddenly grown wheels. I struggled to catch up. When we came to the river he chose to cross lower down, where there were more of the foaming waters, and leaped in his hob-nailed high-rake hill boots from rock to rock without a slip. I, with rubber boots, slipped twice on the wet surfaces but made it across with only one bootful. As if an entire ducking would have mattered – the rain had not let up for an instant. I had been soaked to the skin yesterday and was wetter than a trout now.

'A wild place,' Allan said with a grin.

'Not as wild as grizzly country in Canada,' I said, trying to salve some of my trekking dignity before this fine keeper fifteen years my junior. By the time we got back to the Land Rover my blisters were bleeding and the wet clothes had caused raw sores on my legs. As we drove home we both admitted we would not have done the trek alone on such a day. We talked for a long while, finding much in common. I said that if Eyrie 6 was not deserted and the eggs hatched, it looked my best bet. He said to let him know.

Back in the pinewood, I had to bail out the rain from the half-submerged boat before setting off. Now southerly gales were blasting the loch, making the six-mile journey home hazardous. I reached my bay in twilight with waves pounding on the shore. Slow with fatigue, I failed to swing the bow round far enough as I leaped on to the bank. Waves smashed in over the beam and filled the boat. It took me two hours of bailing and fighting with wooden levers, each end a few inches at a time, to haul the boat out of the water.

I staggered in, with supper for myself and Moobli still to make, after the wettest two days I had ever spent out in the Highlands. I swore that if I could just get *two* good pictures of eagles I'd give them up!

Two days later I was gardening, soft cuckoo calls echoing from the hills and Moobli waiting to chase the odd stone I might throw out, when I heard some odd chuckling calls. High above, eight hooded crows were heading over the loch in the direction of Eyries 6 and 7 in the far hills. It was unusual to see such a flock in the breeding season. Had one located deserted eagle eggs and teamed up with cronies to tackle the eyrie?

The tiring treks continued. When I hiked to check Eyrie 1, it was empty; even the feather had blown away. And the two ravens flew overhead, calling soft '*glop*'s as if laughing. On my 48th birthday I hiked with Moobli over the 1,600-foot hills down to the long river valley, then up to 1,800 feet to check the northern slopes of the highest mountain in the area. There I spied again the two immature eagles I had seen in February airily wheeling round one another. I checked some faces and realised that even if I found an occupied eyrie I was six hard foot miles from home and it would be impossible to find a helper to put me into a hide. My precarious finances made the employment of anyone impossible. Now my isolation, so advantageous for studying most wildlife, was a handicap when it came to eagles. There was a slight, if sad, bonus to the trek. Moobli discovered the decaying body of a stag that had died while sheltering between rocks. I wrapped the smelly head in a plastic bag and packed it home to add to my wildlife collection.

On May 29 I wended my way to Eagle Rock Mountain with Moobli and found Eyrie 3 also unoccupied. As I rested in a heathery alcove I saw an eagle heading north, a good 1,000 feet above the near 3,000-foot peak, in the fast jet glide. With awe I watched it leaning sideways against the north-west wind and travelling at fantastic speed until it vanished over the peak of the highest mountain northwards. I checked my watch. It had covered just under eight miles in four-and-a-half minutes which, if my calculations were correct, meant it had been moving at over 110 mph! And all without a single beat of its wings. This ability is unique among British birds – to use its great broad wings as a yacht uses sails, to tack partly against the wind but with no hull to drag through heavy water. Employing gravity's pull and countless minute adjustments of feathers, the eagle can outrun the wind itself.

The fact that the eagle had apparently come a fair way before reaching the first peak, and showed no signs of stopping over the second, seemed to bend the 17,000 acres maximum territory theory. But the flight had an air of serious intent, as if the bird had been bent on some specific mission.

A phenomenon with golden eagles is that, if a mate perishes during the breeding season, the survivor can often find a replacement, sometimes within days. It has been shown (by the recovery of birds ringed in the nest) that young eagles usually disperse from the home range in which they were born from fifteen to sixty miles away. These immatures and unmated adults take up fringe areas on the edges of occupied ranges, forming a floating pool of seventy to eighty spare eagles in any year. They also tend to lower ground, so young eagles reared on eastern deer forests will gravitate to the grouse moors in winter, for instance, where they are more often shot, trapped or poisoned. The theory is that a bereaved bird may even leave chicks on a warm day, then set off at speed to locate a new mate from the fringe areas to help feed them. Such flight powers and extraordinary long distance eyesight certainly make the theory feasible.

Determined to give Eagle Rock Mountain another good going over, I hiked a few days later right up to the peak and down the far side, traversing between the 800- and 2,000-foot levels of the whole southern face, then plunged into the upper gorge of the burn where the retired keeper had said there was an old eyrie. Scrambling up and down, the sky often blotted out by the foliage of trees that grew from ledges above, I finally found it, or what remained of it – a perfect long ledge, but all that was on it now was a mound of reddish twiggy dust of a nest that had been washed, blown or deliberately pulled out. Well, it might be rebuilt another year.

Even the finding of some nodding water avens, a patch of un-common yellow globe flowers and some starry saxifrages failed to relieve my gloom as we set off for home in the boat after eleven more tough miles. Then the engine conked out and I had to row the last four miles.

On June 8 I decided to have one last try on the mountain. This time we headed down even steeper gorges of a burn on the south side – all we found was a relatively new rockfall under which some thick dead sticks lay half buried, and sadly I noted the demise of Eyrie 9. As I stood there a tiny wren zipped from the cliff foliage just above my head and I found its domed nest where it had been sitting on five eggs. Hell. I come for the mighty eagle only to find the titchy wren!

My best hope now seemed to be Eyrie 4, high in the V-shaped cliff fissure so many miles away, where Lauren and I had found the hen eagle sitting on two eggs. I boated out on June 16 and made the long hike up carrying hide materials. There was no eagle anywhere in the sky. As I edged my head carefully over the eighty-foot cliff, hoping to see the mother brooding, or even the chicks on their own, I was astonished to find the nest empty. The eggs had apparently been stolen. I was even more depressed when, on going below, I found I *could* climb the now-dry gully and that there was a heathered ledge on which I could have built a hide and had a fine safe view of the eyrie. Well, that was that.

As I climbed back down my footing gave way at the bottom and I fell backwards, executing an inefficient Judo breakfall on the hard ground. The binoculars swung round my neck and whacked into a rock, smashing the bridge metal. At least the lenses remained intact – I would just saw them in half and have two monoculars, lighter to carry anyway. As I boated home in misty drizzle I felt that defeat was staring me in the face. My only hope now was Eyrie 6, high on the forbidding cliff in the long glen.

For the next two days I fashioned what I felt was the perfect hide, rejecting the idea of a traditional canvas hide that needed several visits just to install it, each one frightening to the birds. Mentally I put myself in the place of the eagle and worked from there, drawing on Scout experience, infantry camouflage training in the Coldstream Guards, and all the hides I had made for watching the bald eagles in Canada. Using stout green plastic garden netting and hazel wands, I ended up with a semi-rigid green 'tunnel' which could be stuffed with the exact herbage of the area out of sight of the eagles' eyrie. Then it could be towed swiftly to the site and erected in minutes. It could not scare the birds as they would not even notice it. This hide could be adapted to fit any fold in the ground, gap between rocks or odd-shaped ledge. Above all, it would be undetectable to any passing humans unless they actually trod on it, and so could not alert anyone to the existence of an eyrie.

My belief that the hide was light enough to be carried miles on my back was hastily revised on June 20 when I set out on the long uphill slog to Eyrie 6. I was also carrying camouflage netting, hazel wands, groundsheet, lunchpiece, rain suit, sacking, knife, tripod and camera and lenses. At least the extra weight stabilised me, as a long pole does a tight rope walker, as I balanced over the rocks in the rain-swollen river. Keeping low by its banks so the ridge below the eyries obscured my approach, checking through my 'fieldglass' that there were no eagles in the sky, I climbed steeper land to a knoll 300 yards from the cliff, then scanned the ledge. There was no sign of life. Sweating heavily, I stumped with the hide up the almost sheer ground to the final ledge Allan and I had reached before. Both eggs were still in Eyrie 6 but one seemed to have a hole in one end, like a rectangular bite. The whole place again had that mournful deserted air about it.

I took two shots of the lonely nest, ironically finding I could now look down on the river winding over a thousand feet below without as much fear as before. A slight slip on the way down made me grab a sharp rock and I badly gashed my middle finger. I continued down with creaking knees, mind racing with possibilities. I was sure the eagles had left the eyrie before we found it in mid-May. Had the female been shot? The hole in one egg – had it been clipped by a rifle bullet? Perhaps the eggs had been addled and the female, feeling no chick movements, had realised the fact. Perhaps the crows I'd seen, or others, had pecked the egg.

I tramped down the river with Moobli and drove to report the facts to Allan. On the way home I rang Lauren, who had wanted to be my helper at Eyrie 4, and told her of the latest setback. To my surprise, she said that a friend of her family, Greg Hunter, keeper of a large estate a long way from my home, had accidentally found an occupied eyrie on his land. Some folk have all the luck, I thought. As I boated home with Moobli lying in the prow, almost as tired as myself, I felt finally defeated.

Three days later I made what I felt would be the last eagle trek – a nine-miler – to scan the far ridges of Guardian Mountain, but found no eyries. As I headed back along the peaks I found myself looking over a sheer drop of some 1,200 feet into a deep and dramatic glen. But when I saw the great range of mountains on its far side I felt too tired to make the steep descent, check the score of likely cliffs and repeat it all again to get home. I had simply run out of steam. As I turned back I saw Atalanta high in the sky. She was hovering against the strong south-west breeze, not beating her wings like a huge kestrel, just hanging in the wind, totally still. She appeared to have something in her talons. As I took a photo it looked like half a rabbit and I saw her move her feet upwards, her head down, and tear off a morsel to swallow. She was hovering and feeding in mid-air! I didn't know an eagle could hover, never mind feed while doing it.

On a supply trip on June 26 I made an abrupt decision. After getting Greg Hunter's address from Lauren, I drove the many miles to his home. I found him walking off the hills with a huge net which he had been using to catch and tag young deer calves for his annual estate survey. A tall, broad, dark bearded man of twenty-eight, he was not only the estate's keeper and stalker but a knowledgeable naturalist. He too had taken up photography, intending to try for a licence to work an eyrie next year. He seemed impressed with my ideas for a hide, invited me in for a meal and agreed that, provided the eyrie was kept secret and his employers approved, he would help me work it. We arranged to meet again next day. As I boated home I realised that, if we set up the hide, each return visit to it would involve thirteen miles in the boat, a sixty-five mile drive and a five mile hike.

Next day, after banging out against gales, I met Greg again and located the head executive of the estate, who kindly gave us permission. Soon we were hiking out to Eyrie 10. Here the land was lower than mine, rolling hills only half as high, and revealing frequent glimpses of the Atlantic. Here and there jutted grey granite crags rounded by centuries of wind and rain. As we walked with the hide gear, Moobli immediately pally with Greg's German pointer bitch, he told me an odd story. One May day he had been walking a quarter mile from the eyrie when he had seen something white fall from it. Hurrying over, he found it was one of the two chicks, still in the white downy stage, and still alive. He had managed to climb up and put it back with its nest mate, but on a subsequent visit he had found it dead in the nest.

Although two eaglets may hatch out it is uncommon for eagles to rear more than one chick to flying stage. Stories abound in eagle literature of how the stronger chick bullies the weaker, or beats it constantly in the competition for food, and all too frequently the frailer chick dies.

When we reached the eyrie, high on one of the rounded rockfaces, I was surprised to see it had no northerly aspect but faced south west. There was no overhanging rock, the ledge was open to the skies and the nest merely a level layer of old sticks and heather sprigs less than a foot thick. We climbed a steep knoll from which we could look into the nest. At first it appeared to be empty, but Greg, looking through his glasses, announced: 'It's there.' Just then I saw the yellow cere of its large beak as it turned its head. I looked through my glass – the chick was well fledged, about seven-and-a-half weeks old, still in the 'chocolate and cream' stage, its dark brown wings, back and white-tipped tail feathers contrasting beautifully with the creamy white down left on its chest, belly and head. It was crouching low in a far corner like a giant ptarmigan, hiding from the sound of our voices. There was a dead hooded crow in the nest. One of these cunning Highland brigands had not been cunning enough.

To our delight, we found we could build a lying-down hide in the grass of the knoll below a natural overhang which gave some shelter and still see into the nest. Although we could not see either parent in the sky, we made the hide up with threaded grasses and heather fifty yards behind the eyrie rock, then set it in place in minutes. It was undistinguishable from the surrounding terrain at five yards. Perfect place, perfect hide, and when I lay in it I only had to raise my head a few inches to the left and through the telephoto lens I had a clear view of the chick and eyrie some thirty-five yards away. We decided to leave the area for a few days to let the eagles become used to the hide, though I doubted they would even notice it.

On July 1 I boated out under a blazing blue sky and Greg walked me into the hide. Once again we saw no eagles in the sky and could not see the crouching chick. An inexperienced person walking below would not have known there was an eyrie there, never mind a large eaglet. Now there was a new dead hoody in the nest, half plucked by a parent and its side gashed open so the eaglet could feed from it easily. Hooded crows are disliked by some sheep farmers for such alleged crimes as ganging up on sickly lambs or attacking eyes and tongues of ewes which have rolled helplessly on to their backs in a crevice while giving birth. It seemed that this eagle pair were, from their point of view, performing a service in keeping local hoody numbers down. I crawled into the hide and, as Greg walked away, settled down to watch.

The eaglet, head poked just above the nest rim, watched him go and, when satisfied there was no more danger, relaxed. Now it began to behave like a clown. It lay on its side stretching out its disproportionately huge yellow feet and every few minutes flirted out its long right wing across the nest, extended its right foot to full length and opened and closed its yellow toes and dark talons. Then it folded its wing back again with a great heave as if it had grown too fast and was still a little too heavy to move easily. It had a brief rest then rolled over to lie on its back, with neck and head propped up against the rear rock, its beak open and its feet sticking straight up into the air. It looked like a great cockatoo in an uncomfortable deck chair. Really and unconsciously funny.

It kept its beak open most of the time, breathing fast to cool itself, the way a dog does in the afternoon heat. Then it took a long look at the hoody, rolled over and stood up. It put one big foot on each end of the crow, bent its neck and, with straining upward heaves, ripped bits of meat off and swallowed them. Twice it accidentally pulled the body free of its talons and stumbled backwards with wing flaps. But it just patiently lifted its great feet again, clamped them back on the crow and tore off more chunks. After a few minutes it had had its fill, flopped down, white breast first, laid its neck and head flat along the nest sticks as if dead, and had a snooze.

I had been watching for an hour and a half when it woke up and stared up into the sky, turning its head from one side to the other, showing excitement. I judged a parent was flying over the eyrie but probably far up. The eaglet stood up, opened its wings slightly and started giving harsh but oddly weak squeaky calls, '*Keyow, keyow, keyow*', and glaring intently into the distance. I realised the eagle was coming in.

4 · *Ultimate Reality*

Suddenly my lens was filled with the fantastic vision of dark wings as the eagle floated in like a jet honing on to a runway, heat waves shimmering all around it and half a rabbit gripped in the great yellow talons of one foot. Landing with astonishing lightness for so large a bird, it folded the long pinions over its broad tail then stood with a proud parental air as the eaglet immediately gripped the rabbit, mantled its wings forward in a protective tent, and began to feed. I had taken a shot of the eagle coming in and now I got another as it looked round the eyrie – oh, the imperious glare of those blood-orange eyes. Then, without warning, it turned and silently drifted away, and I was left staring, as if at a great masterpiece from which the main character had suddenly been removed.

I thought it would have stayed longer, or fed the chick, and knew I would need to be faster on the button in future. Annoyingly, the eaglet turned its back on me and I had to wait a long time before I could get good side shots of it tearing meat. After feeding for ten minutes, gulping fur and bones too, the eaglet staggered to the left and promptly disappeared behind a rockfold I had not known was there. All I could see then was the tip of its dark hooked beak resting on the nest sticks.

It seemed only minutes before the eaglet squeaked again, and my eye shot to the viewer. A bigger eagle landed with a folding of great wing feathers and began to pace up and down the eyrie like an admiral pacing the quarter deck, looking down at the nest. *This* was clearly the mother and the first one had been the smaller male

61

bringing food. She took ponderous but careful steps, looked at the rabbit and with complete ease, unlike the awkward tuggings of the youngster, tweaked off two pieces and swallowed them. The eaglet was still squeaking away but had made no move to emerge from the rockfold so the mother bird walked across the nest, twisted her head to the right and presented a morsel to the chick. It was a small tender piece but I couldn't see the actual transfer because of the rock. Quiet curses!

For me those moments were like living in a magic unreal paradise. Lying there, the whole world dark except for that living colour through the lens, like looking into a giant and unique television set, I felt privileged, honoured, to be the close unsuspected observer of such magnificent creatures. Unreal? No, this was total, ultimate reality.

Now she tramped back, picked off another juicy bit and, with deliberate steps and intent look, went to present it to the eaglet with great tenderness. I quivered as I took shot after shot – the sunlight playing on her light golden mantle, the powerful folded wings, the red-brown sheen of her feathers, all interlacing, stroking each other, undamaged, and the golden ruddy glare of her piercing eyes. One more piece for herself, then she faced the wind, opened her wings and floated away. She didn't actually jump into the air, just let the breeze take her, the incredible instinctive flight mechanisms playing through all the great feathers, adjusting so quickly and naturally that she was up and moving forwards with no effort at all.

Only then did I relax, feel my heart pounding and find I was breathless from hardly having dared to breathe from the moment she had landed. July 1 – a day never to forget. Then I remembered – it was on July 1 exactly ten years ago to the very day that I had first left the cities to start my wilderness life in Canada. What coincidence, what an extraordinary anniversary. Now, too, all the work to find eagles, the miles of weary foot-slogging over the mountains, finding eyries – inaccessible, deserted, eggs stolen – seemed to have been more than worthwhile.

I seemed only to have been watching half an hour more when I heard the clump of boots and Greg's voice.

'How did ye get on?'

I scrambled out, covered in dust and heather twigs, and told him. I had been in the hide for seven hours. We tramped back to the Land Rover, my legs stiff from being so long immobile, and let out poor old Moobli who had been patiently dozing on the bed in the rear.

Glad to stretch his legs, he cheerfully chased after us as we bounced over bumpy turf back to the little road. After a celebratory dram and supper at Greg's cottage, I drove the long miles, boated home and we arrived at Wildernesse in the near dark of 11.30 p.m. – to find all my four wildcat kittens could now walk well. What an incredible day!

I will now record that season's treks and visits to the far hide in diary form:

July 3. Sunny, but high hazy cloud dulled the landscape from 1.30 p.m. Hide dark and damp and under the huge rock overhang it felt claustrophobic. A rock fall here and nothing would be found of you. The eaglet, less afraid, sat up in the nest watching us refresh the hide vegetation. No action until 6 p.m. when the male eagle came in with another hooded crow. The hungry eaglet almost snatched it from him. The male flew away at once but the chick fed itself easily. More brown feathers were now sprouting through the white down of its neck. Eight hours in the hide.

July 4. By now Moobli was used to Greg, so instead of stoically waiting in the truck he walked in with us and out with Greg. Oddly, on our approach, both eagles flew up from the fields ahead of us, having been obscured by long grasses. Two voles on the eyrie ledge indicated they can thus hunt voles on foot like cats, a surprising discovery. The eyrie had also been refreshed with sprigs of strongly scented bog myrtle. But for the belief that eagles have no sense of smell, one could almost say that they were deodorising the nest of its carrion odours. After half an hour the eaglet began to squeak and tug the nest sticks with his beak, then mother eagle came in with the front half of a rabbit, dropped it and floated away. The chick no longer needed her feeding.

The eaglet grabbed the rabbit with its left foot, striking it hard as if the still-open eyes stimulated it to 'kill' with the talons, then tugged it awkwardly round the nest, hobbling, with many wing flaps. After tugging off furry scraps for a quarter of an hour, the eaglet backed to the edge of the nest, tilted its tail up, with its head almost touching the sticks, and squirted out white excreta with great force – a device to keep the eyrie relatively clean. He – we were reasonably sure from its chunky shape it was a male – dozed for forty minutes, then stood up and began to preen. He flirted his dark white-banded tail feathers out in a turkey-like fan and smoothed each feather over its whole length through his large hooked beak with surprisingly delicate movements. Then he turned his head sideways with his eyes shut, large bulbous blue-white eyelid showing clearly, and scratched it with his right foot like a dog. After that he sat down on tail and hocks, with his big yellow feet sticking out in front. At 6.30 p.m. he stood on the rabbit's chest and tugged flesh from its lips and nose, so it appeared through the lens as if the rabbit was attacking him. At 7.35 p.m. he roused from a doze to give a few breathy squeaks. His mother flew in, looked round the nest, tweaked off a piece of rabbit, swallowed it, glared out to the south and took off. It seemed as if she had become hungry while hunting and returned to see if the eaglet had left anything.

Ten minutes later I heard loud panting and Moobli was outside the hide. Then Greg and a friend arrived to walk me out. They said Moobli had found my old scent a mile away, had galloped off fast, and the female eagle, which they had seen land on the eyrie, had swooped low over the dog, scaring him so much that he had run back to them! Then he had again run down the scent to me. It was interesting that an eagle would swoop down and menace a huge Alsatian. I had been in the hide for eight and a half hours.

July 8. There was an uneaten hooded crow in the eyrie. With Greg's previous observations, this meant the eagles had so far accounted for at least seven hoodies as part of their youngster's diet. Neither eagle came in during my seven hours.

July 9. Seeing a distant eagle, again flying to Eagle Rock Mountain, I trekked it at a lower level and found Eyrie 11. It was above a deep corrie but in a small rockface, a square ledge merely fourteen feet from the ground. The nest appeared to have been torn out, a few thick sticks still on the ledge but many more below, with great wood-rush tufts among them. Grass growing through some tufts indicated the nest had probably been destroyed in March; certainly there was no excreta of young below the ledge. I was disappointed at the tragic find, and the mentality that may have caused it.

July 10. Cloudy sunlight was replaced by dark menacing clouds and south-west gales as we reached the hide. The eaglet was making loud '*kyow*' calls as we arrived, but I saw that a small red deer foreleg had been brought in, probably found as carrion. A small lamb with redly scoured backside sat perched a mere thirty yards above the eyrie, with no ewe in sight. After two hours the eaglet, now almost fully fledged with only small areas of white on chest and rear neck, walked to the deer leg. He stood on one end firmly, so tipping up the other, and ripped off meat slivers with his beak. Then he tried to swallow the whole shin bone, black hooves and all, but it was too

An eight-week-old eaglet feeding from a hooded crow.

The mother sails in with half a rabbit.

She floats away with hardly a wingbeat.

The chick fans its tail like a turkey when preening its feathers.

long and he brought it up again. His crop was almost full anyway, bulging like a giant halved tennis ball. He stood with legs apart and preened his tarsal feathers, quibbling his beak all the way down to his feet with an oddly intent narcissistic air. Then he made a 'turkey tail' again, nibbled at the feather bases, scattering down and specks of waxy sheath, and hauled each feather through his beak, cleaning and smoothing them.

By 4 p.m. heavy rain was falling. The gales increased and whistled through the hide, almost freezing my hands and legs, and water dripped from the rocky overhang, soaking my camouflage jacket. My thighs developed cramps and I had fits of shivering – in July! Finally, despite its long hood, the lens was covered in fine spray which coagulated into large drops and photography became impossible. By this time, the eaglet being about nine weeks old and ready to fly in another week or so, the adults were neither brooding nor feeding it beak to beak and, except to drop in food, spent little time on the eyrie. After seven-and-a-half hours without seeing either adult, Greg came to walk me out. As we left, not only was the scoury lamb still sitting above the eyrie but I discovered another lamb had been lying some forty feet above my head, its ewe fifty yards further away.

Eagles are often accused by sheep farmers of taking lambs, though the more intelligent know by far the larger proportion of lambs seen at eyries are found dead, as carrion. It was interesting that on this estate, where a flock of 3,000 sheep was kept, not one lamb had been brought into Eyrie 10, either killed or found dead, in the two weeks of our intensive observations, nor in the earlier period when Greg had kept an eye on the eyrie for just this purpose. Doubtless the fact that it was a well run estate, employing four full time shepherds so that the flocks were better looked after and few lambs died, had a great deal to do with it. If ever an eagle had an easy live lamb target it was the sick one perched above its own eyrie for over seven hours, yet it remained untouched.

I was now busy catching up with my writing and trying to rear the runt of the wildcat litter called Liane, who I felt would not otherwise survive. Thus the eagle hide was not used again and we removed it, together with all traces of where it had been. The eaglet flew successfully, was seen near the eyrie on July 23 and again, this time with his mother, on August 15. He landed near her on a rock and, although as big as an adult himself, was still squeaking in that silly little voice at her for food.

Apart from a final check of Eyrie 6 in the long green glen on July 18, that first active 'eagle season' ended. The two deserted eggs were still on my mind as my photos showed that what I believed to be a pecked hole in one of them was in fact an image caused by a large twig that had somehow been elevated across the egg's end. I drove down and hiked all the way up to the dark cliff again. Both eggs were still there. It seemed that crows, at least, probably leave eagle eggs severely alone. I was almost certain now that the eggs had been addled and the eagles had given up brooding before we first got there in mid-May.

When my photos had been developed I saw an interesting fact on the one of the male eagle shimmering in out of the sky. There were two primary feathers missing from each wing, so the summer moult had begun at about that time – July 1. As eagles have to feed young in the nest from nine to eleven weeks – depending on hunting success and prey food value – they possibly retain their flight feathers, needed for efficient hunting, longer than most birds and so moult later. By that date the eaglet has only two or three weeks more to spend in the eyrie, and the eagles can afford to start losing a feather or two as they will soon have to catch less food. But they also need to have their full 'sail' area back before winter when hunting is rather harder. I wondered if, to ease flight a little during the moult, they lost feathers evenly from each wing. This theory seemed to be upset when on October 1 I saw Atalanta heading west above the cottage, and that she had lost two primaries from the right wing but only one from the left. This certainly had no effect on her flight.

I wondered if she and Meleager had also bred successfully. Although I was now out on stag treks and saw no more eagles, towards the end of the month I had an answer. I was in the garden, enlarging tree cages, when I heard the raucous '*Kaar*'s of crows – two eagles were swooping low over the east wood, vainly pursued by a pair of hoodies. Closer and closer they came, immense against the strange clear blue of the October sky, and as they passed merely yards above I saw that the front one was Meleager and the rear bird had the white band in the tail and light underwing patches that denote an eaglet. Half a minute later a third eagle came over too – huge Atalanta. She turned and headed south east while Meleager and the youngster carried on to the south west. At this evidence that 'my' pair had indeed bred successfully (they could not be the ones I'd photographed so many miles away) I felt cheated. After helping feed them in the winters and all the weary treks, I had not yet found their working eyrie. At dusk I saw them again, all three circling over the northern ridges, now heading east.

I now knew that securing good photographs of eagles was not the whole point. Far harder and better work lay ahead. Up to date conservation measures need precise information on golden eagles in the Highlands: their diets, nesting, breeding and hunting success, their relationship to stock farming (how many lambs *do* they kill?), plus all factors that affect their lives. Brown and Watson concluded they were in slow decline in 1963, and Brown felt they still were in 1976, due largely to human persecution. My other main aim was to help spread the message of eagle conservation – that with their top-of-the-food-web critical needs, eagles are a key indicator of the welfare of all the 'lesser' wildlife on their territory – in my books, articles and future talks. To do this, I needed to know how many eagles were successful, and why, in a larger area over several years.

When I sent my photography report to the Nature Conservancy Council I expressed these ideas and asked, if they felt the arduous work useful, to let me have not only a photographic but also a special examination licence, which would allow me to find and monitor all the eagle sites in my region. They replied that I should discuss my proposals with Chief Warden Richard Balharry, one of their eagle experts and then approach them again. Unknown to me Geoffrey Kinns, who had often stressed Balharry's excellence as a naturalist, had also said some complimentary things to him about me, so I was surprised when I rang Balharry to hear him say he would be delighted to have my ideas. I explained my *modus operandi* briefly; we agreed that the work was only viable if the eagles were not disturbed, their eyries kept secret, and hides were undetectable to humans. We arranged to meet in the New Year.

Although now busy on a book about my wildcats, I found time for autumn stag treks. On November 4 I was up high with Moobli when we again saw Atalanta, Meleager and their eaglet circling together over the ridges. But it was ten days later that I had the most extraordinary eagle sighting so far.

I was scanning the high northern crests for the red deer which would soon be sheltering in our woods at night and had just located a single hind and her calf on a turfy 'eyebrow' of a plateau at some 800 feet. Suddenly one of the eagles soared over the ridge, wheeled round twice, then with wings upswept and its pinion feathers spread wide, it dived down towards the big calf. I saw white in its tail – it was the eaglet. Jerkily, like a high-stepping pony in a trotting race, the mother hind ran to protect her youngster.

The eaglet fastened its talons into the upper rear of the calf's back and was hauled along flapping as the calf bucked about trying to shake it off. The hind ran close, rearing up and striking with hard downward blows of her forefeet, her long ears held back like those of a cat. When the calf fell over to the right, I thought the eaglet would be crushed like a steeplechase rider under a falling horse, but it let go and hopped ungainly to one side with its long wings beating and took off to the west. As it flew it flicked its right wing down several times, like a giant tern shaking water from its plumage, and a feather fluttered loose. It must have hurt the wing and was lucky not to have had it broken. What an astonishing spectacle.

If I was sorry to have had the fieldglass in my hands instead of my camera, I was even sorrier for the calf that had probably been gashed, and also for the eaglet, for it must have been extremely hungry to tackle a calf weighing about 50lb. Adult eagles are believed to be capable of killing 35lb calves, especially when weak in winter or bogged down in snow, though of course they cannot carry them away. Here was proof that inexperienced young eagles can make dangerous mistakes. I climbed to the small plateau, expecting to find the calf off its feet, but both deer had gone. No sooner had I got halfway back down, however, than the eaglet came circling back, as if ready to have another go, before it vanished beyond the ridges.

This is the most dangerous time in a flying eaglet's life for after spending about three months learning to hunt with its parents (the period can vary) it is gradually left more and more to its own devices. By winter, when small prey spend more time in shelter and the young birds and animals of summer are fully grown, the eaglet that has not learnt to hunt well can die of starvation.

It has been estimated that as many as three-quarters of all eaglets reared to flying stage die before reaching breeding age. And this, of course, does not include failed eggs, weak chicks which die in a twin-chick nest (four cases out of five, estimated Leslie Brown), nor the high proportion of eggs or chicks that perish through human interference. We still do not know exactly how long eagles live in the wild, though there are records of captive birds living to forty-five years. Stories of captives living over a century seem to be based on unreliable evidence. Eagles start to breed at four to five years old. If a pair lived to thirty years in the wild and over, say, twenty years of successful breeding produced a fair estimate of sixteen eaglets to flying stage, it would still be too many to replace one pair. If all survived, in a few years there would not be enough home ranges to go round. Thus the high 'infant mortality' (apart from that caused by humans), while apparently tragic, is one of the controlling factors in eagle populations – and only the most resourceful individuals survive.

Nevertheless I didn't want my nearest eaglet to perish. When I again saw it sitting on a crag above the cottage and looking weak after five days of hail, rain and gales, I boated out on a supply trip and brought back some meaty bones from the butcher's. These I put up on the same plateau without erecting a hide – the eaglet needed the food more than I the photographs.

Through early December winter laid its first harsh chill upon the landscape, the rain and hail replaced by snow and frost, and in the mornings the loch steamed in the freezing air. Icicles clung to rocks in the burn, my primitive water system froze up, forcing me down to the loch for two buckets a day, and the hills were transformed into icebergs. The deer came down to our woods venturing out at dawn to paw away snow from the herbage near the shore with their cloven forefeet. As I chopped firewood, wrote in the near dark with the sun skulking behind the hills, lighting the lamps each day as early as 3.45 p.m., I told myself – as I had in some of the last ten winters without road, electricity, telephone, gas, television and all the comforts we take for granted – 'This is the last!' But of course it wasn't, and if I felt I had it hard, I was in the lap of luxury compared with the wildlife in the area.

On December 21 I saw huge Atalanta circling over the ridges westwards, with nothing below her now but wave upon wave of blanket snow. How many miles did she have to cover in that patient soaring flight before finding food? If I found wilderness winters harder each year while living in a weather proof cottage with some supplies, how must it feel to be an ageing eagle? What was it like, after a life based on physical prowess, when the eyes were no longer keen enough to spot and flush the white blob of a sitting ptarmigan on the white tops, the speed no longer there to pursue and catch the dodging rabbit or hare, and when the talons lost their killing strength? How did one cope when the only hope of survival in the bleak winter was to stay aloft on those great wings which, although fashioned by evolution to carry her for hour upon hour without a single beat, were now beginning to tire, relying for food on the discovery of a sheep or deer carcass, and then to suffer the ig-nominious harassments of ravens and crows?

Compared with the eagles I had nothing to complain about. On New Year's Eve I went into the freezing night, put up my little tent in the woods, cooked supper on a campfire, and tried to resolve to work more intensively on my studies of the great golden eagle. With Moobli snug in the flyleaf of the frosty crackling tent, I slept peacefully through the long night.

5 · *Courtship, Mating and Spectacular Displays*

To my surprise I did not see any of my three eagles again throughout that whole winter, despite numerous treks far from the cottage. I was puzzled, knowing eagles are believed to keep to their territories through the year. I checked my diaries. In the first winter I had seen eagles in the area, in the second not. In the third I had seen them again, but now in the fourth winter they had disappeared once more. I then found an odd phenomenon in my notes – during each of the winters when I had seen the birds, there had also been a high mortality of deer in the vicinity. They had been wetter winters than the others, worse for the deer which constantly lose heat through evaporation, and the weakest among the old and young had begun to die from late November onwards. Some I had hauled up into the hills for the eagles.

It now seemed possible that once the eagles discovered that deer mortality, along with that of sheep, was insufficient to provide them with carrion, they had moved further to the more prolific rabbit areas to the west. This indicated they could be hunting beyond their normal home range, possibly overlapping the ranges of other eagles. In turn this would imply that eagles are tolerant of each other in winter, which would be a useful species' survival instinct. The fact that they could travel ten miles in fewer minutes without energy-wasting wing-flapping lent some strength to the idea.

By this time I had met Roy Dennis, the enthusiastic Highland

71

officer for the Royal Society for the Protection of Birds. Apart from protecting rare birds, tracking down egg and chick thieves and trying to bring illegal poisoners to book, Roy also edited the Scottish Bird Report for the Scottish Ornithological Club and was Chairman of the Highland Ringing Group. He was a keen student of bird movements. He thought these theories reasonably valid. He knew of two ringing recoveries where eaglets from the Glen Affric area had been recovered dead in their first winters in the Spey valley area, a south-easterly migration of some forty-five to fifty miles. He believed that some of the central Highland eagles migrated to the easterly moors in winter where such favourite prey as mountain hare and grouse were more plentiful, and that birds from high icy snow-covered areas like the Ben Nevis range moved south east to Perthshire in harsh winters. The only trouble was that most ringing recoveries were of young birds. He thought it quite feasible that the adults from my area might move slightly south west in similar circumstances, or west to the lower ground in general, where prey was easier to find.

Would they have taken the eaglet with them? Eagles' breeding seasons generally begin in late December and January when both partners spend time round their various eyries, occasionally roosting in them, then refurbishing one or two likely choices for that year with dead twigs and sprays of greenery. Courtship flights, in which the male zooms in with spectacular dives on the female, start in January. By then the eaglet, ignored by its parents, has usually drifted away to occupy the fringe areas not used much by adults, land which may include a road or village or a farm or two. If the eaglet had indeed made a minor migration with its parents in this way it would possibly stay in that area when the parents returned to their home range to start nesting. I realised it would not be essential for adults in harsher winters to be back in late December – they could return in late January or February, with plenty of time to rebuild an eyrie and lay from mid-March to mid-April.

On January 25 I was driving along the coast road below the mountain containing Eyries 4 and 5 when I saw a pair of eagles circling round one another near its peak. I thought it likely Eyrie 5 would be used by them this year. When I reached home I found the first dead deer of that winter in the next bay. It was a weak late-born stag calf. In case any of the eagles were still in the area and I had just failed to see them, I hauled it up to the 400-foot-high shelf I had used before. By February 12 it had been scavenged by a pair

72

of buzzards, crows or ravens, and at night a fox, and I still saw no eagles on treks.

By now the Nature Conservancy Council had said that they would be grateful for a report on the eleven eyries I had found, so on February 20 I took it to Richard Balharry who was then living at Newtonmore. He turned out to be a big, tough, red-bearded Highlander, and a conservationist who knew Highland nature from its broadest aspects. As an accomplished climber, he had also worked as a professional stalker for the Red Deer Commission and as a 'keeper before joining the Conservancy as a warden of the Beinn Eighe reserve. He was now Chief Warden of the whole north-east region of the Highlands and had special responsibility for golden eagles. He greeted me warmly, praised my report beyond its merits and soon revealed a vast knowledge of Highland wildlife, eagles in particular. They had become his favourite bird too, and he had studied them for over twenty years.

We were soon agreeing general principles on working with eagles, and as his wife Adeline prepared supper, he willingly shared his knowledge. He did not fully approve my 'migration in winter' theory but felt that, if carrion were short, the adults probably went over the western edge of their territory on to the lower slopes near the sea where there were more rabbits. True, the eaglet could have cut out around December to find its own fringe area, just drifting, catching what food it could on the way. He knew no records of adults actually driving young from the territory, however. Male eagles would rarely fight during the breeding season, though there was a record of one such engagement in 1940 when both males crashed to the ground, one badly injured with a talon wound through its eye. This occurred when two occupied eyries had been on opposite sides of the same glen. Although eagles depend on eyesight, he had known of one female, blind in one eye, which had still successfully raised eaglets.

One thing to bear in mind, Dick Balharry said, if you're looking for eyries when the chicks are two to three weeks old: while there is no eagle in the nest, one of them will be keeping a close eye on it. With one, usually the male, away hunting, the other could be cruising so high as to be beyond human sight, or else perched on a far ridge, still watching. When a female was sitting tight during the 38 to 44 day incubation period, her male would feed her, sometimes dropping food on the nest, or flying near with prey so that she could fly off to meet him, the food sometimes being transferred in mid-air.

Once the chicks hatched and could be left without brooding, both birds hunted to feed them. He thought males brought some 30 per cent of food actually into the eyrie, sometimes as much as 50 per cent, but the females nearly always did the feeding of the chicks.

'Some males, however, do very little work once the chicks can feed themselves, just bringing in twigs, and the female has to do most of the hunting for the chicks. They vary greatly.' He grinned. 'I had a vocal pair once. The male would go off for long periods, then return with something small like a black-headed gull nestling and feel that would be his lot for the day! He was very proud of himself and preened on nearby branches, then he got hell from his mate. She yelped at him, between the yelp of a terrier and the cry of a common gull, as if telling him to go and get something else!'

Dick thought that eagles seldom lived longer than thirty-five years in the wild, through a lessening ability to hunt as they age, even though they had been proved to live longer in fed captivity. He was impressed by their ability to find a new mate fast if necessary. He had known females in the breeding season, when the male had been shot or had died, to go away and return with a new mate in a matter of days. They went over to the fringe areas occupied by immatures and young adults and somehow picked up a new partner. And he would return with her and help to look after the step-kids!

In his own studies at eyries he had often been surprised by the prey brought in – a 9lb fox was carried up with ease by one female, as Geoffrey Kinns had also witnessed, and he'd known weasels, stoats and a wild goose in nests too. Once he was watching a heron's nest from a treetop hide when an eagle landed and took its pick of the young herons.

'In Wester Ross one eagle brought in water voles more regularly than anything else,' he told me. 'One day it came back with *seven*. Now, how did it catch them all – put one into one set of talons and catch with the other? Catch, kill and pile them one by one? The image of an eagle standing on a burn bank catching voles is mind boggling.'

He felt it likely I would get the licences I wanted that year and added that there was still a great deal to be found out about the golden eagle. 'All we really have is a little information,' he added. 'There is still so much we don't know.'

When I left Dick Balharry I felt fired by new enthusiasm, and the next day I went to see Greg Hunter who again kindly agreed to co-operate with the eagles on his estate. As I drove back below the

Eyrie 4 mountain, I saw the pair of eagles circling above a high ridge. Suddenly the smaller male soared high and dived down on the female, banked, looped up and dived at her again, and this time she twisted slightly as if to touch talons but I don't think contact was made. The male turned again as the female landed on a high rock with her wings kept open slightly. I whipped out the fieldglass. Now he swooped over her once, came back and landed a couple of yards away. He looked at her, stalked heavily towards her, then jumped and landed on her back, but with exaggerated lightness and care. Both birds winnowed their great wings gently for a moment or two before he was away again. She folded her wings, stayed still for a short while, then lazily glided away too. I had witnessed a pair of eagles mating – unfortunately from the seat of a Land Rover.

In due course my eagle licences came through and I felt honoured, delighted and yet fearful. To my surprise, I had been given some 300 square miles of the Lochaber district to cover. Some hard hoofing lay ahead but much cautious and careful work too, for I now had to check all known eyries, find new ones that were occupied and locate one suitable for photography, and do it all without putting any female off her eggs. Again, I checked every rockface through the glass from afar before approaching closer, and also scanned the sky and ridges for watching eagles before looking at an eyrie. My main problem, as Roy Dennis had pointed out, was that whereas in some Highland areas eagles nest in obvious lone crags that only occur occasionally in rolling green hills, in my region there were all too many rockfaces and crags with likely sites.

I won't describe all the weary hikes. Suffice it to say that although I could only work part time, I drove over a thousand miles in that one season and made 33 hard treks on foot specifically for eagles – and covered most of the area I had been given. On March 14, Eyrie 11 had been built up, with fir spray decoration, but contained no eggs. On March 27, Eyrie 1 was untouched and no new eyries were found in a nine-mile trek covering two mountains. But as we headed back I was delighted to see what looked like Meleager come over the mountain crest to the south and perform a tremendous territorial and courtship display.

From high in the sky, when but a tiny speck, he closed his wings and dived down towards us, getting bigger and bigger and lit by the sun into a ball of gold. At the last moment out shot his long wings. He looped up on the wind, slanted down again, closed his wings and hurtled earthwards in another power dive, pulled out of it and soared up again. Several times this spectacular diving and falling was repeated as he headed south west. Then he circled, performed two more gigantic aerial undulations heading north east, sailed to a far peak and landed. I thought there might be an eyrie there and set off for it, but two minutes later he flew again, circled the glen to the west, turned north, went into the wonderful 'jet glide' and vanished from my sight.

This was certainly Meleager, and he was displaying over his territory to show any other eagles his rough boundaries. Atalanta must also have been somewhere in the sky. It was good to know they were back, but this pair were really exasperating! When I reached the peak, no eyrie could I find.

Two days later I was boating home when a large female eagle flew overhead, gliding and flapping along heavily, her talons filled with greenery, but against the brightness of the sky I couldn't identify the foliage, nor did she look as big and dark as Atalanta. Her flight was so straight and purposeful that I knew she must be heading for an eyrie which she and her mate were building up or decorating. I noted the landmarks over which she had flown and when I got back I marked a straight line on the map. It led to some likely high ground on the sea coast. I drove to where the road ended a few days later, but, after an eight-mile hike along the shore ridges, found no new eyrie.

I now had more glimpses of my local pair and once after finding Eyrie 1 was still empty, Atalanta came over us and began floating upwards, not even circling, on a rising thermal. She vanished into the clouds at about 5,000 feet like a silvery ghost.

In mid-April I went to see Greg who had located Eyrie 12 in a high sea cliff, too inaccessible to work, but at least the female was incubating eggs. Later, the pair we had worked last year at Eyrie 10 were found to be nesting again but this time had eggs in a new eyrie (13) some 300 feet above a sandy beach almost at the top of a short cliff. There was nowhere to build a hide and the beach was frequented by the public, so it was an impossible place to work. How I now envied Greg his rabbit-filled area, so good for western eagles. He had seen both pairs all through the winter.

Through May, Eyrie 1 showed no activity, and the long trek to Eyries 6 and 7 showed only one egg in 6 and again no sign of the eagles. I wondered if it was another addled egg. On my forty-ninth birthday, Eyrie 14 was located on a northern sea cliff with one live and one dead chick in it. A half-eaten hooded crow lay on the nest which had been decorated with rowan sprays. Again it would have been a hard place to work, needing an even longer drive and walk-in, and I knew of no helper in the area anyway. I thought this may have been the eyrie toward which the female with greenery in her talons had been flying on March 29, but when I checked the line on the map it seemed too far to the west.

I had a break from eagle treks when Geoffrey Kinns visited me for a few days and we concentrated on badgers and wildcats. When he had left to try for eagles in Skye, I drove down to renew permission to search the Forestry Commission lands. Forester David Jamieson had interesting news. He had seen a pair of eagles flying around some inland rockfaces a few miles north of Eyrie 4. Now this *was* a vital clue, for if there was an eyrie there, it would be dead on the line I had drawn on my map. I decided to try one more hard trek in that area – but it wasn't necessary. As I was buying supplies in early June, Euan, my local butcher, told me his thirteen year-old son Calum had a pal called Tom Stewart who accidentally discovered an eyrie after seeing an eagle fly from it. From his description, it was clearly in the rockfaces David had mentioned. As I wanted only helpers who actually knew of eyries, Euan agreed to ask Tom Stewart to take me to see if it was workable. That day I also called Lauren and we made the long hike up to check Eyries 4 and 5. Eyrie 5 had been built up and there were some fawny white eagle incubating feathers in it, but it seemed as if it was just being used as a roost for there were no sprays of greenery and no eggs. We saw no eagles. Eyrie 4, where the eggs had been stolen last year, was untouched. It looked blackened and torn about by the winter weather. I noted that the heather had grown longer on the ledge opposite the eyrie, so it would be a fairly good place to work if ever the eagles used it again. My vertigo seemed to have lessened a little as I peered over the long drop, while Lauren as before showed no fear at all.

On June 3, I trekked over Eagle Rock Mountain and was disappointed to find Eyrie 11 had again been destroyed, with new sticks lying over the ground below and some hanging from the ledge as if poked out by a long stick. There were no signs of eggshells or down from chicks. On a rockface a quarter mile away, near some fleshy roseroot stems, I found several long downy incubating feathers, as beautiful and soft as ostrich plumes, together with some dead twigs. Perhaps they had come from an eagle which had begun to build up Eyrie 11, had started again on the ledge but had finally gone elsewhere.

Feeling strong, a pair of new boots now worn in, I hiked over to

77

Eyrie 2 – and was astonished to find a downy young eaglet in the nest! It saw me and shuffled on its bulbous yellow scaly 'elbows' into a crevice out of sight, so I didn't even get a photo. Until they can stand at three weeks old, eaglets travel over the nest sticks in this way and the joints of their haunches thicken up like little footballs. By the proximity of Eyries 11 and 2, it seemed clear that both belonged to the same eagles and it was good to know that despite the breaking up of 11, the pair had bred in 2. I hoped the destroyer did not know of the latter eyrie. As I left an eagle flew low overhead. It was the old-looking male and its grey-mantled head glistened oddly in the sunlight. I was glad to have identified him with an eyrie at last, but this too would be a hard place to work. Although Allan Peters would have put me into a hide, because of the deep crevice only part of the nest would be in view.

Over the next few days I checked Eyries 3, 8 and 9 – no new building. I was reasonably sure 3 and 8 also belonged to the pair which owned 2 and 11, but all had to be checked each year. A new eyrie (15) with a healthy chick in it was located between Eyries 12 and 4/5. It was almost surely a third eyrie of the 4/5 pair but for several reasons it was not suitable for working from a hide. My only hope now was Eyrie 16, the one Tom Stewart had located. On June 9 I boated out and drove to Euan's home, immediately received a welcome dram and he sent Calum to fetch Tom.

'You'll have a job going up there and back with him,' Euan's wife Jane warned me. 'He's the fittest hill man in the area and we all call him "The Hare!"' As we talked I noticed young Calum looking at us enviously. 'He's mad keen on wildlife,' said Jane. 'He would so much like to work with you.' I said I didn't think my licence allowed me to show an eyrie to someone who didn't know it and that thirteen was a little too young. Recalling how I had felt at Calum's age when I had worked with a gamekeeper pal of my father's, I promised her I'd try to take Calum with me in a future year.

When Tom Stewart, twenty-three, arrived I saw what Jane meant. Tall, dark-haired, slim, he was a leading player in the local football team and seemed nearly all powerfully muscled legs! Tom agreed to be my helper on his next day off, June 12. Taking me up the Hill would get him fit for the football season, he said.

As we finally set off on the three mile trek, Tom carrying the hide and I my pack with camera, lenses, films and other hide stakes and materials, I soon discovered how Tom had come by his nickname. The first part of the journey was up a steep burn gorge and he leaped from rock to rock without a falter, not hesitating at drops of five feet or more. I had a task keeping up with him.

As we strode across boggy fields of sedge and white tufts of bog cotton, with a few ewes and lambs grazing on hillocks, a large dark eagle I was sure was the mother bird sailed close over us, apparently unperturbed, and vanished over a ridge. I reckoned she would soar back lower down for another look at us as we were not far from the nesting cliff, but she proved to be far more clever. She landed out of sight behind the ridge, then *walked* back to its top, just poking her beak and head round a rock to watch us. Such foresight, plus her large size and dark plumage, told me she was a wise and wily old bird. We would have to be very careful with her.

From 250 yards away I scanned the cliff with the fieldglass and soon located Eyrie 16 which had been well decorated with leafy sprays of rowan. It was an unusual eyrie, halfway up a sixty-foot craggy face and was clearly old, for the nest was perched on top of an eight-foot stack of dead twigs and branches. The whole edifice was held securely in place by dwarf rowans and a birch which sprang from the cliff. Thankful that foliage prevented a clear sight of the drop below, I managed to scramble quickly up to the nest. My rising head was met by a large month-old white downy eaglet which hissed through its open beak and made forward smashing movements with wide outspread wings which were as yet nearly all long white quills with dark feathers sprouting from the ends. This threat display was formidable and I was surprised at the size of its wide head, beak and large dark brown eyes. It was already far bigger than a chicken. There was a quarter-eaten lamb in the eyrie, but from the lack of blood and talon wounds on its body I reckoned it had been found dead. I took four pictures and, not wanting to upset the eaglet further, climbed down quickly.

We had a task finding a place for the hide because from most ledges bulging rock faces prevented a clear view of the eyrie. But soon we found a precarious mossy seat on a rocky projection over which a thick birch tree root grew like a red-brown snake. This rock was screened from anything looking at the cliff by the birch and several small rowans, while beside it was a V-shaped fissure into which I could retire for rests – so I thought. Bearing in mind the mother eagle's intelligence, we built the hide with all the cunning we could muster; indeed, so undetectable was it to the human eye that later we had trouble finding it ourselves. Eagles' eyes can locate a motionless rabbit at a mile, so we took no chances.

We wove leafy branches into the roof and sides, and stuffed the whole edifice with cranberry fronds, wood-rush, moss and masses of long heather to match the surroundings, all roots naturally downwards. In little over an hour I had a seven-by-three-foot greeny-brown cavern between the rock and the cliff side. Because of a protruding rock bluff, the only place I could fit the camera lens so it viewed the eyrie forty-five feet away was in the extreme top corner of the hide. The only way my eye could reach it was by sitting on the uncomfortable birch root and straining my neck upwards. The thirty-foot drop was on to ground that sloped steeply downwards from which sharp granite rocks leered upwards like teeth. While the thirty-foot fall might not kill one outright, the unpreventable continued descent downwards, with the rocks ripping chunks out of one, would certainly complete the job! My only brace against such a fall was to wedge my right foot on to the birch itself, directly overhanging the drop, rest my right elbow on my right knee, and in that strained position sit there. I would just *have* to get used to it.

The most important thing when watching birds from a hide is to be completely sure that they accept it. If the eagles did not now accept what we felt to be a minor masterpiece, I would have no alternative but to remove it quickly and abandon the project. The birds' welfare always comes first. When we walked out and were a quarter mile away the mother eagle appeared, just floating casually over our heads, with no signs of fear. It seemed as if she had never been shot at or harassed by man. We slipped behind a rock and kept watch. She flew over the eyrie, circled and, to our delight, zoomed straight in and with an upward swoop landed on the nest. The hide, apparently, had not been noticed. She had no prey in her talons that we could see but she was clearly going to spend time in the nest, possibly feeding the eaglet from the lamb, but it was too far to see. I now felt it safe to leave the hide. We sneaked back behind the rock and stole away.

Tom agreed to put me into the hide four days later, but when I said I was worried about the lamb in the eyrie, he assured me these eagles were in no danger from a vengeful sheep owner who might believe the eagles had killed it. The man who kept sheep on that land was a friend of his, Allan MacKay, and he admired eagles. I later met Allan and found him a man of fine character.

'I would never hurt an eagle, nor would anyone else around here,' he told me. 'First of all, we don't know how many lambs are found dead already. I have never found eagles to be a threat anyway. It's good to have them on the land.'

In fact that was the *only* lamb that was brought into that eyrie during that season's study and it had almost certainly been found dead.

On a bright sunny June 16 I boated out and Tom walked me up to the hide by 6.30 p.m. Armed with an old cushion to put on the uncomfortable root, I intended to spend the night on the cliff ledge. Very few observers have ever maintained night long vigils over eagles and I wanted to see what they did then. As Tom checked my invisibility from outside, and that the camera lens was obscured by firm vegetation, he departed with the crack: 'Don't drop off to sleep there – or you'll *really* drop off!'

It was interesting to see the eaglet emerge from the crevice into which it had crept on our approach and lift its head above the edge of the nest, watching Tom's retreating form until he was out of sight. Its stubby dark brown tail feathers, tipped with a creamy fringe, had grown over half an inch in three days.

Even with the cushion I soon found the mossy rock perch excruciatingly uncomfortable. The birch root dug into me yet I could not cut it because it was the main support of the small tree which supported the hide, and my right foot was also braced on it. To look through the camera I had to lean right over the sheer drop, braced by a soon-trembling right leg, and push against my knee with my left hand while my right hand stretched up to work the button. I didn't realise until then what a strain it was to maintain just the upper body in a diagonal stretched position for long periods.

After four hours the chick began to call out and I heard the mighty swish of eagle's wings as its mother passed right by the hide. Then through a gap in the vegetation I saw her vast dark form and seven-foot wing span winging away to where the Atlantic swell was thumping into the granite hollows of the cliffs half a mile below. As the sun slowly sank I realised it was setting further to the north west than I had expected and for half an hour it shone straight into the lens, hazing the whole scene with orange. Well, half an hour wasn't much to lose in a long summer day.

Twice more she passed overhead before dusk, the eaglet calling for food for there was none in the nest, but she did not come into the eyrie. These were anxious moments. I was sure she had accepted the hide as she had flown into the eyrie after we had built it, but did she somehow know I was now inside it? If she had seen through our careful ruse, the project would have to be abandoned next morning.

When a cold north-easterly wind began blowing on to the nest and still no adult eagle appeared, I became more worried. Could the half-fledged eaglet stand a cold night alone? Suddenly there was more rushing of giant wings around me, then crashing sounds as if both parents were landing on nearby bushes and not on the eyrie itself. Oddly, the eaglet did not cry out.

Sleep was impossible. Apart from the root-covered rock seat the only space was the narrow V-shaped fissure between it and the cliff face. This too was divided into two levels, so I had about two-and-a-half feet of slanting rock on which to wedge myself. I could only lie in a cramped position on my right side with legs bunched up, the cushion under my hip bones, and use my heather-stuffed pack, which suddenly seemed all buckles, as a rough pillow. I was afraid of falling if I turned over while half asleep, so I tied a rope round my waist and the birch root.

Expecting a summer night, I was ill-prepared for the cold north-easterly wind which blew through the vegetation of the hide. I shivered until dawn, which luckily was only four hours away. The excited calling of a male cuckoo, followed by the metallic bubbling trill of a female, roused me from my semi-comatose state. Then I heard both birds fly past the hide, calling with odd wind-notes '*Hoh hoh, ha ha hah*', as if they were laughing at the joke of laying an egg in the nest of some unsuspecting meadow pipits. I silently sidled over to the viewer.

Only the eaglet was in the nest, looking cold and miserable, as if it had not been brooded all night. Why do eagles often build on such chill north-east faces, as was the general belief? Surely, a more southerly eyrie, despite hot sun for a few hours (when the sun *did* shine), would be better. When the light increased I soon realised they had chosen well. At this latitude in summer the sun rose more in the north-east, flooding the eyrie with early heat when it was most needed, after a cold night. And when the sun was at its hottest, there was no need for the mother to shield the young eaglet, for it would then be shining *behind* the cliff and the hill, leaving the eyrie in shadow. North-east winds were in fact rare in summer and the eyrie was also shielded from the main south-westerly rain-bearing winds. At sunset the eyrie was again given a brief warming by the sinking sun, so this really was a good place. Again, I thought it showed a wise old bird. (In fact I was to learn over the years that eagles build their nests in the most suitable places and it is largely an accident of glaciation that more suitable cliffs have a northerly aspect.)

I had just sunk down for a rest in the fissure after two hours on the

rock when suddenly the eaglet started to call '*k'yew k'yew*' – a shorter
cry than the first year's eaglet – while staring intently up behind me.
While I knew I could not be seen, I resisted the temptation to move
fast to the viewer in case the movement might somehow be detected
by the flying eagle. Above all now, I wanted them to feel safe in
coming in. There was a sound of great braking wings, a faint
brushing of foliage, then silence. I waited a few seconds before
slowly easing myself on to the rocky seat. Only the eaglet was there.

Ten minutes later I again heard a slight brush of foliage, my eye
reached the viewer, and there on the eyrie but behind the chick was
the mother eagle! Her upper plumage was paler than last year's
female's had been, with more brassy tips to her wing coverts, and the
hazy sunshine lit her up like a golden statue. She had come in from
the far side of the eyrie so I had not heard the swish of her wings. To
the chick's disappointment, she had brought no food. I hesitated to
push the button until she was in a better position but she just glared
down, seized the bones and skin of a rabbit in one set of talons from
the well of the nest, crouched and jumped as my camera clicked,
then, as if it weighed nothing, floated away to drop them several
hundred yards away. This eagle was keeping the eyrie clean.

For the next two hours the eaglet betrayed its hunger by yanking
strips of bark from the small branches on the nest edge. It preened,
quibbled its beak right along its back so it looked headless, then
flirted the stubs of its tail feathers and pulled its beak upwards
through them as if to stimulate their growth.

I was leaning back on one elbow, easing the pain of the root in my
rear, when the eaglet called out again. Now the herbage-stuffed sides
of the hide were buffeted by a miniature whirlwind – an eagle going
past like a bullet – but when I jack-knifed up to the viewer I was only
in time to see the glaring orange eyes of a smaller eagle, clearly the
male, as he turned on the nest rim and took off, a fraction of a second
before the click of my shutter. He had brought in half a rabbit, and
the eaglet fixed it with a hypnotic stare, grabbed it with both sets of
talons and began to rip off pieces to swallow. It fed for about twenty
minutes, with many heavy stampings of its feet to keep the rabbit
down against the strong pulls of its beak and neck muscles. Then it
backed resolutely towards the rim, lifted its stubby tail feathers high
and forcibly squirted a jet of white faeces many yards clear. After that
it walked to a niche below the cliff, flopped on to its breast and went
to sleep.

I left at noon, limbs aching and with leg cramps making it hard to climb down. When I was a quarter mile away the mother eagle flew over the eyrie ridge, floated in two circles above me and sailed off to the west. She seemed unperturbed. I had been in the hide for sixteen hours and all I had was one shot of an adult eagle – a fuzzy, useless shot as it turned out, for she had been moving too fast for the shutter speed. I had missed the male altogether. Still, I felt quite proud at having spent the night on that lonely cliff ledge.

When I reported to Dick Balharry, he said it was clear that the eagles had accepted the hide well and I need not be too worried about the adults not coming into the nest at night. Once the chick is a month old and sprouting the adult feathers, the mother may only brood it during especially cold, windy or wet nights.

Two more days of eyrie checking followed. There was now one healthy chick in Eyrie 12. Greg Hunter had been watching it from a distance and had been astonished to see one of the parent birds fly in with a nestling kestrel in its talons – and the kestrel mother flying all round the eagle, kicking up hell with high pitched calls at this murder of her offspring. Predator apparently preyed upon by a larger predator. Later a hooded crow nestling was also brought into his eyrie. We had found with the pair at Eyrie 10 last year that the eagles in this coastal area took many hoodies, so mitigating their image in the eyes of the more diehard sheep farmers. Eyrie 15 also still had a healthy chick in it. But there was no cause for joy when Eyrie 13 was checked, the new eyrie of our last year's pair. A hill fire – started either by a shepherd burning off long heather or a careless tourist – had burned right to the edge of the cliff and partly destroyed the nest. There was no sign of eggshells or chicks, so it was possible that they had been taken before the fire anyway. However, at least we knew of occupied eyries that contained five chicks between them.

On June 19 I boated out early to hike up to Eyrie 16 again. On the way in we accidentally startled the mother eagle from an old ewe carcass on which she had been feeding just inside an oak wood. She took off to the south and no eagle appeared in the sky on the long walk in. I spent nine hours in the hide which started as cold as an icebox and ended up hotter than an incubator. Neither of the adults came in. The eaglet had a full crop, however, and had been feeding from a fresh half rabbit. At this stage the half-feathered eaglet, well capable of rending its own food at five weeks old, is often left for over nine hours at a time. Lonely, confined to a single eyrie and ledge for day after day, week after week, it often gets bored.

This one coped with ennui in comical ways – it spread its wings, basking in the sun with its neck stretched over the twigs like a snake, or it lay on its side like a dog, constantly stretching out its disproportionately large yellow talons, like bunches of small bananas. The eaglet clearly had acute hearing. When some red deer hinds cropping grasses passed beneath, it craned its neck over the nest rim to watch them with great interest. Sometimes it cocked an eye upwards to look at scolding wrens. Trying to watch big buzzing bluebottle flies, it screwed its head round completely upside down, as if trying to wring its own neck. Although it often peered at the ants crawling up its legs, it made no effort to pick them off – just something one has to put up with in life! Three times the eaglet called out, looking up intently into the sky where one of its parents was probably passing above. It seemed that, even if not bringing in more food, eagles checked their bairns were all right from the sky roughly every two hours.

As I left I felt keenly disappointed. I had boated, driven and hiked a long way, and worked hard, for just one fuzzy picture of an adult eagle. Clearly nine hours, or even sixteen, in the hide were not long enough. From now on I would have to make far longer visits, become masochistic towards all of the discomforts, and spend more nights out on the ledge. Some naturalists believe the eagle doesn't become fully operative until mid-morning when the warm thermals begin to rise from the sun-heated land. I wanted to see what they did at night and at dawn. In other words, if I was to find out more, I would literally have to *live with the eagles*.

6 · Living with Eagles

Midsummer Day dawned into a sky as bright as polished brass, but when I boated out, south-west winds were building up into a strong gale. I was all prepared for a really long stay, with an old sleeping bag, a strip of plastic foam to ease the pain of the short uneven rock fissure, a can of orange juice, a pint of milk, sandwiches and a sheet of plastic to ward off rain. All this as well as camera, films and lenses. I gave Tom the smaller pack and away he went like a great hare. Towards the top of the hill I flagged and said: 'Hold on a bit, Tom. This pack's heavy and if I get too sweated up I'll be colder at night.' Tom promptly handed me the lighter pack and seized mine.

We briefly titivated the hide with fresh vegetation – it is important not to let it degenerate into an obvious withered brown clump – and after Tom had checked that the lens was well hidden, I was inside alone by 6 p.m. Almost immediately the gale abated and midges flocked to my helpless form. Luckily I had brought a repellent, though it would have been too smelly to use when working badgers or foxes at the den. The eaglet had no food in the nest and was bothered by the midges too, flicking its head back and sideways with violent movements against its wing shoulders. It looked more like a young eagle now – although it still had much white on chest, belly and in its longer tail and wing feathers, small brown feathers were now speckling the white of its head and neck.

As the sky slowly darkened and still neither parent had come in, I felt more worried. Had one or other been shot or met with an accident, I might have to feed the eaglet on meat and rabbits to rear it to flying stage, I thought. At 11.15 p.m. in the near dark I was sipping the orange juice and nibbling a sandwich when I heard a slight brushing noise, as if from the occasional small wave washing the beach far below. Moving slowly, I peered through the viewer.

The vast form of the mother eagle was standing at the back of the nest, dwarfing her large chick, making it look like a sparrow. She had flown in and landed her eleven pound bulk and folded her heavy long wing feathers in total silence. This, plus the fact that the chick had not called out as it did during the day at her approach and after her arrival, could indicate a protective instinct, perhaps inherited from the days when such night prowling predators as wolf and lynx formerly inhabited Britain. Even a large fox or a wildcat would be able to steal a lone eaglet in an accessible eyrie at night. The great eagle looked tired, blinking her large eyes more slowly than in the day, and I saw her beautifully arched neck moving as she peered in all directions, finally checking she was safe. But again she had brought no food.

When it was so dark I could barely make out anything through the lens, I was astonished to see her stand up and the eaglet crawl under her wings and body before she settled down upon it. So even when the chick was well feathered at over six weeks old the mother would still brood it at night. Then I witnessed something I had never seen recorded – she twisted her neck and tucked her head back under her left wing, like a roosting duck, and went to sleep. The golden mantle of the doubled-over neck looked like a thick crown atop her body which now resembled the shape of a wide dark boat. I watched them until my knee trembled on the birch trunk as it supported my weight above the drop, which in the dark I thankfully could not see. But she was back, and at ease.

A fine end to Midsummer Day after all.

All night, as I lay crouched up in the sleeping bag, at least tolerably warm, I suffered nightmares about falling from cliffs during brief fits of dozing.

June 22. Well before daybreak with the sky lightening to the north east, I moved with stiff aching slowness like a toy doll that had not been wound up for a hundred years, easing my legs into position on the root-covered rock. I was scared of every rustle of my clothes and daren't allow any debris or even dust to fall from the ledge in case she woke up. This took a full ten minutes. The eagle was still sitting there, head under her wing, like a great black boat at anchor. Wrens whirred about my head, cuckoos began to call.

The eagle awoke, looked round the surrounding terrain sleepily, then, like a human reluctant to face another hard working day, she pushed her head back under the 'covers', biting into her back feathers with her beak as if to secure it there. Finding she could sleep no more, she took it out again and stood up.

Now she preened her chick's white breast, quivering her huge beak up and down as it stood high, as if on tiptoe, and twittered with bliss, a sound as high-pitched as that of a blue tit. The chick tried to return the favours and preened its mother's rear head feathers. Twice it nibbled her beak, as if telling her it was hungry. Suddenly the eagle stopped, looked about her, frowsted her neck feathers up like a cockatoo, stretched one foot sideways and flirted her huge, banded brown tail round to touch the talons with the outer feathers like a giant fan, and stretched out each wing in turn to overhang the broad nest. As the light was too poor for photos I refrained from clicking the shutter. I was afraid the noise in the pre-dawn silence would scare her off. I would wait and get one good shot of them both together when the sun peeped over the horizon.

She dozed again briefly, but as the sun emerged to my right she woke again, looked twice about her and decided it was time for work. She craned her neck, making an intent long-sighted stare as if seeing something on the land far away, and I knew she was going then. I took one shot of her – she did not seem to hear the shutter – as she took two steps to the edge of the nest, leaned off gently with the wind playing through her flight feathers, and was gone.

I'll never forget the moment I took that picture – the eyrie bathed in golden light, the intent look in her eye, the intricate brassy patterns on plumage that from a distance appeared drab brown, the sheen of her yellow-gold mantle, and how the words of an old hymn went through my mind: 'Heaven's morning breaks. And earth's vain shadows flee...' It was still the only good picture I had taken after all the work that year but what a unique hour of watching it had been!

It seemed as if the eaglet was now capable of lasting two days without food; that at such an early age it was already becoming used to the feast-or-famine regimen which is the eagle's lot in life, as it is for many large predators. Doubtless when adult in the wild, it would have to endure far longer foodless periods than that. Zoo eagles have been known to last three weeks without food after a good feed, but of course they don't use the energy of a wild hunting eagle.

The sun warmed the eyrie and the hide too, then disappeared above the cliff behind me at around 10.30 a.m. Suddenly the chick began to cry out with neck outstretched. The mother swished in again, this time with a tiny woodmouse. When she landed the chick was already in the solicitation posture, head down almost on the nest twigs, wings out and mantling, and squeaking like a pigeon squab. It appeared almost to attack her in its hunger and swallowed the mouse with one head-tossing gulp as she left again. I had just withdrawn from the strenuous hang-over-drop position when an eagle swished in again. I pressed the air release bulb for an 'insurance' shot, but by the time I had slow-motioned myself to the viewer, it had gone again. Later, the photo showed it had been the smaller male but he had brought no food.

By now I had worked out that, if the eaglet was looking high into the sky and squeaking quietly, it had spied a parent checking the eyrie from above. Louder squeaks and stretched neck with intently staring eyes meant one was coming in from a fair distance. If the eaglet was dozing and didn't cry out, I could tell from the sound of the eagle's wings what was happening – '*wush wush wush*' and becoming fainter meant it was passing close by the hide and the eyrie but not coming in; a slight air sound (and a possible glimpse of a shadow passing the hide) meant one was sailing in from behind me; and a sudden rapid '*swish swish swish*' meant a parent was almost in and was braking to land from immediately in front of the nest. I had always believed that eagles did not fly in woods in case of damage to their long wings, and when I first saw this eyrie I had thought that flying into this ledge, with small trees growing up from it, would present problems. But both eagles skilfully closed their wings to get through the gaps, barely brushing the foliage.

At 2 p.m., after passing to and fro above the hide with rushing wind sounds on several eyrie checks, the eaglet squeaking with perplexed looks as it followed each pass, the mother came in with the front shin bone of a red deer hind. When the chick did not eat, she flew away. The eaglet did not tackle the bone for two hours but looked at it as if trying to decide whether it was food or not. Then all alone, by trial and error, it learned to stand on one end with a foot, and rake and rip the meat and hair off lengthways with its bill.

There was no more action for several hours. I was learning that eagles tend to have a siesta when the sun is at its height, as do many of their prey animals. They sit in shady places between cliff rocks or perch under foliage in trees. I was glad when Tom came to walk me out. I climbed down stiffly, bones creaking and joints aching, like an old man. I still had only three good shots of adult eagles, not much to show for so much work and time. I was also worried the eaglet may not be getting enough food, that the parents were having a spell of poor hunting, and that I ought to keep a close check. Accordingly, I went in again the very next day.

June 23. This time I bought half a pound of stewing steak and a sheep's heart from the butcher's before meeting Tom who was anxious to get going. He had forgone an invitation to watch the Scotland–Brazil football match on a portable television twenty miles away on a hill where reception was clear, just to put me in.

'Oh, I'll get a lift and still be up there in time if we hurry,' he said. So we did that, and I felt my fifty years then!

As we stormed, sweating, up the gorge and hill, we saw the mother eagle sailing over ridges a mile away to the south, but the male was nowhere to be seen. I wondered if the pair were finding it harder because there were less rabbits about. I had not found a single one killed on the roads this season, whereas normally I found several on drives to eyries. Taking advantage of the parents' absence, I climbed up to the eyrie and threw in the steak and heart. The heart went up awkwardly and landed on the big eaglet's foot, but its instinct not to fall out was strong and it clutched the nest sticks hard, not giving ground to the sudden arrival of the strange object.

When I had set up the camera and Tom had bounded away down the hill, I saw the eaglet had fastened its talons into the heart and was rending it for dear life! The north-east facing eyrie was dark on this cloudy day, so I decided to bump up the ASA speed of my camera film from the normal 200 to 600. (It then has to be specially processed.) But I found I could not read the dials in the close space. From now on I would have to bring the reading glasses I should have worn at the age of twenty-one, but hadn't. It seemed ironic I should discover my eyesight suffering the normal afflictions of middle age when doing something so abnormal as spending nights out on eagle cliff ledges.

At sundown I was sipping a can of orange juice when a fawny brown streak shot up from below the hide and swooped on to the eyrie. I slowly moved to the viewer – just in time to see the mother eagle pick up my piece of steak, show it to the snickering eaglet, then drop it down again, as if saying: 'This is not poisoned, kid. So eat it!' At that both she and the youngster began pulling the meat with their dark hooked beaks – as if she wanted to strengthen her youngster with a tug of war. I took a shot. Either she didn't hear the click or it didn't bother her. I took another as she left quite casually. The eaglet then swallowed more morsels of meat.

At dusk the mother came in again, this time with a quarter-plucked hooded crow. Although eagles pluck prey almost naked for very young chicks, and feed them slivers beak to beak, it seemed she had now decided hers was old enough to cope with the remaining feathers on its own – as it would have to do in later life. As always, the eaglet prostrated itself, half-fledged wings out and squeaking, but it didn't feed. Although its mother now stood over it, as though it were a naughty child, it simply wasn't hungry. It was so full of my sheep heart, which the mother had not seen, and later the steak, which the mother had probably forgotten as she had not brought it in, that its crop was distended, making it resemble a busty showgirl. The simile was apt, for by its large size I felt sure the chick was a female. Eagles must keep a mental picture of how much their young have eaten and when they need more.

By now the light was so bad that even a fifteenth of a second did not register on the camera's light meter. The mother left again, brushing through the small trees with no fear of wing damage. Perhaps she would feel that the chick was now old enough for her to roost away for the night, but as I slipped into the sleeping bag there was a brief wing flapping outside. It was now well after dark – though in summer in the Highlands it did not become pitch black – and she had after all come back to brood the eaglet.

I was now finding out that eagles can fly and hunt when it is so dark that a man could hardly see to walk. And that when feeding chicks in summer, they will hunt for eighteen or nineteen hours a day. An eagle's night vision, while probably not as developed as an owl's, is finer than most birds of prey, coinciding with the pre-dawn and post-sunset periods when most small mammal prey is abroad. Perhaps they use near-dark to shroud their approach to such birds as grouse too.

I actually slept a little that night, but again I had an odd dream. I had been locked out of a penthouse apartment, was balanced precariously above city streets on high tree branches, yet daren't move for fear of falling!

June 24. I woke before dawn, saw dark grey-mauve clouds on the horizon and knew there would be no dawn sunlight on the eyrie today. I manoeuvred cautiously back into position. The mother eagle was standing facing me with the chick between us. Perfect! Although the meter needle barely quivered at half a second, I took five shots of them. They would be too dark but would convey a true impression of eagles in the nest at dawn – or how they looked to the human eye. It was better than cheating by putting tame eagles into wild backgrounds.

As I watched the mother looking tenderly down at the eaglet, warm in the nest's shallow bowl, I felt oddly moved. She gave the impression of immense calm and reserved power, yet showing a look of real 'love' for her baby. The great cruiser of the skies stilled at last, as if in a painting by Millais. Once she lifted her head and yawned sleepily with her beak wide open, and the eaglet, seeing this, caught the urge too and yawned in the same way. Several times the mother glared straight down the lens as if she could see my eye at the far end, a disconcerting stare. If she had twigged the presence of some being in the hide, due to the meat supply, she at least felt it was friendly. After twenty minutes more, the pains in my knees and arms excruciating, and long before the sun emerged from the horizon clouds, she looked out with her usual intentness, took two steps and just sailed away. She always looked as if she had spied some specific prey and was just going out to pick it up, but I knew it likely she would cover many mountain miles before returning, and that I had a long wait ahead.

After a long preening period the chick decided it would have a go at the unplucked crow. Lifting its feet carefully so as not to trip on the nest twigs, it set them firmly on each end and tore off little feathered pieces and swallowed them. By now its wings were covered with dark brown feathers which glinted greeny-gold in the sun, the tail plumes were over four inches long, and more dark feathers had appeared on neck and chest, giving it a real 'chocolate and cream' look down its former snowy front. There were bald patches in the white down on the back of its thick yellow legs from constantly squatting on the nest twigs. While some eagles line nests with moss, wood-rush and grass tufts, this pair had not. And as for decorative and sanitary greenery, they seemed satisfied with a few new sprigs of heather.

Not until 2.15 p.m. did the chick, now hungry again, begin to squeak. I was just in time to photograph the male eagle landing with talons out, primary feathers all separated from each other before the wings folded, with a sprig of green heather in his beak. I will never forget the chick's look of disappointment, its crop empty, its eyes fixed on the inedible sprig.

'Is that all you can bring, Dad? I'm damn well starving!'

The male quickly flew away with the heather and returned twenty minutes later with a bigger sprig, more to his liking, which he

dropped on the far side of the nest. But not before I had my best shot
of an eagle and chick so far, with him standing high and proud, eyes
bigger in proportion to his head than the female's. He was a smaller,
lighter-coloured bird, but really sleek and strong, his legs thickly
muscled. Once, when he turned to face me, they looked slightly
bandy.

Ten minutes later I heard a noisy rush of wings and was astonished
by a rocketing thwack. He had thumped right down on top of the
hide, his black talons and yellow toes bunching only inches from my
head as they grasped for footing. My heart pounded as I thought he
was attacking the hide or myself, but all he wanted was another
heather spray. When he flew off again almost immediately, I saw he
had taken a large twig from the hide's roof. He wheeled round in a
small circle, landed on the nest, dropped it and flew off again. What
an astonishing experience! It was also a great compliment to Tom's
and my work, for of course, he would not have landed had he
suspected a human lurking inside. I felt really proud.

Fifteen minutes later in came mother, this time with a small black
water vole in her beak, which the eaglet instantly grabbed with its
beak and swallowed head first. Then the mother stood near her child
with a soft maternal look, unlike the usual imperious demeanour,
before flying away again. Later she came in with a headless young
grouse, stayed briefly to check that the eaglet was feeding well, and I
recorded its squeakings on a small recorder I'd carried in the previous
day. After that both eagles would be having their afternoon siesta,
and so I left the hide. I had spent twenty-two more hours on the
cliff ledge and had been well rewarded.

I was feeling good now, legs toughened up from all the treks,
writer's winter midriff gone, and when Tom and I toiled up the hill
again on June 26 I hardly noticed the hard three miles. It was a dull
day with drizzle showers. During a seven hour stay, the eagles did
not come in but the chick ate from an unplucked hoody and a whole
furred rabbit.

On June 29, with Tom away at football practice, his brother Iain
kindly walked me up for my fifth night on the ledge. He was as fast
on the hill as his younger brother. A strong north-westerly wind
was blowing and rainclouds that had been threatening all day began
releasing their liquid burden as we set off. The hide was dank,
gloomy and cold as I stripped off my sodden shower suit and got into
position. When Iain left, he gave the pre-arranged whistle that told
me one of the adults was flying near the eyrie. The eaglet now looked

93

less vulturine as the dark feathers on its white neck and head had increased, and the white of its chest had been reduced to a narrow bar. All the back plumage had grown but the tail and wing feathers were still short.

I had been on the cursed root for only twenty minutes when the mother came in with a small red deer foreleg. As the eaglet went for it, still making the obeisance posture although now nearly as big as its mother, I saw that both birds had drawn the grey-white nictitating membranes over their eyes. This semi-transparent 'third eyelid' has many uses, apart from cleansing the eyes. It can also act as a shield against strong sunlight, against hailstones when flying, and as protection from injury when actually struggling with prey. I had seen the eaglet use it in tugs of war with its mother, and even for protection against a slip of its own talons when scratching its head like a cat. As soon as the eaglet began dragging the leg round the eyrie, as if to strengthen its legs and talons, the mother flew off again.

Once more she returned in the near dark but this time she did not brood the youngster. Instead she roosted, head behind wing, beside it all night. The eaglet looked miserable, drops of water dripping from the end of its hooked beak. It was having a hard schooling now in the inclement Highland weather. I had no sleep in the rocky fissure either, as it was a bitter night and rain seeped through the hide netting and herbage above me. I huddled in the bag under a tent made from the plastic sheeting, but water ran down tiny gullies and emptied into eye or ear at odd moments. The only warmth in the cold wind came from my own breath, so I had to keep lifting the plastic slightly to avoid suffocation. Eagle ridge? It was more like an eagle fridge.

June 30. I roused and slid shivering into position before the eagles woke. Now the camera eyepiece kept steaming up from the heat of my face in the damp cold air! I kept poking it clean with a handkerchief wrapped round a pencil and saw the eagle wake. She looked as gloomy as a human on seeing yet another dark and rainy day, kept her neck feathers frowsted out, yawned a few times, then with an air of 'Hell. Duty calls', stepped off the nest and beat away into the rainy twilight. As she went the eaglet actually called after her, the first time I had witnessed that, almost as if saying 'Don't leave me in this, Mum!' Where would the eagles hunt in such awful weather?

At 8 a.m., the rain having stopped, the sun emerged and flooded the eyrie with welcome light and warmth, just as an eagle swished in from the north west. It was the male, with a great heather sprig, standing like a man with a pipe in his mouth, but after dropping it in front of the eaglet he straightaway took off again. At 10.30 the eaglet cheeped loudly and in came the mother. She deposited half a rabbit on the nest, turned and took off as my camera clicked – on her back! She had probably caught the rabbit after it had emerged from a burrow when the rain stopped.

Now the camera viewer became filled with action. In came the male with a dry ash twig, and as he looked for a good place to put it he nearly swept the eaglet off its feet with the longer end. Again his legs looked rather bandy. Half an hour later the mother swept in with a dead young curlew. She had been hunting on the marshy part of the shore, a good place for such birds after the rains. She then spotted the heather sprig the male had brought in, apparently decided it was not suitable or up to standard, seized it in her bill and flew off with it. The eaglet, crop full, grabbed the curlew but after a few tugs and swallows left it to the buzzing flies. Ten minutes later, in came the male with more heather, folded his wings and tramped about like a naval officer inspecting his decks, decided it was not the right shape and flew off with it again. This male was bringing little prey into the eyrie himself, his visits more limited to maintaining the Home Beautiful.

By now, with the sleeping bag soaked through and almost every limb aching, I had run through two films and felt I'd had enough. So I was relieved when, after twenty-two hours, Tom Stewart arrived and I creakily followed him out.

When we took the hide down on July 3 after another stay in it, the eaglet was in fine shape. In about a month it had grown from mainly downy white chick to a proud well feathered young eagle. It now stood straight up in the nest, not hiding from us any more. I climbed up with a rabbit as a parting present. The eaglet started to rend it as we dismantled the hide and left the site pristine. As we tramped away with heavy loads the mother came sailing low over our heads, knowing now we meant her no harm.

The rest of my spare time that season was spent checking the other eyries: July 9 – Eyrie 1 unused. July 10 – eaglet gone from Eyrie 14 though nest seemed totally undisturbed. July 13 – eaglet gone from Eyrie 2 but again no disturbance of nest or its surrounds. Saw two eagles flying over distant ridge, one with white in the tail was probably the eaglet. Also found Eyrie 17, only thirty yards from Eyrie 2 but in a low recess and looking as if it had not been used for several years. July 15 – 'our' eaglet in Eyrie 16 now fully fledged and almost ready to fly. Did not approach close for fear of putting it to premature flight. July 19 – I was told rough positions of Eyrie 18 and a possible site (19) in a far glen by a landowner who knew there had been no action in Eyrie 18 this year. July 20 – both eaglets in Eyries 12 and 15 were reared successfully and seen flying. July 22 – reliable professional stalker witness told me of Eyrie 20 with healthy fledged eaglet in seldom-visited cliff face, but just out of my area. I had enough square miles to cover and it was too late to check now anyway. July 25 – checked Eyries 6 and 7. One unhatched egg still in 6. Theory that egg could be survivor from last year's two was confirmed by Dick Balharry who had known of addled eggs lasting for more than a year in failed eyries, untouched by crows and ravens.

Summary of breeding success that season: three eaglets definite-ly flew successfully from Eyries 12, 15 and 16, and were all seen between August 6th and 14th. Eaglet in 2 probably flew safely but eaglet in 14 could be doubtful. Eyrie 20 was also probably successful. Thus, it would be fair to assume at least FOUR eaglets flew successfully from the region. Possibly five. A good year.

After I had sent in my detailed report, I received an appreciative letter from the Nature Conservancy Council and later a heart-warming one from Chief Warden Dick Balharry, who congratulated me for being so busy, adding that a good portion of my findings was new data and 'the whole report is a valuable one'. He reflected my own wish that we meet for discussions and said he would walk in to see me one winter day – a change from the fair weather visitors of summer.

On October 21 Moobli and I were up in the high hills, photographing red deer stags in the rut with their harems of hinds. The stag shooting season had just ended and several grallochs were left lying on the hills. We had just rounded a high knoll when I saw several ravens and crows wheeling in the air above a heathery plateau, too far ahead for photos. But there, on two grallochs, were *three* eagles – male, female and a large eaglet every bit as big as its mother! They saw us at the same moment and took off. It could not possibly be the family from Eyrie 16, the distance was much too great. Again, I felt the exasperating certainty that Atalanta and Meleager had bred successfully nearer my home, in an eyrie I still had not yet found. I hoped that they would spend the winter near us this year, and that I could help them again by hauling any deer that died in the woods up to the open hills.

In my second season – at five-and-a-half weeks old the eaglet calls anxiously for food.
The dizzying and spectacular view from an eagle's eyrie.

At dusk, the eleven-pound
mother returns without prey.

The eyrie bathed in golden
light at dawn.

The male brought in a twig
but the chick was wanting
food.

The mother watched over the
eaglet while it was feeding.

She removed an unwanted heather twig from the eyrie.

At eight weeks, the eaglet did not tolerate a close approach.

7 · *Almost Touching the Void*

We were boating out on a supply trip when suddenly I saw huge Atalanta flying low over the loch shore just a hundred yards inland. Another large eagle came flying behind her, almost hitting into her tail. At the last moment Atalanta made a rolling wing-flapping turn on her back and grabbed the talons of the other. This was not the mating season and golden eagles rarely actually touch talons in these symbolic food-passing aerobatics, but as they went past I saw that the upper bird had all the white-patch plumage in wings and tail of the immature. It was the eaglet. Both birds continued to fly in this way, Atalanta upside down, and both were flapping hard as if hauling away from one another, and tugging with their talons.

It seemed that the mother was teaching the youngster to grab, clutch and pull with the talons while in mid air, that she was really making it fly and heave at the same time. And all the while smaller Meleager flew behind, swooping from side to side but on the same flight path, as if checking that all was well. Eagles catch most of their prey on the ground after fairly low flight, spotting prey and making a quick wheeling attack. But if they spy prey when soaring high, a fast stooping glide soon brings them low enough to level out and try to make a surprise attack, often coming upon the prey unseen. Occasionally eagles can catch bird prey in mid-air – one, quoted by Leslie Brown (see Bibliography) was seen to outfly grouse downwind, dive below them, then turn up and seize one grouse from below with a foot. I was sure Atalanta was teaching the eaglet how to hunt this way and this talon-tugging was part of the process. It was quite unmistakable, and it was superb.

On October 31 there was an even rarer occurrence. I was out in the garden, scanning the high hills for deer with the fieldglass, when I saw what at first looked like the eaglet heading over high from the west. But as I looked I saw it was even larger and darker and its whole tail was blazing white in the sun. Its flight was also more ponderous than a golden eagle's. I was sure it was a white tailed sea eagle, a species which has been extinct as a breeding bird in Britain since 1916, and that it had probably flown from the island of Rhum where the Nature Conservancy Council were trying to re-establish them with young birds from Norway. (Later a sea eagle was found shot dead some miles away, and I learned one indeed had escaped from Rhum earlier that autumn. Sickened as I was that die-hards still exist who would shoot a rare eagle, when Dick Balharry was subsequently investigating this, my sighting helped to establish that it could have been the same bird.)

When I found the first dead deer of the winter, a six-year-old hind washed up in the burn in late November, I hauled her carcass up to 400 feet for the eagles. On a trek on December 4, however, it seemed I had wasted my time. I found a huge dead stag, with bad neck wounds and blood in its throat, lying in a small burn a quarter of a mile from the cottage, then a second dead hind on the ridges above the long wood a mile away. I had seen Atalanta and Meleager circling there the day before. There was no need for me to haul carcasses up for a good while now as deer carrion keeps relatively fresh for a month in cold weather and now there was plenty up high. Three days later I saw both parents circling ridges three miles to the west, but the eaglet was not with them. Some accounts say eaglets leave their parents in October, but to my mind that seems a little early for a large creature that has to learn to kill.

Next day I had finished photographing a golden sunset when Moobli gave a bark and there, coming through the west wood after a six-and-a-half mile hike, was the back-packing form of Dick Balharry. He had had a 'magic walk' he said, had seen a swimming otter and both parent eagles. He thought it likely that they would be spending less time with the eaglet now.

As we later feasted on venison and I indulged in the rare luxury of log fires in both main rooms, we had a good crack about eagles and other Highland wildlife. He shared more of his eagle lore, and doubted that the feathers I'd seen on the rockface near the destroyed Eyrie 11 *had* been the start of a new eyrie. Eagles often roosted near their eyries, on a crag or a dwarf tree, and the feathers came from the birds preening. He told me something I didn't know. In eagle literature there are many references to one eaglet being bigger than the other because the initially laid egg hatches first, thus one eaglet gets a good start over the other and often kills its weaker sibling. Dick had been studying eagles for twenty years and had found that there can be two to four days between the laying of the eggs. Usually the mother does not start to incubate them until the last egg has been laid, or even a few days after that. Thus the chicks do not start to develop in the eggs until she warms them enough by sitting seriously. Of course one can hatch marginally before the other and get a start on the first few feeds, but it is natural for one chick – often the female – to be bigger anyway. It is true, however, that some eagles do incubate seriously after laying the first egg, and in these few cases there can be two to three days' gap between hatching. In either instance, in the competition for food the weaker gets less, suffers a few irritated stabs from the stronger one's beak and often perishes. If it survives for three weeks or so, and the parents are hunting reasonably well, both chicks could be reared to flying stage. Clearly, however, it cannot be a large preponderance of female chicks that survive what Seton Gordon (see Bibliography) called these 'Cain and Abel' battles or there would not be enough males to go round. The ecological purpose, if there is one, of the deaths of weaker chicks in eagle nests is, as Leslie Brown once wrote, 'obscure'. Dick also believed the mortality rate among chicks that had flown successfully could be as high as 75 per cent, usually during their first winter when they have cut out on their own and have not yet learned to hunt and find carrion efficiently.

Next day we drove a long way, parked at the end of a rough track and hiked three miles into the land mass south of my home, where Dick showed me Eyrie 21, a five-foot-wide and deep stick nest on a triangular shelf high on a sheer bulging rock face. As he climbed up like a spider and peered into the nest above the sheer drop, fearless of the height, I confessed to my vertigo problems, adding that I was probably not the best man in the world to be working eagles.

'Nonsense,' he said cheerfully. 'It means you won't be climbing into too many eyries and won't take silly chances!'

As we left, he indicated another old eyrie (22) belonging to the same pair and I agreed to check them both next year as well as the others. I liked the way he trekked, long relaxed strides, our paces matching naturally. He even walked sometimes with his hands behind his back, as I had often been teased for so doing myself. Once we found a small twisted scat on a mossy rock.

'Pine marten,' said Dick, picking it up and pointing out its characteristic sweet smell. 'They don't need trees, can survive on the hills if plenty of mice, voles and birds are about.'

I told him that I had seen only one wild pine marten in my area, crossing a single track road two miles from where we were standing. Before we parted, he pulled his car up above a loch and indicated Eyrie 23 – at some 700 feet up cliffs above a steep gorge. It was not strictly in my area but I said I would check it if he wished.

The winter that ensued was the coldest, snowiest but also the driest I had so far known in the Highlands, but after making a cottage heater from a forty-four gallon oil drum, an invention learned from an old Scots-Indian in Canada, I passed it in more comfort than usual, despite having to spend a whole day each week cutting and hauling dead logs. I wasn't seeing the local eagles on winter treks now. Rather than sit and mope on Christmas Day I set out with Moobli on the hardest hike for weeks. I always felt better after hard exertion on the Hill, and if it is true that a man is partly what he eats and partly what he thinks, it also helped my mental processes. We headed along the loch shore, up a long river valley, then turned to climb a steep killer of a hill to over 1,700 feet. I had to cling on to dwarf trees to get up some of the almost sheer faces.

We emerged on to the peak and there below us lay a vast expanse of undulating tawny hills, precipitous crags and high cliffs, the loch winding like a silver scarf between them to the sun-filled west. On the steep slopes, herds of red deer blended with russet clumps of dead bracken, barely distinguishable but for their white-buff rump patches. I saw the two adult eagles heading towards us and Meleager banked, climbed and dived down by Atalanta's side, so close to us that I heard the wind rushing through his pinions. The whole scene was so wonderful it took the rest of my breath away. What a privilege it was to be up there among nature at its wildest. Without the ability to appreciate such beauty and the desire to work towards conserving it, I thought, man is little more than a beast.

Here I was once more on the roof of the world, amid timelessness, mystery, the unknown, and ancient silence, as if I were standing in the real 'cathedral of God'. We have suffered from loosening our roots in the natural world and losing the sense of wonder, deepened intuition and perception that naturally occur when we see nature's most extraordinary and beautiful phenomena. We are humbled by such glimpses of glorious creation and the mind opens, the soul becomes inspired at last. I felt then that our final attitude to the last of the natural world is an important barometer of our state of mind as a species. We humans evolved from original creation with superior gifts of intelligence, foresight, communal invention and the unique ability to love spiritually beyond ourselves, to become the world's most dominant species. Yet each dominant species before us perished when it could not adapt to changing conditions. Today it is we who are changing environmental conditions, often to our own detriment, and at a pace with which many habitats cannot cope.

Eleven civilisations before ours foundered when they cut their roots to the land, lost awareness of universal nature, and affluence bred decadence; thus it has long proved insufficient to dominate alone. Animals have no choice beyond survival but man does have choice and he must use his unique gifts now to play the role for which he has truly evolved, as responsible custodian of the last wild places, not merely their exploiter. We can never escape the inherent responsibility our genius bestows upon us. We must learn to love and conserve what is inspiring and beautiful, not only what is economically profitable.

As I walked on, the certainty came that if we do not exercise that choice, help to transfigure the callous side of nature, so often reflected in our own natures, by compassion and acts of intelligent conservation, we will begin to die spiritually – are not the signs now all around us? – and then create a hell on earth for ourselves before we too pass along the same route to extinction. We shall be yet another of God's failed species (if we believe in God), just another failure of evolution (if we do not). To love in the *universal* sense is not the refuge-seeking philosophy of the romantic. It is the necessary ethic of our own survival.

As we later descended the steep gorge of the burn near home, Moobli scented a deer calf carcass that had fallen on to a ledge. I climbed down, managed to lift it out, then hauled it to the heathery shelf 400 feet above the cottage. The dead stag and hind above the long wood had little left on their bones now; foxes, ravens and crows having competed with the eagles for the carrion. This new calf might help to keep the eagles close, for I still had hopes that they would use Eyrie 1. Three days later I left my desk to trot up the steep hill behind for exercise, when I was startled to see the eaglet on the carcass. Its white tail and wing patches showed as it tore out tufts of hair and flapped to keep balance when it fell back slightly.

It saw me, jumped and flew slowly to a rock some seventy yards further on. It wobbled in the air, and when it landed, it had to take some steps forward to arrest its impetus. It was weak. It was on its own but still on the home range where clearly it was being tolerated by its parents; perhaps it was too feeble to fly far. I was sorry not to have had my camera with me but rejected the idea of setting up the hide again. It needed the food more than I needed pictures.

I spent New Year's Eve as usual sleeping out in the woods, but this time all round me sounded the cannon and tympany of a winter storm. The loch seethed and snarled its waves upon the broken shore, the wind rocked the bare trees, making the trunks creak and sending down showers of twigs and an occasional branch. I chose an open clearing to avoid the risk of being spiked in the night. Slanting blasts of rain hit the tent like sprays of bullets but I felt at peace amid the storm for I had finished the first draft of a new book that day. My first two books about the natural world had now been published, and after eleven-and-a-half years of living in remote wild places I was at last beginning to haul back on the hedonistic city years of early manhood and fulfilling the instincts I'd had as a boy.

When I took the tent down in the morning I saw the eaglet again, flying like a vast kite over the bare tree tops. Alone like me, I thought. I *was* alone too – for Moobli had sneaked back to the house and spent the night sleeping in the kitchen.

On wintry treks through January and February I caught glimpses of Atalanta and also of the eaglet but they were never together now. On February 25, my hopes that the adults would use Eyrie 1 rose when I saw Atalanta circling above it for nearly a quarter of an hour. Was she waiting to be joined by Meleager? I realised I had not seen him once since Christmas Day. I crouched among some trees above the burn to watch, but then she turned and flapped heavily to the south against a fair wind, until she vanished into cloud at some 3,500 feet. Again it was clear that the loch was no territorial boundary – or maybe she had gone to look for Meleager.

Next day I was working on the final draft of my new book when Moobli, beneath my chair, whined slightly. A red deer calf had come out of the east wood and now appeared to be nervous at being so close to the cottage, sniffing the rainy air with wide dilating nostrils. Telling Moobli to keep back, I went out with the camera. The calf jumped back in fear but moved only slowly back through the wood. It looked shaky on its slender long legs. Over the years, sick deer have often come near the cottage before dying, as if instinctively seeking help from the occupants whom they have often watched with interest while grazing the nearby ridges. Some we managed to

save, with diluted milk and glucose and nutritious garden vegetables, but most of them died. This one, clearly an orphan whose
mother had died or been shot, also seemed to have come for help,
but then the close sight of us triggered the stronger instinctive fear
of humans. Well, I would try to catch and treat it. I went indoors and
changed into wellingtons, but by the time I got back it had gone. On
command, Moobli set his nose low and tracked it to the swollen
burn. We forded the rushing water and Moobli searched again before
heading nose-high to the north-eastern escarpments. We soon
located the calf once more.

'Turn it, Moobli. Don't hurt it.' Knowing the command well,
off he loped. He soon caught up with it and without barking or
trying to bite he herded it, running groggily, back to me. Suddenly
it fell and became stuck under a dead branch that bridged two rocks
on a downward slope. Holding its rump and neck I walked it back
but the ground was rough and twice it fell down in water pools. It
was a hind calf, thin and light for its size, about sixty pounds, and I
had no trouble getting her on to my back in a fireman's lift. The wet
from her coat soaked through my clothes and it was tricky fording
the burn with her weight, but I got over without falling and took
her into the warm kitchen. As I heard the familiar rattle in her
throat denoting the late stages of pneumonia I knew there was little
hope. I dried her with a towel and got half a pint of warmed milk
down her, then left her on a bed of dry hay. By late afternoon, the
vegetables were untouched and she was dead. One cannot save
them all. Sadly, I removed the rear haunches for Moobli and my
young wildcat Liane, and heaved the rest up high for the eagles.

On the last day of the month I saw Atalanta soaring above Eyrie 1.
On this cloudy calm day, she had to flap more than usual, her wings
appearing to be fashioned in two slow-moving hinged pieces which
unfolded as she altered wing shape and stroked the air. So different
from the flight of a buzzard that flaps faster, more often, and seems
to have stiffer wings. Next day I opened up the carcass with an axe
so that the broken whitish inner skin and dark flesh showed up well
to any eagle above it.

For two days nothing went near it, then on the third I hiked up to
find two great white splashes by a hard tuft near the carcass. The
lower two ribs had been torn through and a hole some eight inches
across had been made over the flank. The heart and most of the lungs
had gone, typical eagles' work. As we examined further, Atalanta
came sailing overhead, her head turned briefly as if to say 'Leave it

alone!', but she made no alteration in her flight and floated casually out of sight behind the eastern ridges. I wondered then if she knew it was I who had been hauling up these feasts during the hard winters. Although I kept sporadic watch from the rear window in early mornings, I never caught any eagle actually on the calf. By March 4 a pair of buzzards had located it, also for twilight feeds. Then it was ripped apart by foxes – Moobli tracking one to a temporary den in a huge cairn of rocks.

Heavy snowfalls now whitened the hills but after they had passed there were long periods when the sun shone with new warmth, the small birds started to sing in the woods and I began to look forward to the new eagle season – once more to ground the great birds, capture their superb symmetry in my lens, observe that extraordinary ability to soar beyond sight, seemingly to heaven itself, in mere seconds. On a brief trip south I optimistically invested in a new Olympus camera with a 300mm lens and motordrive. When my new licences came through from the Nature Conservancy Council, I saw that I had been given the entire Lochaber region to cover. Greg Hunter had successfully applied to monitor the eyries on the estate for which he worked and he kindly agreed to give me his statistics. Now I was free to search new areas further inland as well as the eyries Dick Balharry had shown me in the winter. But first I wanted to locate an eyrie for Atalanta.

So the boat trips, drives and long, weary but exciting foot treks began again. Frequently we tramped up to what appeared from a distance to be likely rockfaces, only to find they were no more than a series of small faces, five or six feet high, with ledges eight or ten feet wide between them – like great grass-covered steps – where no eagle would nest. By the end of April it was clear that Eyrie 1 was not being used and I had found no new ones. On one trek, examining a white-splashed rock, Atalanta flew languidly overhead for a good flight photo. Although Eyrie 16 had been freshly built up, I doubted that the eagles would use it again this year. A favourite site can be used two years running but usually only in areas (unlike mine) where sites are few. I thought it more likely that the pair were breeding in another eyrie.

On April 12 I was in the garden, throwing sticks for Moobli to chase, when Atalanta came winging over the loch from the south, pursued at last by her mate. As she flew low over us, her great long wings bending supply upwards, the difference in size between the male and the female – not always obvious when eagles are seen apart

– became clear. I also noticed that he was a lighter-coloured bird. He swooped down upon her and passed close by. She turned over sideways but no talon contact was made. I rushed indoors for the camera but in those few seconds they were already far away over the peaks to the north east.

Three days later we were crossing the burn when we startled Meleager from a fresh deer calf carcass hidden among some dead brown bracken. Once more a hole had been made partly through the ribcage and the heart and lungs had been removed. A long mountain hike to the north east next day produced only a few shots of antlerless stags but no new eyries. What an exasperating couple they were.

We trekked to near Eyries 4 and 5 on April 24, but on seeing a pair of eagles in the air close to the clifftop ledge of 4 and recalling how the eggs had disappeared from this nest two years earlier, I decided not to go in close. They would certainly have seen us. Through my glass it appeared the eyrie had not been built up, but if there were eggs it would be better to check after they had hatched in May, to go in on a warm dry day when the birds were away and the risk of desertion was almost nil.

I had to work hard on my book for the next few days but on April 30 I was making a final abortive check on Eyrie 1 when Atalanta came gliding along, saw us and far from swerving actually circled round low over us before sailing leisurely away to the east. Only thirty yards up, she showed no fear at all and I was almost sure now she knew I had been the winter provider. Another long search for a new eyrie in my immediate area proved fruitless.

On May 6, filled with hope and my pack containing the new camera equipment and hide materials, I set off on the trek to Eyrie 16 with Tom Stewart, who had again generously agreed to be my helper. Although the nest had been built up even more and some tufts of great wood-rush lay in the nest bowl, there were no eggs or chicks in it, nor did we see an eagle. We searched the entire cliff face, and found another nest (Eyrie 24), but it proved a mess of decaying sticks and looked totally deserted.

I boated out with some apprehension on May 10 to meet for the first time one of Scotland's most famous men – mountaineer, photographer, ornithologist and leading conservationist, Tom Weir. Tom had written an enthusiastic review of my wildcat book in *The Scots Magazine* and I had written briefly to thank him. He wanted to visit me and write a piece in the magazine about my work in the wilds, an honour to which I agreed. As I walked to the post office to keep our date I was expecting to meet a tall, rangy, powerful grizzled character, possibly on the lines of the 'Glencoe fox', mountaineer Hamish MacInnes.

I was surprised to be greeted by a short man, not slim, wearing baggy knickerbockers stuffed into long wool socks. He had gimlet green eyes, balding head and looked to me like no great athlete. My plan had been to invite the great mountaineer to come with me to check Eyries 2 and 17 on the lone crag some twenty miles away but now it did not seem such a good idea. I put it to him anyway.

'Er, I should really check an eagle eyrie,' I said, 'but it's a long drive from here and then a steep climb up to about 900 feet. I expect you've had enough for one day.'

Tom, who had just driven all the way from Loch Lomond, smiled. 'Fine. I'm not tired at all. In fact I could do with a bit of exercise.'

As he put his boots on, whistled to the dunlin on the loch shore, which obligingly replied, and then climbed into my Land Rover, I thought unkindly, 'Yes, you could, pal.' How was this old guy going to get up the Hill?

As we drove through the passes his questions were exceptionally perceptive, but when we took off on foot through the tussocks and uneven runnels up the steep wooded ride I took it slowly to give the old boy a chance. I looked back after four hundred yards – he was still there. I put on some speed, then suddenly – I don't know how it happened – he was in front of me and heading up even faster! As he didn't know where the eyries were I slipped to the right when he took a zigzag to the left and with an effort just managed to get in front again. I had new respect for this man's ability to 'hack' the hill.

Then, as I puffed along, head down, he said, 'There she is!' He had been able to climb the rough sheer ground and still look up, and had seen the eagle before I had! There, winging casually away to the east, went a large female eagle.

'You've brought me luck,' I said. 'One of the eyries must be in use.'

When we got to the bulging crag, we tried to climb through a gap between the cliff face and a ten-foot high rock slab to look down into Eyrie 2, but the gap was too narrow. I went up on the main ledge but couldn't get all the way. He tried too, got a little further than I had but said it was dangerous – too much loose stuff. Tom then led the way to the west over a hard rock jutting from the face, which I had difficulty surmounting to join him. From above it we were looking into Eyrie 17, which was empty and untouched. Now there were

106

only two ways to Eyrie 2 – one up a long slanting crevice which ended in a sheer outward-bulging face which I knew I couldn't climb because I had tried on previous visits; the other lay forty yards to the west, up an easy bit before traversing along the dwarf tree-lined ledges to a shelf from which one could see into the eyrie at eye level.

Tom set off up the steep slanting crevice. 'You'll not make it up there, Tom. I've tried.'

'Well, I'll have a go,' he replied.

'I'm going the way I normally do,' I said, and headed off down and to the west. I had only gone thirty yards when a faint cry came back to me through the smirring mist.

'Two eggs!'

Had I misheard? No. He *had* climbed directly up to the eyrie! My heart pounding with effort, mind racing with astonishment and shame, I hurried along below the cliff, up the easy bit, then had a terrible job working my way along the almost sheer face through the dwarf trees, with sheer drops where rocks had recently fallen away, to the spot I had reached last year. It took me a good five minutes.

Tom Weir was standing on a precarious tiny ledge right above the eyrie, one hand braced on a small slanting rowan tree over the perilous drop, and peering right into the nest. 'Two eggs,' he said again, smiling happily. I got to the end of my shelf, craned out as far as I dared and also saw the ends of the two eggs, but I was thunderstruck. He had climbed, without equipment, over virtually overhanging rock. What an incredible character for sixty-three! He had completely outclimbed me, thirteen years his junior. I felt a great respect for him then.

Not wanting the eggs to get cold we left quickly and from 250 yards away saw the eagle return to the nest. My respect for Tom Weir increased during the two days he spent at Wildernesse as I realised he was a master of all things to do with the ecology and conservation in the wild Highlands, for which work – although he didn't tell me – I found out later he had been awarded the MBE. In the years since I have counted myself fortunate to be one of the friends of this astonishingly hardy, gifted man. And whenever I have felt like flagging on the eagle work, or felt I might be getting too old for the treks, the image of Tom Weir has come into my mind to goad me on.

Finding the two eggs in Eyrie 2 was the first time I had experienced eagles nesting in the same eyrie two years running. It could be a site to photograph once the eggs had hatched for there was a high heathery ridge some forty feet from the nest which would be ideal for a hide. The trouble was the deep cleft, into which eaglets would often creep, such as after being fed. But it would be a good place for interesting flight shots, as Tom pointed out. I decided to check the other two eyries first.

By May 12, the pair from Eyrie 12 had twin chicks in a new eyrie on a ledge twenty yards away from last year's on the difficult sea cliff, and the pair from 10 two years ago, which suffered the heather fire in the low eyrie (13) last year, also had just-hatched twin chicks but in a third eyrie. Greg Hunter, under his own licence, was monitoring this pair himself. He told me he had been walking in the glen below Eyrie 4 when he had seen an eagle fly out of it. As it was in the area I was checking, he had not investigated further.

It rained during the next few days and I didn't want to risk putting an eagle off its nest, but when May 17 dawned in a clear sky, I boated out, rang Lauren who again agreed to help, and together we trekked the 1,300 feet up to Eyrie 4. I crept towards the triangular ledge above the formidable drop and peeped over. Mother eagle was sitting on the nest right next to a downy white chick about ten days old. I backed up, but her head turned, a glassy orange eye stared into mine and then she was winging away over the glen, a great dark brown mottled bird flying like a hawk with fast silent wingbeats. As the chick stretched flat on the nest, sensing danger, I saw that there was also an unhatched egg beside it and, with disappointment, a dead lamb. It was small, had been half plucked and had some blood on it, so I had to admit it had possibly been killed by the eagles. The eyrie was unusual for there were very few sticks on it, the whole ledge being covered with great wood-rush, so that anyone looking up from below would not know there was an eyrie there. I wondered if this pair had evolved this shallow, almost non-existent nest as a protective device. After all, this was the eyrie from which the eggs had disappeared two years ago. At least the wood-rush was softer and warmer than a stick bowl.

As Lauren and I left the cliff and went to check Eyrie 5 – naturally unoccupied – the eagle circled above her nest and chick, now being warmed by the sun sinking to the north west, ready to land again when we were out of sight.

That night I drove the long winding road and up the old track to the long glen which contained Eyries 6 and 7, arriving at exactly midnight. Tired as I was, I couldn't sleep for half an hour because Moobli, who had run the last mile behind the Land Rover, panted so hard it shook like a vibrator!

I woke at 5 a.m., donned the sweaty gear from yesterday, and with Moobli at my heels climbed up to the dark forbidding cliff. When I saw an eagle sailing past the high rocky buttress I thought it might have come off chicks, but neither nest had fresh herbage decoration or even preened feathers on them. They were not in use. Not surprising after two years of addled eggs, I thought. While clambering down, I was thinking how I'd fallen up here last year when my footing gave way again – only a frantic twist and clutch at a craggy projection of mica schist kept my slithering fall to four feet and possibly saved my life. As it was, I gashed the ball of my right thumb badly. We trekked for another two miles, then the six miles back without finding any new eyries. Back at the truck I washed my sore feet in a burn. A trekking man needs to take care of his feet – they're the only ones he'll get!

By now eleven eyries had been checked, containing five chicks (seven if Eyrie 2 had hatched both eggs) and one unhatched egg. There were eleven more eyries to look at, two of which, 18 and 19, I had yet to find. Right now, however, I had to start work with a hide and it seemed a choice between 2 and 4. Despite the deep cleft, Eyrie 2 had the long heathery ridge opposite, ideal for a hide, and was only a one-mile hike to 900 feet, as opposed to the three-miler to 1,300 feet to Eyrie 4. I would try 2.

On the way to ask Allan Peters if he would help me again, I checked Eyrie 9, but there was still no sign of new building after the rockfall. Allan had interesting news. A few days earlier, about a mile from Eyrie 2, he had seen a female eagle on a rock, and the male flying above had swooped down and landed right on her back briefly, fluttering his wings to maintain balance, then away both birds had flown. He too had now witnessed the act of mating. It was interesting to know that eagles would still do so after the eggs had been laid.

On my fiftieth birthday, Allan and I hiked up carrying the hide, its stakes and other materials in warm sunshine. We checked the eyrie but it appeared to be empty. To our surprise, as we reached the heathery ledge a female eagle flew out of the nest, turned east over the top of the cliff, then re-emerged a quarter of a mile to the west, where she was joined by the male. He was the old-looking one with the greyish mantle which shone almost white in the sunlight. He was still alive then. Together they sailed southwards and vanished over a ridge.

I wanted to check the nest, make sure the chicks had hatched, but was worried about the time it would take as we also had to create the hide and I didn't want to keep the mother away for too long. To my surprise, Allan swarmed up the almost sheer wood-rush-covered face to above the eyrie in some twenty seconds, a route neither I nor Tom Weir had taken! He said that all he could see was some white feathery down. We could only assume the eggs had hatched – there would probably have been something wrong if they had not by now, near the end of May – and that the chicks had crept deep into the cleft. Quickly we built the hide, covering the sides with long grey moss and thick heather sprays. In an hour it was done, a very good hide indeed, bridging the edge of one ledge with the one above it, indistinguishable from the surrounding terrain.

As we left and reached the steep woods, we were gratified to see the mother eagle sail in and land on the eyrie. All seemed well.

I will tell of the hide visits in diary form.

May 28. When I reached Allan's house he was out, having been called to a forest fire started by a tourist. He returned half an hour later, covered in ash and smoke smuts, and I felt bad about his taking me up to the hide, but he insisted on keeping his promise. As we plugged up the steep slope with full packs he broke the news that a local foxhound pack would be hunting from the bottom of the same hill next morning. Just my luck, I thought, to have them head up and go straight past eyrie and hide. As we emerged from the woods an eagle sailed above the eyrie, but had not come off it, and vanished.

I squeezed into the hide, a narrow damp tunnel, and Allan left. I found I'd forgotten my strip of foam and had to lie on a mere plastic sheet spread over the bare earth and rocks. To counteract the possibility of rolling off the sloping ledge during a doze, I pushed a stake into the earth and tied a rope from it round my waist. Tiny rocky ridges in the area of my hips and side knee bones produced excruciating pains in any position after half an hour.

The eagle did not return until nearly dusk. I was lying down after a spell of looking through the lens when I heard two loud swishes. I was in time to see her dark rear and tail disappearing into the cleft but I didn't try to take a picture. She had been away a long time. Was she on chicks or just returning from habit, to roost? Had the eggs indeed been taken before we put up the hide? It was a rough night.

May 29. At dawn I was roused from a brief doze by the soft calls of cuckoos, the tinkling songs of robins, the cheery notes of chaffinches and the piping of thrushes from the woods below. Occasionally there came the harsh '*raowl*' bark of a fox. But nothing moved on the half portion of the nest that I could see. Suddenly I heard cars driving far below, clanking and banging as one by one they went over the loose timbers of a wooden bridge. The slamming of doors was followed by the loud baying of the hounds; then I heard savage human cries too as the huntsmen set off after the pack. Hounds have been bred to bay so that the hunt can follow from a distance, but why all the human yells too? In the serene silence after dawn it sounded utterly alien, primitive, falsely festive, and lunatic. All the birdsong ceased. I heard loud swishes and saw the eagle shoot out from the nest and wing away, doubtless as terrified as any fox, which would have heard that racket a mile away.

The eagle did not return all morning, and when I heard the clumping of Allan's boots as he arrived to take me out in the early afternoon, I felt bitterly disappointed. Not only at not having a single picture after twenty agonising hours in the hide overnight but by the thought that there might be something wrong with the eyrie. While the fox hunt racket may have put the eagle off the nest, surely it wasn't enough to cause her to desert if she did have chicks. We checked from above but again could see nothing except white down clinging to twigs. These, I now realised, could have come from the eagle's own incubating plumage, not from chicks at all. I would leave the eyrie alone a few days, hoping for the best.

May 31. I hiked up Eagle Rock Mountain with Moobli, and after seeing some white excreta splashes below Eyrie 11 (although it didn't appear to have been built up afresh) I forced myself to climb across the sheer cliff above the nest shelf. Biting my lip, a pang of hope helping me to overcome the fear above the sheer drop, I looked over. There were a few new sticks on it, plus more downy feathers, but no sign of chicks or prey. I was almost sure now that this was a third eyrie of pair 2, for it was only one-and-a-half miles from it, and was probably being used as a roost place by the male. At least it hadn't been further destroyed this year. As I climbed down I saw the grey-headed male and the female flying over the mountain towards Eyrie 2, a heartening sight. Maybe there *were* chicks in that deep cleft. I also checked Eyrie 3 that day, but it showed no signs of occupation.

June 3. Allan and I hiked up to the hide again but saw no eagles on the way. We now had to check the nest thoroughly, and somehow I managed to reach the high ledge too. There were the remains of a dead hoody on a little shelf above the nest, but neither of us could see anything in the well except a few bits of down. If the eggs had hatched and the eagles had deserted, where were the dead chicks? I noticed some moss and bark had been rubbed off the rowan tree that grew above the nest – this could have been done by a rope. Yet there was no disturbance on the nest itself. It would have had to be an expert climber with pro equipment to have held on with one hand while removing eggs or chicks without treading on the nest twigs with a foot. Just in case there *were* chicks crouching in the far corner of the crevice we could not quite see, I went into the hide again with foreboding. Another uncomfortable night as it also began to rain. Sleep impossible.

June 4. After 22 more hours in the hide, Allan came to walk me out. I had not once seen an eagle come to the eyrie or heard one go past. Sick at heart, Allan as disappointed as I was, we sadly removed the hide. Leaving the area as we found it, we abandoned the project. When I reported to Dick Balharry, he said I had no need to reproach myself. As the mother eagle had come in the first time I was in the hide, and we had also seen her land on the eyrie the day we built it, then it was clearly not the hide or its building which had caused any desertion. It sounded to him as if the eggs had gone before observations started, since we had not seen them since May 10. He reminded me how we'd found pine marten scats on our December trek in that area, and asked if there were any near Eyrie 2. In fact I had seen a pine marten cross the road a mile from the eyrie and the foresters had several times seen martens in the woods below it. Dick thought it was possible the eggs were addled, and as they had not hatched out on time, the eagle's incubation of them had become looser. While crows did not usually attempt to prey on eagle eggs, pine martens were certainly capable of it. (It wasn't until later in the summer that we partly solved the mystery of Eyrie 2.) On the night we took the hide down I returned home exhausted and filled with depression.

All next day, as south-west gales swept the hills and loch and rain doused the land, I felt like quitting on the eagle work, a feeling not alleviated when I discovered Eyrie 14 was unused on June 6. But either I have a stubborn streak or suffer from masochism, for I recalled a motto that a famous screen actor had once told me – 'A winner never quits. A quitter never wins' – and decided to persevere. After all, I had promised the government to check as many eyries as possible in Lochaber. My fascination with eagles themselves had not wavered, and I didn't want to have to admit failure at the end of the season. Now my only hope for good nesting observations this year seemed to be Eyrie 4, far away on the sheer cliff. I duly obtained permission from the landowner.

112

I heard locally that the farmer who grazed his sheep on the land round the eyrie disliked eagles as he believed they took many of his younger lambs. I took little comfort from Eyrie 4 being a ledge that could not be seen from below. Most shepherds I knew who went out on hard gatherings and after foxes had a very good idea of the wildlife on their lands. The trouble was that this was the eyrie from which the eggs had disappeared two years before. I would have to secure the farmer's co-operation somehow. Then I heard an opposite view – that the farmer and his father were quite proud of having eagles on their land, regarded them as *their* eagles. I could work from there, I decided. To hell with gossip and rumours anyway. I had been wrongly judged this way myself.

I should explain here that I soon realised I would get nowhere by being the militant conservationist, or by pointing out to those who might feel they had a reason to destroy eagles that it was illegal, and the fines were heavy, or that they lacked ecological understanding. From landowners to farmers, keepers, crofters, or men who just kept a few sheep part time on land – all would resent a stranger, even a well intentioned stranger, suggesting what their attitudes to eagles or any wildlife should be. I would gain more co-operation for my work, and possibly also for the eagles, by approaching them as an interested if somewhat aged 'student', anxious to know what they knew of eagles, to present the evidence truly, and to encourage a share in my own belief that it was an honour and an achievement to have such magnificent rare birds feel safe on their lands. It was also clear that while vast tracts of land remain in private hands, nature conservation can *only* be successful through friendly co-operation, for only a tiny fraction of the Highlands, less than one per cent, is yet in actual wildlife reserves.

While it may seem that conservation of eagles or other rare wildlife is thus at the mercy of a particular owner or occupier's whim – as indeed it largely is, laws often being unenforceable over wild un-inhabited terrain – there is no way round these problems under the present land holding system other than by friendly approach, good humoured and reasoned arguments, and assurances that they will know the results of your findings – on *their* eagles. Also, it helped for me to give away costly colour pictures, copies of my books if wanted, a bottle of whisky here and there, or an illustrated talk to family and friends. None of my actual helpers would ever have accepted payment but I found little ways in which to reward them.

When I drove down to see farmer John Ritchie I was not sure what to expect. I found him mending farm machinery in his garden with a small wiry fisherman who had bright blue eyes and was repairing a net. John was burly, dark-haired, with a cheerful face and a cautious but gentle manner. There was a beautiful white boat down in the bay. Trying to be friendly, I said, 'Is that your boat down there? It looks a fine craft.'

'Och no,' said the fisherman. 'If that was my boat I'd not be needing to mend this bloody net. I'd be using it for the hay!'

I looked at him. He looked at me. I looked at John. He smiled. Suddenly I found myself laughing, for the remark seemed extremely funny. The little man laughed too, slapped his knee, then John joined in the guffaws. The ice was broken. I told John I would greatly appreciate him letting me photograph *his* eagles and wouldn't do it if he objected. I'd give him a good colour picture of them if he wanted, tell him my findings and I would never reveal his site to anyone.

'Aye, all right,' he said. 'Ye'll probably find them up there. I don't think they do much harm, the eagles. Aye, you go and have a look.' I'm glad to say John (a bachelor like myself) and I became good friends later. When I left, I rang Lauren with the good news.

We were delayed a few days by rainy weather but she and I were finally on the long tramp, carrying the hide and gear up to Eyrie 4. I felt apprehensive at seeing no eagle in the sky, and thought that the chick might have gone. We dumped the hide below the cliff, climbed up the long way, then with one foot well back as an anchor, I peered over the drop on to the eyrie ledge. The eaglet was still there! Nearly six weeks old now, it had sprouted most of its chocolate brown wing and tail feathers, but its head, neck and chest were still covered in the second thick coat of white down, giving it a vulturine look. In the nest was half a rabbit, a headless semi-plucked grouse and a small lamb foreleg, almost certainly found as carrion. And so was the still unhatched egg, rather dirtied. At least this pair was hunting well.

We climbed back down and in the hot sunshine, well away from the eyrie cliff so as not to alarm the eaglet or a watching adult, we stuffed the hide full of herbage to match the ledge on which it had to sit. Then, thankful that the growing wood-rush, bilberry and crowberry foliage made the drop appear less dangerous, we climbed up to the ledge and hauled the hide up by rope. What a job it was to bend and fit all the hazel support wands into place on the ledge which was only four feet long. Luckily there was a craggy projection to the right of my head into which I could fit the front stakes. This rock also helped the illusion that there was not a forty foot sheer drop below.

114

With Lauren plucking vegetation and me threading it into place from inside, we soon had it finished. Once again, the only way I could mount the camera to see round a rock bluff into the eyrie sixty feet away was in the upper right hand corner of the hide, but at least I now had the motor drive equipment and could look through the eyepiece for longer than last year without fatigue by jamming my elbow on the rock as support for my chest.

This eaglet seemed different from the others for it apparently had no fear of us, watching our movements with interest as it stood up straight. It fed itself as we worked, as if it had been used to humans all its life.

June 14. In fine sun Lauren walked me up to the hide and left me in it by 3 p.m. The eaglet was feeding from half a rabbit so it appeared the eagles had accepted the almost undetectable hide. After dark neither eagle appeared on the eyrie. I felt worried. It was hard to sleep here too for I could not straighten my legs in the sleeping bag without half of them hanging over the void. Being only four feet long, the ledge could only contain my head, body and half my thighs. I could rest on my back with my lower legs dangling over the edge under the hide's rear flap but after a while their weight tended to drag me and the slippery bag towards the drop. If I didn't keep hauling myself back with my hands, I could, in sleep, slide too far – and be away down the cliff in the bag like an Egyptian mummy, or more aptly perhaps, like a coffin into a crematorial incinerator! I had to doze doubled up to one side or the other, and jam myself in with a knee. I must be crazy, I thought.

June 15. Before dawn a shower sent drips into the hide and it was bitterly cold. The eaglet spent the night crouched between a clump of wood-rush and the cliff face. A north west facing eyrie, it was not warmed by the rising sun as Eyrie 16 had been and it was darker too. During the morning a parent eagle '*wush woos*'ed by several times, about once an hour, but I daren't risk flight shots until I was sure no suspicions of the hide remained. Suddenly there came an abrupt '*swish swish*', a slight thump, but when I got to the viewer the eyrie was empty except for the eaglet and a new baby rabbit. It had just been quickly dumped and the eaglet, which immediately began to tug at it, hadn't uttered a single cheep. It had a weaker '*keyow*' call than last year's chick anyway, much breathier, so it wasn't going to be much use as an alarm system.

Twice more an eagle flew overhead, knowing that after bringing in prey, she need only check the eaglet from the air during her ranging hunting flight. By the time Lauren came to take me out, I'd spent twenty hours in the hide, legs so stiff I could hardly climb down.

June 17. Another hot blue day for the long walk/climb after the usual boat and Land Rover trips. As we crossed the bogs below for the final ascent, the female eagle was flying to the north east. She landed behind a ridge and then walked back to a high rock from round which she peered out at us. The same trick as the Eyrie 16 mother! As we walked on a gull dived down towards her twice with loud shrieks but she took no notice. Then she flew off and sailed in hunting circles over the bogs, making smaller circles inside larger ones if something of interest caught her eye. She then went into a long glide and we saw her disappear over the far peaks a good ten miles westwards, right through the home ranges of pairs 12 and 10! Once again it seemed that the range boundaries of eagles are not rigid, even in the breeding season, though she probably kept well clear of the other two pairs' nesting sites.

After our long climb, she re-appeared from the west, but we waited until she headed south over the sea before I entered the hide. Not until 5 p.m. did the sun shine from behind clouds on to the nest. I saw that the eaglet had half a baby rabbit and a golden plover's head and remains beside it. With its crop full it was not hungry but it took great interest in some ewes and lambs passing below, listening with cocked white head to the snickering bleats of the lambs as they ran to the ewes' calls for a suck of milk.

Further away, in the marshy land, I heard the faint '*kipe kipe*' of a calling snipe, and the soft double notes of the cuckoo, less vocal after the laying season. As the sun was setting, the eaglet lay on the nest edge, beak open and panting like a dog in the heat. Several times I heard a sharp '*woof woof*' of eagle wings, different from those I had previously heard, so possibly those of the smaller male. But he was landing on rocks above the eyrie and once directly above the hide itself. Not once did the eaglet call out.

Again the mother did not return to brood the eaglet at night and it sank down, looking lonely in the nest cup. I was exhausted after all the treks and dozed occasionally, now held in against the 'coffin' fall by a rope to a stake wedged between the rocky projection and the cliff face. I had a horrible nightmare – that I was at a party in a skyscraper and after showing friends how to climb a sheer wall with tiny crevices and get through a foot-wide skylight, I found myself perched on some unstable telephone wires above the concrete

116

pavement, and someone shut the skylight so I couldn't get back! When I woke and realised where I was, I felt the usual brief panic – which way was I facing? On which side was the sheer drop? And until I worked it out when full consciousness returned, I dared not move! Four nights out on cliff ledges this year and not a single photo to show for it. I swore I would never work eagles again after this year. It was altogether too difficult.

8 · Growing Up

I woke from a fitful doze to find the hide bathed in a strange white light. There was mist everywhere, so thick that even through the lens I could barely make out the form of the eyrie on the opposite cliff. When I peered through the heather sprigs to the west and out over the void, I couldn't see the bogs of the corrie below or any of the land or hills. I felt shrouded in a cold ethereal world of vapour, isolated from all life high up on that lonely cliff face.

I heard a noisy '*wush wush*', then the faster flapping of an eagle landing. I shot back to the viewer just in time to see the huge mother eagle alighting on the nest rim with the chick standing facing her. Again it did not call out, probably because it had not seen her coming. It bent down and swallowed a single haunch of a baby rabbit, then looked disappointed that its mother had brought nothing more. It astonished me that the eagle could fly in such thick mist, as much as when I had discovered that they could fly and hunt in the near dark. I clicked off five pictures singly with the motor drive trigger, although I could hardly see the birds through the white haze and felt sure that the light shining through the million mist droplets had distorted the meter reading anyway. She stayed about a quarter of a minute, peering round the nest at prey remains, assessing what was left, and looking towards me with exaggerated 'double take' movements of her head and neck, like a big brown pigeon. Then she turned and sailed away.

As she left I noticed that she immediately dropped low. In mist the eagle flies lower than usual, scouring the ground from just a few

118

yards above, hoping to surprise its prey on to which it thumps down with amazing aerobatic skill. Low flying has the advantage of stealth and a sudden arrival. Its prey cannot see it coming. What surprised me most was that she sailed right over the heads of two small lambs, which had been bleating immediately below the eyrie, without even looking down – yet she knew her chick was hungry.

When the mist cleared at about 10.30 a.m., and I thought that at last I would get some good pictures, I suddenly heard human voices. Far below a man with a bright blue backpack and a boy were walking along a deer path below the cliff. They took forty minutes to clear the area and all the time their voices came back as clearly as if carrying over still water. It was enough to keep the adults off the nest.

An hour later I heard the swish of eagle wings above the hide and moved to the viewer, but no parent came in. A few minutes later I heard the loud '*keeya*' screams of gulls from a ridge above the hide. As we had seen the mother harassed by a common gull on the walk in, it could be that some were doing it again now. Would they also mob an inexperienced eaglet? Possibly she would not come into the eyrie for a while so as to avoid giving away the position of her chick to these mobbing birds.

By the time Lauren came to collect me after 6 p.m. neither adult had appeared again. I staggered after her with aching hips and painful knee joints. After thirty-one more hours in the hide, four nights and eight days on cliff ledges, I was sure I still hadn't one good photo of eagles this year. (In fact the misty shots turned out to be interestingly atmospheric.) I felt cheered by Moobli's boisterous welcome after what had also been *his* longest eagle wait in the truck. As usual his iron tanks showed no great urge to obey a call of nature, which impressed me as much as his incredible stoicism. Of course he had had three mile runs by the boat on the way out and food and water in the truck as well as my own bed to laze upon. But as we boated home, with Moobli charging along the shore again, I felt tired and just about beaten. I could hardly face the long treks I had yet to make to check the other eyries too.

A day of desk work refreshed me and on June 20, despite misty drizzle, Moobli and I boated out, drove the long miles, and set off on the hike to Eyries 21 and 22. My shower suit had begun to leak and my clothes were soaked in several places before we reached 22. The eyrie showed no signs of use. I tried to go over the top of the sheer rockface of Eyrie 21 so that I could look down into the nest but the ground sloped steeply to the top of the cliff and was slippery with the rain. I went back down and climbed up until I was level – no excreta or sign of chicks. Drops of water hung from every stick of the nest and it looked deserted.

The landowner of Eyrie 18 and the old possible site 19 in the far steep glen in which I had not yet set foot had kindly written to say that, although he had seen a pair of eagles there earlier in the season, he knew the eyries had not been used for several years. He thought the birds were nesting in a mountain away to the north, if at all. On June 22, another misty drizzler, we drove to the start of the glen and began the ten mile return trek. It was the steepest, rockiest glen I had so far searched. As I scanned innumerable faces with my left eye through the glass, my right eye developed a twitch and its vision became blurred, from being screwed up so much.

I located the old site of 19, just a few old sticks on a ledge at some 1,200 feet. Finally there was only one big rounded buttress left near the end of the glen, quite low at some 800 feet. While walking below it, Moobli scented out a rotting deer calf foreleg between rocks, crawling with red-necked sexton beetles. A hopeful sign. I scanned the buttress and at first saw nothing, then suddenly into the lens came the shape of a huge nest, the old sticks as dark grey as the granite behind them. It was on a thrusting shelf some forty feet up, protected from above by beetling crags. Withered brown leaves on thick rowan branches showed where the nest had been decorated earlier in the year but there was no white excreta. Had the eggs or chicks been stolen? We had seen no flying eagles during the hike. I climbed up some of the steep grassy ledges, then saw a layer of white across the nest. A lamb? Through the glass I saw it was the shed fleece of an adult sheep! It was not as white or curly as the short 'astrakhan' coat of a lamb, and was far bigger. If ewes are not sheared in summer, they slough off their old winter wool in swathes, but this was the first time I had known an eagle take such a fleece to line its nest. Now the heavy rain obscured vision and although I kept wiping the glass clean I could make out nothing else in the nest. I dragged my soaked self back out of the glen, wishing that I could be as happy as Moobli for whom the walk alone was more than enough, and slogged home.

The following night I had an extraordinary dream in which I'd been condemned to wander eternally in eagle glens, scanning countless cliffs, scrambling over innumerable rocks. I found myself once again standing below Eyrie 18. For some reason, I began *talking* upwards to the eyrie, imitating the '*keyow*' calls of eaglets. Suddenly a huge and shining silver eaglet, gleaming in the sunlight like a metallic statue, came out on to the rim of the nest to peer down at me with glittering golden eyes. I woke up then, but all next day I could not put the dream out of my mind.

When June 24 dawned in a clear sky, I decided Eyrie 18 merited a second look. I was feeling fit after all the treks and, carrying only camera and lens in a rucksack, I stormed over the hills with Moobli. It was a hard trek, involving some 12,000 feet of ups and downs, but this time I decided to go in from the top of the buttress. As we drew near the edge I was fearful of looking over the great drop and had just decided to go back to where I'd stood before when Moobli got a strong scent, went to the edge and looked over. I wasn't going to be beaten by a dog so, steeling myself, one foot braced well back, I leaned over. There were many downy white feathers in the nest behind the screen of the old sheep fleece, and much white excreta had been ejected behind it. Although I could not see all of it, the nest was at least seven feet across. In it were the remains of an adult ptarmigan and two full grown headless rabbits. Because there were no rabbits within three miles, they must have been carried far, and this was the carrion Moobli had scented. I could not see an eaglet.

I climbed down to exactly where I had been in the dream and, feeling extremely foolish, started to imitate chick calls and talk softly upwards, saying I knew an eaglet was in there, that I meant it no harm but would it please show itself so I could go away happy and leave it alone. Lo and behold, a well-fledged eaglet with its wing, head and tail feathers almost fully grown, appeared on the edge of the nest! It peered down at us, large brown eyes filled with curiosity, then it turned and tramped back into the recess.

When I wrote later to inform the landowner that he had a fine eaglet in the eyrie and expressed the hope that he would ensure its protection, I did not mention the dream. If I had told anyone I'd found an eaglet with the aid of a dream and a dog's scenting ability, I felt any reclusive image I might have gained after eight-and-a-half years of isolated living in the Highlands would have been given an unwanted cranky twist.

Inspired by the find of the new eaglet, I felt that my run of bad luck could be about to turn, so got Lauren once more to put me in the cliff ledge hide at Eyrie 4. As we hiked in, a shower preceded us, drenching the long grasses so that my dubbined boots were soaked through by the time we reached the cliff. We first checked the nest from above – the chick was lying on its side with one yellow leg stretched and its white head, speckled with new brown feathers, lay across the nest with eyes closed. There was no prey in the nest and at first I thought it was dead. Maybe its mother had deserted. But then it moved, heaving a great sigh like a tired dog. When I squeaked, it instantly pulled in the leg, rolled on to its stomach and looked up.

Now I had to make sure that the parents were still feeding it, so despite cold wet feet and the fact that both hide and ledge had been soaked in recent rains, I climbed in for another night. A few minutes after Lauren had left, wraiths of mist wafted past the hide, temporarily blotting out the eyrie. I heard an eagle flying past, as if just checking up, and quietly unrolled the sleeping bag, meaning to get warm before the cold of the night. Then I heard the snickering bleats of lambs and through the misty patches saw three of them walking with two ewes only thirty yards below the eyrie. I removed my wet boots and wrung out my soggy trouser ends and my socks. I finished pulling the socks on again and was easing my feet into the bag when I heard the swishings of an eagle braking before landing on the eyrie in a following wind. I was out of position but snaked my right hand up to squeeze the motor drive trigger. Nothing happened. The clip of the battery pack had somehow broken, and the pack had slid down an inch. I nearly strained my back getting both hands high enough to push the batteries back into position, but I managed one shot through the mist as the male eagle turned and left the nest. Far from attacking, he too sailed over the lambs without turning his head. When I looked out, the two ewes were standing over two of their bairns but the third could have been picked up easily. My experience so far with three pairs of eagles was proving the scientific studies to be correct – killing of healthy live lambs was indeed rare.

While the father eagle had been in the eyrie the eaglet had been twittering like a tit. I saw its half full white crop – so it *had* eaten earlier – quivering with the effort. The male had brought in a totally unplucked crow and the eaglet didn't seem to know what to do with it. It peered all round the hoody, hopped on it twice then jumped off and sank down beside it for a nap. The mist cleared completely twenty minutes after the eagle had gone and carefully I took the camera off its clamp to wipe the mist droplets off the lens. As I did this I heard a faint air noise, a shadow passed the hide, the eaglet gave two weak '*keyow*'s and I was just in time to see the big female eagle turn and leave the nest. She could come in almost without a sound – and would, I thought bitterly, the moment I had the camera off its clamp! Through the lens I saw she had brought in a young curlew, but the eaglet made no attempt to eat.

As dusk fell she came in again, sat down beside the chick and lifted her heavy nearest wing as if to encourage it to come close. The light was poor as I tripped off photos at a full second's exposure. She was a lovely sight with her wide head, the great arches behind the eyes showing the power of the head and neck as she looked towards me face-on. No other British bird has this. Her golden mane feathers all ended in sharply curved tips, like an otter's spiky coat after leaving the water, all slipping smoothly over each other with every movement of her head. The creamy incubating plumage of her underside flowed everywhere near the eaglet, looking so warm and soft and inviting that I almost wished I could change places. There was also much white in the bases of her tail feathers. My suspicion that this might be the same pair that used Eyrie 16 last year was now dispelled for there had been no white at all on that large dark female. This looked a much younger bird. She preened the chick's feathers with her great beak as it looked down at her feet, twittering with pleasure. Then as its mother lay half on her side the eaglet preened her, working its beak all along her rear side feathers. One white feather came out on the tip of the eaglet's beak and the expression on its face as it saw the wind float it away was one of surprise.

After a while the mother pushed the chick up on to its feet and from her own lying position began to tug at the crow and eat pieces herself. Twice she turned her head sideways to give the chick a piece. Then she stood up, and walking with exaggerated care, like a great slow parrot, she sat down in the well of the nest, leaving the chick on the side. It seemed odd behaviour. It was marvellous that she had come to spend the night with the eaglet but it seemed she was not actually going to brood it, possibly because it was now too big.

My throat developed horrible tickles but I dared not cough! I withdrew inside the sleeping bag and tried to clear my throat muffled by a thick scarf. When I checked again I was just in time to see the mother eagle stand up and let the eaglet sneak in below her. She then sat much higher, half standing, actually on the eaglet, so that I could see all her body and dark tail. It was almost as if she had sat in the well of the nest to warm it for her youngster. Then she frowsted out all her head and neck feathers, her eyes blinked slower and all her movements slowed down as she relaxed after the hard day. Finally she thrust her head back behind one wing and slept.

I dozed for brief periods, still waking in slight panic when I forgot which side the sheer drop was, quivering with cold some of the time and glad that I had brought gloves.

Well before dawn, in the blue twilight, the eagle woke up and preened her wing and tail feathers for a quarter of an hour. She looked out twice, took two steps to the edge and floated away. She had had only four hours' sleep, and half standing at that, keeping her chick warm. How hard eagles work – a full four months from laying the eggs just to rear one eaglet to flying stage. Then they have to teach it to hunt for at least three more months.

Four hours later the chick squeaked, and in came the mother with a huge sprig of green heather which she waved airily like a semaphore flag, as if making sure not to hit the eaglet. It was the first time that I had known the female to bring in greenery. I got two shots, then waited as she spread her wings and took off after dropping the twig. She came straight for the camera, as vast as a dark umbrella, gnarled yellow talons clenched like grapnel hooks below, eyes glaring from beneath wide imperious eyebrows, and passed over my head. And as she went the eaglet stared after her with a yearning look which bespoke envy, as if thinking 'Oh, I wish I could do that and leave this boring ledge.'

The next few hours were filled with action. The sun at last came over the clifftop at 2 p.m., filling the hide with green fairy lights through the gaps in the covering herbage, though the eyrie itself was still in shadow. I had just lain down to ease my back pain after a long watch when the chick began calling. In swept the mother with a headless grouse, dropped it as I pressed the trigger, turned and sailed away again. The eaglet, having forty winks itself, had not seen her until the last moment. I had only five exposures left on the film and was resting my head on the rock, in the right position for once, when twelve minutes later I heard a faint rush of air and looked through the lens. Mother eagle, coming in with a strong following wind, had a task slowing up. She clutched at the eyrie sticks to arrest her forward impetus, turned her beak sideways so as not to crash into the eaglet and uplifted her tail so high that she looked like a Victorian girl whose many skirts had been blown right over her head. Again I saw how many white feathers she had in her tail – she was certainly not the Eyrie 16 mother.

She had come in with one intent – to feed her chick which had not touched the curlew or the new grouse after the bits of crow she had fed it last night. Unfortunately the eaglet kept its back to me and I had to wait for the right beak to beak shots, knowing that I had only a few frames left. She fed it nine tiny slivers, all tweaked off the grouse with consummate ease and offered with great delicacy to

124

the youngster. Then the film ran out. At last I knew that I had *some* good photos after five nights out on dangerous ledges. Changing the film wasted valuable seconds for I dared not let the lens quiver, and as I was doing it both birds turned sideways for what would have been perfect shots. By the time the new film was in, and I'd ricked a back muscle when moving up to the viewer, the mother had gone.

After the mist and showers, some prey which had kept low in the bad weather had now come out once more, thus the eagles had caught curlew and grouse easily in just a few hours' hunting time. An hour later the eaglet crouched forward and launched a crescendo of squeaks in the classic manner. In came mother, but not to stay this time. Instead she picked up the remains of the hooded crow and I took pictures of her momentarily hanging in the air with it before she took it away. This eagle was scrupulous over keeping the nest clean.

At 5 p.m., after twenty-nine more hours on the ledge, I creaked down the cliff, aching all over. My right knee hurt every time it bent going downhill. The long cold damp nights in awkward positions, this one with wet socks and wet trousers twisted round my legs, were not the best way to keep one's joints healthy. But I was rewarded with pictures of a family of four young wrens flitting on to rocks, not daring to let go again of the rough surfaces in the high winds, opening their beaks hopefully every time mother went near. She was trying to get them off the rocks and out of danger in the deep heather. She kept flying near me, leading me on with loud '*zik zik*' alarm calls. It was the first time I had ever known a wren to act as decoy to protect her young.

*

By the end of June, Eyrie 15 was clearly not being used but a healthy eaglet was accidentally found by a friend of mine in a new eyrie (25) in cliffs above a loch several miles south of the eyrie I was working. However, it was not in my area. Greg Hunter had two surviving eaglets in the two eyries he was watching. So, despite the odd loss of eggs or chicks at Eyrie 2, we still had five known occupied eyries with eaglets – another good year.

On July 4 I trekked round Eagle Rock Mountain, found no new eyries and discovered that more of the debris and old sticks of Eyrie 8 had disappeared. It was washing out slowly in the winter rains and winds.

Two days later, with Lauren unable to take time off, I decided to risk walking up to the Eyrie 4 hide alone. Now that the eaglet was almost full grown and feathered its parents were leaving it alone for a day or longer at a time, and I could slip into the hide unnoticed. I camped out overnight, then slogged the three miles up to the high eyrie at 5 a.m. just before the sun rose beyond its cliffs. I had a double load in the pack now – two cameras, three lenses, battery pack, motor drive, tree clamp, fieldglass, rain gear, sleeping bag, sandwiches, pint of milk, apple and orange, and a dead rabbit. The latter I intended to leave below the eyrie in the hope that the mother would take it up and I could get a shot of her landing with it.

By the time I was halfway through the final steep ascent, the 40lb pack felt like lead as I had forgotten to clip on its waistband. The mother eagle was riding the cold north winds high above the nest, just hanging in the sky and not hovering with wing flaps like a kestrel. She went into a fast glide north-westwards as I came up the hill, her long wings curved back like a swallow's. When I reached the top of the cliff, the smaller male came over in the same flight path, a full two miles behind his mate. As if his gaze was fixed upon her alone, he sailed after her and also disappeared from my view.

The wind was blowing a gale on the exposed cliff top and I was scared of being blown over on to the eyrie, on which I would merely bounce horribly before going to my death. So I braced one leg well back before looking over. The eaglet was still there, asleep with its head tucked behind its right wing. The nest was devoid of prey – a good sign as it meant that the adults might soon be back with something.

The eaglet was covered in dark brown plumage now, wings and tail feathers almost fully grown. When it woke and peered up at me, I saw that its head was also fully feathered, with a hint of gold in the mantle. Because of its large size I felt sure it was a female. I climbed back down, set the rabbit on a prominent rock and scrambled into the hide in the bitter winds.

I found the angle too steep to focus the second camera on the rabbit without fixing it to the edge of the hide ledge. This was impossible without special clamps. Neither could I camouflage even so small an object without my movements being detected if one of the eagles came by. I should have worked it out carefully earlier. Well, I was reasonably sure that the mother eagle would not take the rabbit anyway.

I had been in the hide for only half an hour when the eaglet cheeped. I switched on to 'Automatic' and pulled the motor drive trigger as the mother landed on the nest with *my* rabbit. Nothing happened. I had forgotten to twist the battery pack's switch on to 'Sequence', but I managed one shot before she took off again. The eaglet fed for half an hour, plucking away the fluff with fast professional right-handed flicks to be carried away on the wind. It tugged off chunks of meat between wide straddled legs and swallowed them. Once her crop was full, thrusting white through the new brown breast feathers, she preened herself sitting down. And she kept her back to the wind so that many of her rear feathers were blown conveniently upwards. Below the folded wings I saw that the tail still had some three inches of white waxy sheaths below the brown feathered tips. An hour later I heard a double wing flap, and the male eagle was on the eyrie. He had brought in a headless wood pigeon. How had he caught it? He could have taken a full-fledged squab from a nest. Being smaller than his mate, he would be more manoeuvrable on the edges of a conifer wood. Or maybe he had dropped on a feeding adult after a stealthy flight behind the cover of a rock, vegetation clump or a ridge. Although eagles have been known to take grouse on the wing, I doubted he could have taken the smaller, faster flying, stamina-filled pigeon in this way. The bird was not plucked and the eagle made no effort to feed his daughter.

A few minutes after he had gone, the eaglet cheeped and in flashed the big mother; she looked around, seemed satisfied that her mate had done his bit that morning, and took off again.

The eaglet had now spent nearly nine weeks on that high ledge, screened from all views but the north west by the high lichened cliff faces towering above the nest, and with the long gaps between her parents' visits now, she suffered from boredom. At midday the mother eagle went over to check that all was still well, then I knew I was in for a long wait. She and her mate would now catnap in the early afternoon heat, perched in cliff tree foliage or under a shady overhang, resting from the hours of hunting and digesting their own meals. That they don't use the eyrie for daytime roosting could be due to several factors – a defensive instinct that tells them *two* large eagles on an eyrie are more likely to be seen by the enemy, 'man', than a single eaglet; the fact that the nest is fouled by prey remains and inefficiently ejected excreta, so that they prefer a fresh roost; an instinct to acclimatise the eaglet to the long isolated periods it will spend as an adult; and to induce in it a desire to leave the eyrie when it is nearly ready to fly. Doubtless by this stage they are getting fed up with catching and carrying prey, sometimes long distances, to feed the big brat which should be reaching the time when it will accompany them on hunts!

After dozing, the eaglet awoke to preen herself and performed some vigorous wing-flapping exercises, making her muscles strong. She jumped up and down like a trampoline dancer, clutching and letting go of the heavier twigs and grabbing the nest edge for dear life if ever she felt about to go off into the dangerous void below. Sometimes she just held her great long wings open, showing the white patches, the sunlight glistening on the thick curved edges, feeling how the air currents lifted her up if she dropped her 'rear flaps' or pushed her down if she raised them. She was getting the feel of the winds that would soon be her natural element through all the grand new virgin feathers. Then she folded them in again, stamped on rabbit or pigeon and, still tossing away fluff or grey plumage, rended the meat.

At about 4 p.m. the mother came in again, this time with a slightly plucked young ptarmigan. She landed so fast that the eaglet barely had time to squeak before she was down. I heard ravens calling above but neither mother nor eaglet showed any concern. She left almost immediately and the youngster gazed after her longingly.

By now the eaglet had become used to my comings and goings, and it also responded to a quiet whistle with its normal '*keyow*' squeak, but cut down in resonance, sounding more like '*fischoo fischoo*'. You can get fond of an eaglet as you share opposite ledges for weeks on end – after all, it is your only companion. If I had come back to find it killed, it would have been like the murder of a friend or a beloved child. As I left the hide after only thirteen hours, my shortest stay that year, the eaglet stood bolt upright and watched me go, still squeaking in response to my quiet whistles. I limped down the steep inclines, my right knee again giving hell. When I reached the far track a good mile away, I could see her standing in the late sun in the centre of the eyrie, like a little black statue staring after me all the way. She looked very lonely.

I wanted to rest my painful knee for a few days but it didn't work out that way. Two of the young foxes I was keeping escaped and long searches with Moobli followed. Finally, one by one, he tracked them down by scent and cornered them in thick bracken, long enough for me to grab them by tail and neck. Oddly, after the fast running the knee seemed better, but it was July 14 before I got back to the eagles.

Upon hearing that a nest robber had been convicted in Fort William for stealing eggs from two eyries on the land to the south of my area, I decided to make one more last check of Eyrie 2. I climbed

In my third season – while cleaning the nest, the mother removes
a crow's remains
The eaglet watches enviously as its parent soars away.

The nine-week-old eaglet is getting the feel of the wind, and will soon fly.

The eaglet charges off on its first flight.   And circles to sail past its nest.

the steep ride with the hot evening sun kept off me by a belt of conifers, and at last managed the hard climb straight up to the eyrie that Allan Peters had made earlier. To my astonishment, I found one broken half shell and one full length half shell of the eagles' eggs on a small shelf directly beneath the nest. Certainly no chicks had ever hatched from them for they would have been more broken up than this. It was possible that they had been addled anyway. They could have been poked out of the nest with a long stick before we built the hide, thus the eagle I had seen had returned only out of habit and to roost. Or they could have been nibbled and sucked by pine martens after falling from the nest. I would never know for sure. I wrapped the long piece of shell in dogswood mercury and took it to show Allan, to whom I also gave a show of my best eagle pictures to date, plus a photo for himself – all he would take for his fine help in the late spring. Our only consolation for Eyrie 2 was that the eggs had not been stolen, so maybe it was still not known by any thief.

That night I camped out and woke at 5 a.m. on July 15. After giving Moobli a two-mile exercise run along the deserted single track roads, I hiked up the steepest but shortest route to the torture chamber hide opposite Eyrie 4. I saw no eagles in the sky. By now the eaglet was a beautiful young eagle. Her plumage was a deep chocolate brown all over, with the white in her lower wing and tail feathers showing only when the wind ruffled them. She had a single rabbit leg in the nest.

She spent much time flapping hard, hopping from one leg to the other, clinging with talons to the nest sticks as if strengthening sinews of wing and leg together. I felt she was really ready to go. At about 3 p.m. I had just changed films and was curled up for a rest when she began to '*keyow*' louder than usual. I shot up to the viewer in time to see the male coming in with wings held high, talons extended towards the nest, one of them holding what looked like two mice. The odd thing was that he was coming down almost vertically and facing not the cliff face, but outwards over the nest, as if he had done some magic reverse twist in the air. He touched the nest by the crying eaglet daintily with his feet, let go the prey, sprang up like a ballet dancer and, bringing the wings down in a single beat, flattened out and was away again. As I pressed the button I saw his eyes glaring into the distance, his mighty wings wide spread, his yellow feet retracting like a plane's undercarriage, and the eaglet staring after him with what seemed great envy on her face. As he shot past the camera I saw what looked like one of the mice tumbling down the almost sheer face below the nest. The eaglet looked with apparent disappointment at the remaining mouse, gulped it in one swallow, then began to rend the rabbit leg.

From the loudness of the eaglet's calls and the speed with which her father had dumped the prey, it was clear that the parents were deliberately just making a swift drop off once or twice a day, doubtless feeling that the eaglet should make an effort to fly. After a short sleep, the young eagle peered over the nest edge, then far into the horizon, and indulged in more vigorous flapping exercises than ever. Twice, one of the parents went past the eyrie, missing the hide by only a yard or two with the '*wush wush wush*' of wings growing fainter as it faded into the distance. Each time the eaglet saw a parent coming, it cried out for food, then stared in dismay as it became clear the eagle wasn't coming in. At dusk the eaglet settled down to sleep, jerking her wings fitfully like a peeved child. Neither parent came in all night as I lay huddled in the bag in the usual cramped positions.

Next morning the mother eagle flew past several times, once swerving in close, just above the eaglet, as if almost trying to drive it out. Each time she passed, the eaglet screamed for more food and flapped its wings in anticipation. I was sure the mother was trying to tempt her youngster out, for she had something in her talons on the last two runs, though she was moving so fast I couldn't make out what it was.

The west wind began to increase and the young eagle now made use of it for more buoyancy and made violent flapping charges right across the eyrie, only to clutch the rim branches at the last second before shooting into space. Then just before midday she looked up twice, high into the sky, head twisted almost upside down. I was sure she could see her mother high up there in the ethereal blue canopy.

It was apparently the trigger that was needed. Suddenly I heard a furious flapping and was just in time to photograph the eaglet charging across the nest from the furthest crevice, wings beating like the sails of a broken windmill in a storm. Then away she went. My camera was fixed by its clamp, but desperate to witness an eaglet's first flight, I could do nothing but slide out of the hide. I almost fell down the cliff but I clutched the wood-rush tufts, dug in my heels, and watched her.

She wobbled at first, tail switching unstably to left and right. Then the great wings stabilised as she instinctively felt her flight powers and began to soar to the west. A gust of wind caught her, again a violent flapping and tail switching, then she soared once more, veering to south west, to south, before banking to the south east. She was travelling at such speed that I was afraid she would become a victim of the wind. As she shot eastwards and vanished round some bluffs I was terrified she'd be dashed into the rockfaces further along.

I shot back into the hide, banging my right knee cap on to the rocky ledge, undid the camera equipment, stuffed it all into the pack and slither-climbed down the almost sheer gully. The mother eagle was hanging above the eyrie, slightly to the north, and had clearly seen the eaglet go. And seeing her had helped its decision to fly. But so worried was I that the inexperienced youngster might have come to grief, I staggered over the heathered boulders, oblivious to the increased pain in my knee, anxious to make sure she was all right. As I passed below the eyrie I found the 'mouse' that had dropped down: it was a dead field vole.

Finally I spotted the eaglet standing normally on a small rocky ridge at about a thousand feet, with the rockfaces I was worried about still a good way beyond her. They also made her difficult to see for she was not on a skyline. As I lay in thick heather to watch, the mother flew off to the north. I waited twenty minutes. When the eagle came back much lower over the ridges, the eaglet saw her and '*keyow*'ed like mad for about half a minute. The mother flew close over it as if for inspection, then soared away to the north east again. I got out of there quickly. Clearly an adult eagle can locate a flown youngster easily, especially if it can hunt tiny creatures like voles, but for man in such rugged hills it can be a hopeless task. I had been lucky. As I topped the last ridge before the final descent to the Land Rover I saw the mother fly back and head down to where the eaglet had been standing. It should be all right now.

As I drove and boated home I felt relieved and elated, despite the pains in my knee and a feeling of desperate tiredness. I noted in my diary: 'After a bad start, this year has proved to be the best, with the best flight shots so far. I observed an eaglet almost from hatching to its actual first flight. With a fine mother and good hunting success by its parents, it had plenty of food and flew in only nine-and-a-half weeks from hatching. I doubt I will work eagles again as too dangerous and strenuous at fifty years old – some of that energy could be expended on actually earning a living!' It never occurred to me then that I might still be at it fifteen years later, nor that I would write not one but eventually three books about eagles.

Three days later I went back, climbed above the eyrie to over 1,400 feet and was rewarded by seeing the mother eagle gliding slowly overhead against a drizzly north-west breeze. Not more than half a mile behind came the eaglet. I could see her white tail and wing patches clearly but she was flapping more often and heavily than her mother. To my surprise, she appeared to see me for she dived quite expertly, circled round below the eyrie, giving me a good flight picture from above her, then soared away in the direction her mother had taken. What a fine climax to the season – I had never captured a flying eaglet at close quarters before. That night I gave Lauren a pair of new hill boots for her help and rang sheep farmer John Ritchie and Greg Hunter. The three of us met for drinks and good talk at a local inn. When I told the truth about the single lamb I thought the eagles could have actually killed, though it had been small and might have died anyway, John took it sportingly. 'We'll have a dram on the lamb!' he said. While he accepted a bottle of the best, two of my books and a big eagle colour print as my tribute to his co-operation, he has since regaled me with such fine hospitality at his farmhouse that I still feel in his debt! Somehow I drove and boated home after the celebratory evening, fed the foxes and young wildcat, gave Moobli a second portion of supper, and collapsed into bed after a can of soup for myself at 4.30 a.m.

Two days later I saw huge Atalanta, the female who haunted the land around my home and whose occupied eyrie I had never yet found, fly across the loch and vanish beyond some trees in front of a 150-foot-high rockface which reared above a small glen. She did not reappear. 'Don't tell me she has an eyrie there!' I groaned aloud, thinking of the long boat trips, 50 mile drives and long six mile treks to the eyrie I had observed that year. I boated over and searched. It was hard going, all forestry plantations where two-foot deep bulldozed drainage ditches beneath the scratchy sitka spruces were often hidden by tussock crowns, bracken and heather, and it would have been easy to break a leg. I found no new eyrie, however. She must have flown in just to perch awhile.

I rested my legs for a few days as I caught up on neglected work at my desk, but with conscience pricking, I set off in sunny hazy weather on July 30 with bored Moobli to check that the chick had flown safely from Eyrie 18. It was as ever the hardest trek of all, a real killer involving some 12,000 feet of ups and downs there and back, and my only hope – a frail one – was to glimpse the eaglet flying. Unless (eaglets can die during their first weeks away from the nest), I found its body. As we slogged upwards, wheatear and meadow pipit families flitting on rocks all round us, I saw five golden plovers flying with deep wingbeats, the first I'd seen in these particular hills.

We headed north east on the last descent so as not to lose height before striking north west again to above the eyrie. Suddenly I was astonished to see the eaglet fly from a ridge to the right and disappear over the eyrie cliff. There, among the new chocolate plumage were the unmistakable white underwing patches and white tail band – and the darn camera was still in my pack! As it drifted over us, it called loudly, '*Keyow, keyow, keyow*' as if confirming it was the eaglet. It was good to know this chick was flying well too. As we walked above the eyrie, on which it had not landed, and I checked for a possible future hide site, the eaglet appeared to our left and again circled our heads. This time I had the camera out. As the meter was playing tricks I banged off five hand held shots, switching shutter speed from a 1,000th to a 250th between each push of the button – a tricky operation, to make sure of at least one good shot. Now, as the wind swept up the glen towards the eyrie, I noticed the old sheep fleece was not only still there but appeared to have been arranged on the windward side of the nest. Had it been put there deliberately by the eagles to keep winds off the eaglet? It seemed a possibility.

I looked up again for the eaglet and there in the sky at the end of the glen, as if waiting for the youngster as it headed towards them, were both the parent birds. Clearly they could locate each other by sight at least four miles on a clear day. As we came below the eyrie, Moobli scented the air and turned back. I followed and we found a roosting perch of the adults forty yards south of the nest – a stripped dry rowan tree growing at right angles to the cliff. There were white mutes everywhere, many preened feathers clung to the heather and grasses and two large regurgitated four-inch long pellets – containing rabbit fur, small bones and what looked like a grouse's beak – lay among them. The hard trek had been well worthwhile.

A week later we boated out and hiked up to Eyrie 4 to take down the hide. As I tore out the covering vegetation and left the whole site as pristine as before, I again saw the eaglet and her mother flying together some five hundred yards to the north. I hoped she and her mate would teach it to hunt well for its first winter would be critical.

On our way home I paid a call on a friend, who worked on a neighbouring farm and was the long-lost nephew of the old French-Canadian log craftsman who had helped me build my log cabin in Canada over ten years before. Meeting him in the Highlands had been a thousand to one coincidence. Now he told me of an extraordinary sighting he'd had some days earlier. He had seen a large eagle and a white-patched eaglet flying over the loch from the south when a small flock of common gulls arrived and began to mob the eaglet, swooping so close that they almost forced it into the loch. Suddenly a smaller eagle had flown in, clearly the male, and had actually struck one of the gulls, seemingly with bunched talons like a fist, and knocked it into the trees above the shore. The gull had not re-appeared. As the other gulls dispersed, the eaglet landed on a high rock, its mother circled over it, and both flew out of sight, followed by the male.

I wondered if these eagles were Atalanta and Meleager, and if they had again reared an eaglet in an eyrie I had yet to find. Or were they the pair that had used Eyrie 18 this year? (It took me three more years to establish that this was indeed the situation.)

It had been the finest year so far for eagles locally. I had seen and photographed the two chicks from Eyries 4 and 18 flying successfully, the two from pairs 10 and 12 were also on the wing and had been seen flying with their parents on several occasions by Greg Hunter, and there was the healthy eaglet found in Eyrie 25 in the land to the south west at the end of June. Just before I prepared my detailed report for the Nature Conservancy Council, I met Dr Ray Hewson, a scientific officer with the Ministry of Agriculture, who had been studying foxes in the region. He also had discovered a healthy eaglet in a new eyrie (26) in the land to the south, a few miles from Eyrie 25. In addition, a friend told me he had seen five eagles flying together in that vicinity only a few days ago, two of them with white bands in their tails. From his description it seemed he had spotted them between the two eyries. He was a keen amateur ornithologist, not a man to confuse eagles with buzzards, and it was clear he had not only seen the two eaglets flying but two separate eagle families behaving amicably toward each other, on the same home range, or at least on the edges of their mutual territories.

Again here was evidence that the territorial instincts of eagles lessen after the breeding season. This was a fascinating question on which I was personally to gain more evidence in future years. On checking through my diaries, I found I had by now trekked over a thousand mountain miles on foot for eagles and had spent over three hundred hours in eagle hides, mostly overnight on cliff ledges. While I doubted my ability, financially and physically, to carry out so much work next year, I also knew my early fascination with the great eagles remained undimmed.

9 · *Hard Times*

A series of catastrophes during that autumn, and through what proved to be the harshest winter in the Highlands for sixteen years, not only impaired my eagle studies but had me doubting whether to carry on with the wilderness life at all. It was as if some malevolent deity were trying to oust me and send me back to normal civilised life.

En route home in early September, after a brief research trip south, two young foxes from those that I had been studying all summer escaped in odd circumstances, so ending the fox project.

After the 600-mile drive from Sussex, my boat engine which I had put in for service, flatly refused to start as I sat in the loaded boat in the near dark facing the six-and-a-half water miles to my home. For the next few supply trips I had to row most of the thirteen miles out and back, until a different mechanic found that the head had been put back wrongly and fixed it.

A worse shock on my return was the total disappearance of Liane, the young wildcat I had tamed and who had been with us for two-and-a-half years. The mystery was never solved, though I hoped she'd gone off with a visiting wild tom. After so rare and close a relationship, I found her absence depressing.

On September 30, after days of heavy rain, I heard a loud crash as I sat at my desk. A tree had fallen across my water pipe, holed it and sent it hanging over the thundering waterfall writhing like a snake in its death throes. It took a day to repair and re-set it.

On October 4 I was racing over rough ground after Moobli, who I

135

thought was on Liane's scent, when my right foot hit sideways with great impact on a tussock. I heard a nasty cracking sound and felt a terrible pain. I was virtually immobilised and in pain for the next eight days. My one-time remark to those who asked what would I ever do if I broke a leg 'out there', that I would hop down to the boat and launch it on my knees, was now thrown back in my face, for only with a supreme effort and the use of a stick could I reach the shore at all. Such was the pain that I could not move the boat a foot, never mind launch it. Finally, when I could get out, I had to drive with my left foot on the accelerator to hospital in Fort William for treatment.

No bones were broken, the doctor told me after an X-Ray, as he bound the ankle with a sticky bandage that held it almost as rigid as a plaster cast, but it was a very bad sprain and tendons had been torn. I ought to be able to trek the Hill again in time but the ankle might always be weak. I felt as if nature and the harsh terrain had bestowed – as upon an old stag – judgement upon me. Well, I thought, my eagle days are probably over but at least I could do something for them with my writing.

I had long been concerned over one aspect of eagle conservation in the western Highlands – that of the alleged predation by eagles on live lambs. I had found only four lambs on eyries during the studies of three pairs of eagles at the eyrie in the last three years, only one of which I was reasonably certain had been killed by the birds. But I could understand the anger of a farmer who felt he *was* losing lambs to eagles – it was all very well naturalists preaching eagle conservation but they weren't losing money after hard hill gatherings and weeks of work in the lambing season.

As one farmer indeed said to me: 'If we just got the occasional fiver from the government, at least it would show *something* was being done. Otherwise it's the farmer alone who bears the brunt of supporting rare wildlife like eagles.' I also bore in mind the destruction over two years of Eyrie 11, the loss of Eyrie 13 in a hill fire, and the possible poking out of eggs this year in Eyrie 2.

I decided to sound out the Nature Conservancy Council on the issue. When I sent in my eagle report, having heard the R.S.P.B. had once operated a scheme for paying fees to farmers who had successful eaglets on their lands, I suggested it might be a good idea to start a small compensation scheme for killed lambs. I said I wouldn't mind operating such a scheme in my area, if it was thought to be a wise idea. At least it might help encourage the few 'die-hards' left to leave nesting eagles alone.

On October 15, feeling guilty that this was the first year I hadn't made treks to observe stags and hinds in the rutting season, fearful that the ankle would remain weak if I didn't exercise it, I hiked with Moobli up to 1,500 feet and covered a slow four steep miles with the help of a stick. We found several stags with hinds but didn't stalk them well as I was too worried about where I was putting my foot. The doctor had also said if I ricked the ankle in the same way again I could do grave permanent damage, but when I reached home, the throbbing foot once more up on a chair by my desk, I felt happier. Maybe once the leg had healed my run of troubles would be over and I would be back on the Hill as good as before.

Two days later came the worst shock of all, one that was to plunge me in and out of recurrent nightmare for a year and a half. Around 11 p.m. I saw torchlights flashing in the darkness out on the cold but calm loch. Wondering what was happening, I shouted 'Who is it?' out of the front door, then dodged out of a side door to make a wide sortie through the trees until my eyes were used to the dark. When I came upon the boat, I found my friend from the neighbouring farm with a companion. The police had asked them to deliver a telegram. Its message was stark and simple.

'Stepmother dying. Father incapable. Imperative you come.' It was signed by friends of my father and stepmother.

I began to pack immediately, knowing in my heart what probably lay ahead. Thirteen years earlier my father and stepmother had retired to southern Spain, where they built a villa overlooking a spectacular Mediterranean view but seven kilometres away from the nearest shops. Next day I boated out, drove south to deliver Moobli to friends in Worthing, in Sussex, and caught the first available flight from Heathrow. When I arrived at the villa after a seventy-five mile taxi ride from Alicante, it was to find that my stepmother had died on the night I received the cable. The funeral was already over and my father was ill and bedridden. Two groups of friends, taking turns to look after him, looked haggard and were relieved at my arrival.

For the next month, hobbling with a stick myself, I struggled to get my father back on his feet, cope with a defunct car, shopping, cooking, laundry, plumbing repairs, complicated business affairs, and set about the long process of getting Spanish probate on my stepmother's estate because almost everything had been put into her name. Somehow I snatched an odd hour to finish a new book for its Christmas deadline, though I also had to cope with thirsty well-wishers who arrived to help cheer my father up.

It seemed like a missive from another world when a Nature Conservancy Council letter dated October 20 was sent out with other mail. '. . . it was gratifying to note that the golden eagles had a fairly successful year. No doubt if you intend to continue your work next year you will make the normal application at the appropriate time.' But, as I had feared, the reverse bounty scheme I had suggested was not supported. 'The question of a bounty scheme to compensate sheep farmers is a highly charged political one and would have to be adopted on a national basis rather than in a piecemeal fashion. However, past experience suggests that a scheme of this sort is open to wide abuse, and for these and other reasons I cannot see any practical means of adopting a bounty scheme – even if the various Government Departments were in agreement on this delicate question. However, I am copying your letter and this reply to Mr Balharry and you may feel the matter is worth pursuing with him.'

Well, I would, when I got home, *if* I ever got home again, but right now there were more urgent matters. The only good thing during all this was that the sun was good for my ankle and by November 3 I was able to take my first hard run over the deserted mountain roads and cut up my walking stick to help the nightly fires in my father's lounge.

In the middle of November my elder sister bravely flew in all the way from Lesotho, in Africa – where her husband, a Canadian cultural attaché, was on an extended tour – to look after our father for a month. It was now clear that he could not be left alone in Spain. There was no old folks' home in the region, and he resolutely refused to live with me in the remote, cold, wet Highlands. The only solution was to bring him back to a nursing home in Worthing where he had lived for several happy years and had friends. I flew back, tied up his business affairs, looked over some likely places in Worthing, picked up Moobli and dashed back to the Highlands to try and finish my book on time. I felt exhausted on arrival and found I had lost over a stone in weight.

On November 24 I was working at my desk when the drizzly clouds rolled away and a low sun shone through a dark blue sky. I went out for an exercise run and saw a young eagle come winging from the west and swoop up to land on a skyline rock. It landed shakily, looked weak, and after I'd gone in for the camera, I saw three red deer hinds only a few yards from it. One of the hinds walked deliberately up to the eaglet and stretched out her long thin reptilian head, as if sniffing at the huge bird. My camera clicked.

The startled eaglet took off and wafted past the high rockfaces to the north east. What an odd sight! Usually red deer fear eagles and will scatter at their close approach but I wondered if this old hind knew it was just an inexperienced eaglet and weak too. Next day I set off in snow showers for a late trek and had just photographed a hind looking comical after a small cliff snow fall had left a dollop of white on her muzzle, when I saw the eaglet again. It was sitting on the same skyline rock which it seemed to be using as a spy post. Through the fieldglass I saw that its head was following the movements of the deer. Maybe it was waiting hopefully for a sick one to drop, a late-born calf perhaps.

I tried to stalk it from behind a lower ridge, but when I peered round, the eaglet had gone. However, I managed to photograph eagle tracks in the snow, over six-and-a-half inches long. Just as I put the camera away again, the eaglet went past above me southwards, flapping its great long wings slowly. I felt sorry for it as it seemed to have been left by Atalanta and Meleager and was engaged in a lonely fight for existence, dependent on the death of another creature for its own survival in the bitter cold landscape. A reminder of the harsher face of nature and creation, I thought. But then *all* animal life consumes other life on this earth in order to live itself.

Next morning on our walk round the woods Moobli scented out a freshly dead old grey-muzzled hind that had sought a last resting place between two fallen pines. I cut off the haunches for him then heaved the rest of the carcass up to the broad ledge at 400 feet, taking care with my right ankle which still gave painful twinges under stress. The eaglet was clearly very hungry and had kept a sharp eye on the area for at dusk I saw through the glass that it was on the carcass and rending it fast, going up and down like a miniature oil derrick!

I was delighted to have helped it so directly in this way but I rejected the idea of setting up a hide. I was battling to finish the book and solve my father's affairs. I was not feeling so robust that I felt I could cope with a night in the bitter snow. Besides, it was more important that the eaglet ate than I get photos. I did, however, find time to answer the Nature Conservancy Council regarding the reverse-bounty idea.

'... I am surprised to hear the question of compensating sheep farmers is a complex "political" one. I just felt if it worked in one area in a small way that might be taken as a pattern for a scheme for the Highlands. Certainly I can see the possibilities of abuse though much would depend upon how firm, and tactful, the operator was perhaps. At the moment it seems it is an occasional eyrie that is abused...

'It is indeed a delicate problem, for a greater interest stirred up towards it may not have wholly beneficial results, and there is the possibility of grievance among those who were not compensated. But there must be some good ways of encouraging folk who have eagles and other rare and valuable wildlife on their grounds to take greater interest and act more as custodians!'

In the next few days I saw the young eagle twice more. It seemed in far better shape now, flapping faster on the few occasions it needed to and landing more efficiently. It pleased me that the hind carcass may have just turned the tide in favour of its survival. I didn't once see Atalanta or Meleager at this time, and again I felt they had moved to the lower ground to the south west where there were rabbits.

Finally, I completed the book, bottled all remaining garden vegetables for my return, filled the woodshed with logs, and after delivering poor old Moobli to Worthing again, I flew back to Spain on December 9 to relieve my sister.

My father had continued to improve but new problems loomed. He wanted to stay in Spain but I could find no-one to look after him. Finally, after a relapse during which a local doctor convinced my father that he had to return to Britain where he could be looked after, I succeeded in bringing him back by plane to Gatwick and a Britain struck by blizzards on January 27. Next day, with a friend, I took him to a pleasant nursing home near the Worthing seafront, close to a pub that had once been his favourite haunt and arranged for him to receive any little luxuries he wanted. I stayed in the town with Moobli for several days until my father seemed settled, then finally returned to my disrupted life and Scotland.

Moobli ran three miles over the harsh terrain beside the boat, had a brief sleep in the cottage, then demanded I throw sticks for him to chase, as glad to be back on his home ground as I was.

*

Heavy rains and south-westerly gales replaced the snows and sleet of late February, and when the snow-capped peaks and ledges began to melt, the sudden onslaught of the combined waters set all the burns thundering down the hills in gushing veins of white and tawny falls. The loch level rose two feet overnight and when I went out it was to see waves crashing over the flooded stern of the big boat, so it was see-sawing madly up and down on its trolley.

The smaller boat was filled with water and banging its keel on half buried rocks. As I winched up the big boat a split pin sheared, one trolley wheel came off and the boat collapsed on to the wooden runway. I raced up to the woodshed for a long two-inch by four-inch spar but my attempt to lever it up again only sent the opposite wheel sliding off the runway and into a rut. The boat was now immovable and still being flooded by waves thumping into its stern. I set down a rock on which to lever the boat's left side up but the rock sank and wedged itself in the mud and trapped the lever under the boat. As I jerked to get the lever free my hand slipped and a large splinter went into my palm. When I tightened the winch wire to breaking point and then hauled the boat bodily as well, it did slide up the runway, only to have the trolley's axle hit the wedged rock. I cursed aloud with frustration and the bitter cold.

I raced up to the house for a crowbar. While I worked with it to get the rock free, every wave slapped into a recess in the bank below and sent a spout of icy water into my face and down my chest. Finally I heaved the boat off the trolley on to wooden runners and repaired the trolley wheel with a new split pin. Afterwards I couldn't lift the 500lb boat and its water cargo back on to the trolley. I would have to wait until the loch calmed down and I could slide both boat and trolley into deeper water and float the boat back on. I spent another half hour baling out the smaller boat with a bucket, then hauled it bodily out of reach and up to more wooden runners. It was 12.30 p.m. before I had finished. 'Just par for a stormy winter's day,' I thought, contrasting it with the soft life in sunny Spain as I walked up to the cottage. Then I saw an extraordinary sight.

Atalanta and what I took to be Meleager were flying above the ridges to the north east and suddenly she circled and dived on him. Wet, slow with cold, I rushed for the Pentax with the 640 mm lens, found the film at an end, fitted a new one and dashed out again. They were nearer now and I took shot after shot. I was astonished to see that the male had faint creamy patches under his wings, which also seemed thinner than Meleager's had been. This was clearly not him but a much younger bird, smaller and even more lightly coloured. And it was not the eaglet either. Had Meleager perished in this, the harshest winter in the Highlands for many years? It seemed possible.

Atalanta was still doing most of the diving and the male was turning *his* claws upwards. I wondered if she, being a middle aged or even old bird with this new younger male, was showing him the ropes! Once, however, Atalanta landed and the new male dived

141

down, beat his wings hard, landed near her, then on her gently, needing no instruction it seemed in the performance of mating duties. They were now three quarters of a mile away and hard to see clearly. In the viewer they were just small black blobs, but I felt excitement that I had some kind of a picture of mating eagles at last.

But what had happened to Meleager? If he had died, here was proof that eagles could replace lost mates quite quickly, and also that an adult will sometimes team up with an immature or sub-adult. If her new mate with the creamy wing patches, small though they were, was a sub-adult, could he have mated with her successfully?

The next time I met Greg Hunter, after driving to his home in another blizzard which caused even the solid Land Rover to slide about, he said he too had witnessed something unusual that winter. He saw a peregrine falcon fly past a soaring golden eagle, not too close, and when the eagle spotted the falcon (reputedly the fastest flying bird in Europe) for some reason it decided to give chase. With a few hard beats the eagle had gained speed, hit into the right half-sideways air stream and in a fast glide had caught up with the peregrine, pursuing it so closely that the falcon had had to swerve and dive about. At that point the eagle had seemed to lose interest.

'And I didn't have my camera with me!' Greg ended with a crestfallen look.

He had applied for a licence to photograph his local eagles again and asked if I had too. I said I didn't think I would this year.

'Why not?'

I didn't want to load on to a friend all my problems in Spain, or the fact that I was months behind with my work and that my earnings had dwindled. I knew, but didn't say, that I would have to go to Spain again to sell my father's villa and bring his belongings back to England. That being so, how could I afford the time, or energy, for the hundreds of miles that needed to be trekked?

'I guess I'm running out of steam,' I said.

Greg grinned. 'You'll be doing them again,' he said. I replied that I just might, if the pair bred again at Eyrie 16, the best I knew for hide work. But I doubted if I would be able to check all the other eyries over the 350 square miles.

On my way home next day I met one of my neighbouring farmers. We had never had a long talk before so when he invited me in for a cup of tea I gladly accepted. We were soon in conversation about farming and wildlife conservation. It had long been my belief that farmers are an essential key to nature conservation as they

142

occupy and work some eighty per cent of Britain's land, and that government should offer more encouragement to them in this field. As he was also actively concerned with the foxhound pack I wanted to hear his views. He expressed them with insight, explaining that he and other sheep farmers were not out to eradicate foxes, merely to control their numbers so that lamb killing was reduced to a minimum.

He said he reckoned there were still farmers who would kill eagles if they felt they had good reason, who believed that some eagles killed many lambs. He asked my opinion. I said I had not yet compared all my notes but knew of only two lambs (Greg Hunter had just told me he had found only one in his studies) that had been killed by eagles. I said I'd seen eagles fly out over lambs when they had not brought any food into eyries for over thirty hours, and not even look down. A good ewe would attack a hungry eagle after its lamb with a bunt or two.

'Or stand over it,' he added. He said that, from the economic point of view alone, some farmers believed it might be better to wipe out all eagles and all foxes.

'Oh, I can't agree with that,' I rejoined. 'We all have to learn to share land with wildlife, especially rare species. There are two-and-a-quarter million sheep in Scotland and only about 280 pairs* of eagles. It's quite wrong to devastate the natural world, especially rarer creatures like eagles, purely for one aspect of farming, like sheep which have to be subsidised anyway.' I added that both foxes and eagles did some good, even from the farmer's view. Foxes kill many voles, which are host to a tick that transmits louping ill to hill sheep, and which also eat grass and ring young trees. Eagles also took voles and killed foxes – cubs were not uncommonly found at eyries.

If his estimate that a fox family took about eight lambs in the critical first three weeks of lambing was correct, then an eagle which took a fox was indirectly saving the lives of possibly thirty lambs or more over the fox's lifetime. And both foxes and eagles took many rabbits, a favourite food, which compete with sheep for grass.

We talked for two hours, ranging over many aspects of wildlife and farming, and I told him I was already discussing the question of compensation in rare cases of eagles actually killing lambs. I knew him to be an excellent and hard working farmer and learned much from what he had to say. I think we both came away with respect for

* The number believed at that time, in 1979. After more accurate surveys in the early '90s there were known to be about 420 pairs and 70 to 80 inmates.

each other's point of view. And I was more than ever sure that the active co-operation of farmers, owners and all land occupiers had to be won before really efficient conservation is possible. Recent tougher legislation had helped, but if unenforceable, as it largely is over such wild uninhabited country, it is basically ineffective.

I took up the compensation question with Dick Balharry, but he too felt the scheme would be open to wide abuse. The N.C.C. was already drastically under-funded, so where would the money come from? We agreed to meet and discuss it in depth at a later date.

On March 5 I was in the garden photographing a tame red deer hind and her calf coming out of the west wood, when the new male eagle came over the north-eastern ridges, followed by Atalanta. I dashed indoors for the big lens but when I got outside again, they had gone. I waited in the cold westerly winds for a few minutes and saw Atalanta heading back, flapping as she zig-zagged along the rock-faces. Now the male was following her and down he swooped, missing her by a foot or so. They soared slowly on the high wind, wings well back like Delta jets, over Eyrie 1 and disappeared. I went in to warm my hands but something made me go out again after a few minutes.

Now Atalanta was flying east above my top fence with a raven – no, a male buzzard – after her. They soared along not far apart and were joined by the male eagle, which dived on the buzzard. The latter just turned slightly, zoomed down and then back up near the hill slope and reversed the tactics. It seemed to be a kind of play, as if they were all having fun, for now Atalanta also turned and dived down between her new partner and the buzzard, both appearing to feel the rush of air. There was no attempt to strike by any party. I noticed again that the male eagle's plumage was lighter than Atalanta's.

The three drifted along together below the north-east ridges, then vanished over a crest. The next thing I knew there were four birds – the female buzzard had also joined in – and they all soared along slowly together, just changing positions occasionally, two eagles, two buzzards, and they finally drifted over high towards the west. I had never seen the like of it but must have taken some good shots with all four birds in frame. What would expert ornithologists make of that?

I never had the chance to prove this sighting, nor the actual mating of the eagles taken earlier. In my haste I had fitted the new film badly. After development I found it had not gone through the camera although the numbers had mounted up on the dial. But I didn't know this on the day I saw the eagles being so 'friendly' with the buzzards. Inspired by the sight, I thought 'I *will* continue the eagle studies for one more year.' I would make time somehow. When I sent my licence applications to monitor the eyries and breeding success, and to photograph the Lochaber eagles, however, I said I would only photograph from a hide if I was sure I could better the pictures I already had and could find out more useful information. I felt even more righteous that day, for I found a dead deer calf in the burn and hauled it up to the high ledge for the eagles.

I wondered now about the eaglet I had last seen on November 24. Had it perished in the cold winter or just moved out of the territory? I had the answer two days later on the way back from a supply trip. As my boat drew in, I saw the eaglet fly off from where I'd hauled the carcass and land with a wide upsweep of its white-patched wings on a high rock. It watched Moobli panting along the shore and myself unloading the boat. When I turned again a slight shower fell and I saw a tightly curved rainbow bathe the eaglet in brilliant light. While I carried supplies up the slope it advanced before me until it shone upon the cottage with a beautiful radiance. Images shot through my mind – rainbow, pot of gold, rainbow on golden eagle, rainbow from eagle to my cottage – it seemed a sign from the sky that I *must* work with eagles again this year. And what a picture! I raced indoors for the camera but by the time I had fitted the right lens the eaglet had gone and I had to be content with the moving rainbow, now shining on the nearest islet.

Heavy snowfalls delayed my eagle treks until March 11, but on that day Moobli and I set off amid sleet flurries on a nine-miler, up the long river valley to the east. We were working along steep wooded slopes at some 400 feet and I had just photographed the pair of ravens which nested in a high cliff there when the new male eagle came beating against the wind from south of the loch. Instantly the two ravens shot off with high '*pruk pruk*' cries to mob it. To my surprise, the eagle dropped low through the trees until it reached a lower part of the ridge and disappeared over it. Again, my previous belief that eagles won't fly in woods in case they damage their long wings was undermined, for this male had done it quite naturally. True, the trees were fairly wide apart, which he had clearly seen for himself. Again it was obvious that the loch was not a natural boundary and, I noted, he was heading towards Eyrie 1.

We found no eyries above the river valley nor saw any more

eagles. A few days later I hiked up to Eyrie 1 and found a few dead sticks below it. At first I thought the male might have taken them in as if saying, 'How about using this one? I've done it up a bit!' And the lady had said 'No!' But when I saw that the nest looked smaller than last year I realised the sticks had been blown off it by winds; the nearest eyrie to me was breaking up.

On March 18 I decided to get the 'killer trek' over soon and set off with Moobli on the 12,000 feet of ups and downs to Eyries 18 and 19. I went west of all the peaks and knolls as the north-east wind was giving my right ear frostbite. Hell, it was cold! All the burns were frozen, with icicles clinging to rocks, making it hazardous to cross, but pretty little icefalls framed by the witch's broom of a rowan tree, a solitary stunted oak, or a clifftop were a reward to the eye. On the high sunless north-facing slopes, the snow slides were steep and frozen so hard that it was difficult stamping in footholds to cross them – especially doing it with my left foot, as my right was still giving off twinges. I really needed an ice axe to be safe. However, having gone so far I was not about to turn back.

Stamping hard on one patch, my foot hit solid ice and I lost balance and was away like a human toboggan, sliding down on my backside. Only frantic kicking and digging in with my heels and fingers arrested my slide towards a precipice. After I had edged my way gingerly off the patch I found the seat of my pants almost ripped out by the rough frozen particles. I envied the way Moobli managed his great hairy hulk across these steep snow sheets. The rough pads on his huge feet matched the rough icy surfaces in a way no human footgear could without crampons.

I did not expect Eyrie 18 to be used again after the successful eaglet the previous year and was not surprised when it showed no signs of activity. Eyrie 19 was also untouched and more twigs had been blown away.

It is likely that such a hard winter inhibits eagle breeding for the birds need to be in good condition to lay their big fertile eggs and incubate them successfully. Maybe this pair would not breed this year, and if this was one of Atalanta's eyries it was possible that her new male was still too immature, despite my seeing them mating. Between 10 and 25 per cent of pairs do not breed in any given year. Eagles occasionally take a year off. I saw none on this occasion.

Our next trek was an eight-miler to find a new eyrie for Atalanta. This was also unsuccessful. Two days later I saw two eagles flying over the hills near Eyries 2 and 17 and my hopes rose there. But I couldn't check for a while as my new book was due out and I had to complete some radio interviews at the publisher's request. On April 8 we covered eight more miles of the land to the north east, but found no new eyries. This time I felt a bit weak on the high trek back, and even Moobli had developed a slight limp in his rear left leg.

By now trouble was brewing in Spain over the sale of my father's villa as a French group were claiming they had paid half the price, blithely ignoring the fact of a go-between making off to Switzerland with their money. I had to go back there to secure a deal, and also to rescue my father's belongings.

On my way south on April 19 I trekked up to Eyries 2 and 17 but found no activity in either. The grey mantled male had been an old bird and after the hard winter could be either not in breeding condition or dead. I saw no sign of either eagle. It was a sad start to the season but I had more urgent problems ahead. I had the Land Rover serviced, drove down to Southampton, caught the ferry to St Malo, then bowled down through France and the Pyrenees to south-eastern Spain.

Much had to be overcome. Days dragged by in lawyers' offices until finally the villa was sold. Tired after the long drives, nights spent sleeping in the truck and the interminable daytime wranglings, I took a few days off.

To keep fit, I walked and jogged through the dusty sandstone mountains. I climbed one 3,200-foot mountain and at the top found an old eagle pellet and the near-fresh green leg of a coot. I had seen coots swimming on the many salt flats on the drive down the coast and it seemed there was still a sea eagle in the area where once they flourished but were now said to be extinct. There was no other likely explanation for a coot's leg being on top of a mountain. Interesting, but I did not actually see any sea eagles, and all the find did was to underline how much I was missing the beloved Highlands and my own eagles.

As I set off on the long journey back, having already driven 2,402 miles from my home loch, I decided to take a different route and go through the Ordesa National Park in the Spanish Pyrenees which, I had been told, was a good wildlife area. I struck up through Alicante, Valencia, Teruel and Zaragoza, and took the smaller road through Huesca so that I could cross the border at Candanchu. Suddenly I found myself in a dream country – emerald lakes, towering conifer trees, rushing streams, and even a weft or two of wraith-like mist which took the heat from the midday sun. I was only a few miles from the border, the great crags of the Pyrenees dominating the distant skyline. I turned a wooded bend in the road and there ahead were three massive cliff faces of red and grey rock, one to the west and two to the east, great towering buttresses over 2,000 feet in height and sheer for most of the way up. Below them stretched green fields fed by streams, and I saw a rabbit or two hopping along near the grassy banks.

I was just thinking 'There could be eagles here' when one came beating along beside the truck, merely eighty yards away! I stopped, leaped out with the camera and took some shots of the golden eagle as it obligingly circled in the sunlight. Then I saw a buzzard, then another eagle. And as I looked up into the sky I saw more huge birds high up, drifting towards the western massif. To my astonishment I counted seventeen huge raptors in the air, eleven of which I identified as golden eagles.* Others were even larger, with bigger wings and longer outspread 'fingers' – lammergeiers, otherwise known as European vultures. I gasped as one lammergeier looped down and flew past with talons extended, the sun shining on its coppery nape, and took more shots. It was like being in an eagle lover's paradise, all these great raptors drifting about in a dream around the peaks, floating like shadows past the great faces where there must be eyries. I did not know then, though the idea was already taking root at the back of my mind, that I would spend five years in this extraordinary country and write a book (which I called *In Spain's Secret Wilderness*) about my encounters there with wolves and bears, with the European lynx, with imperial eagles, great lammergeiers and black vultures with nine-foot wingspans.

I was worried now about getting across the border with all the gear I had on board, so I did not tarry long. To my surprise, the Spanish police took one look at the old Land Rover and the odd pieces of furniture roped to the roof rack and laughed. Without even leaving their office, they waved me through!

I got back to Worthing on May 24 and next day made a deal with the matron of my father's nursing home. For an increased fee she let me remove two beds from a three-bedded room on the ground floor. I installed all his favourite furnishings, carpets, ornaments, clocks, globe bar and made the room as much a 'home from home' as possible. When I brought him down from his small upstairs room, he was delighted and said he now felt truly at home. That night, my

* I discovered later that most of them were griffon vultures, of which at the time I had had no experience.

148

own 51st birthday he reminded me, we went out for a celebratory supper with a friend. I stayed with him three more days, completed his business, and finally reached my home loch with Moobli on June 1.

I now felt beaten into the ground. I was even more behind with my work, and the thought of starting out on hard eagle treks at this late stage seemed out of the question. The wilderness gods, it seemed, had a different view.

10 · *Care on a Cliff Edge*

As I walked into the new café beside the post office after collecting my mail, I met my butcher Euan, his wife Jane and their young son Calum coming out. Calum, who had been so keen to help me work with the eagles at Eyrie 16 two years ago when he was only thirteen, had now grown as tall as myself and was a boy no longer. He shyly but eagerly imparted some interesting news. A few days back he had been looking for fox dens with sheep owner Allan Mackay when he saw an eagle fly out of the cliff and at once thought the eyrie was being used this year. He said he had just left school and had spare time on his hands. The keenness shone in his face.

I made a quick decision. I had thought Eyrie 16 would be occupied again this year and it had always been the best to work anyway. A few days at home and I would be as good as new. Tom Stewart was now working as a forester and could no longer be my helper. I said I would work the eyrie with Calum this year, if he liked.

'Ay,' he said with typical Highlander reserve. 'That would be fine.'

What a grand homecoming, I thought, as I puttered down the loch in the fully laden boat and Moobli, fat and out of practice, trotting rather than galloping along the last two miles of the rough shore.

On the next fine day, June 6, Calum and I set off with hide and hazel wands up to Eyrie 16, Calum zipping along on his trial bike while I blundered along in the Land Rover to where the road petered out. The hill seemed somewhat steeper than it had two years ago.

First, I climbed up to check the nest. As my head came level, a fine

150

month-old eaglet reared up from the bilberry-lined well, hissing like a snake with its tongue up and forward, glaring with huge brown eyes in defensive fear and anger. Its body was covered with white down but as it dashed its immature wings forward, the first flight feathers sprouting from grey waxy sheaths, they made an odd clattering sound. I wanted to see if there was any prey but without upsetting the chick any more, so we climbed to the cliff top and looked down. I saw a plucked grouse in the nest and next to it a dead cormorant fledgling, the first I had ever found in a golden eagle eyrie. Cormorants nested locally on cliff ledges, so it was an interesting possibility that this pair were exploiting the sea shore niche once used by the white-tailed sea eagle, extinct since 1916 as a wild breeding species in Britain.

On the far side of the eaglet, which was now glaring up at us, lay a small white scrap, the body of a dead eagle chick, now being trodden into the nest sticks. It must have died within three or four days of hatching.

We hastened to where we had left the hide among long heather 150 yards from the cliff and worked like madmen to stuff the green sprigs all over its outer shell. The female came sailing overhead, the same big, cunning yet imperturbable mother. It was good to know she was still alive and breeding. We waited until she was out of sight, lugged the hefty stuffed hide up to the old rocky ledge with its V-shaped fissure – the cursed red-brown birch root on the mossy rock seat was even thicker! – and soon had it tied into place among the slightly bigger dwarf trees that sprouted from the face. We built it so that I had to lean out still further over the sheer drop than before, with my right foot braced on the birch trunk. But now I had a remote control cable – instead of having to get both eye and hand up to the camera in the top corner of the hide, I only had to crane my neck to get an eye up there, thus it was slightly more comfortable.

On our way out we found one of the eagles' perching posts, used for feeding, dismembering and plucking prey before taking it to the eyrie, 150 yards south east of the cliff. On the high rock were a ptarmigan leg, the desiccated forelegs of a red deer calf and a lamb, plus a hooded crow and, unusually, some herring gull feathers. Not far from this site was a small twisted birch tree which, judging by the huge fat cigar-shaped regurgitated pellets and white dashes beneath, was a favourite roost of the male. I later found he used it at night when the female was brooding the chick.

I will record that season's observations from the hide in diary form.

June 9. Moobli had a five mile run along the shore so he was tired after his meal and would rest stoically while I spent the night in the hide. Calum brought a rabbit he'd shot and a sheep's head from the butcher's, but I didn't think it a good idea to encourage eagles to eat sheep heads or to take pictures of one doing it, so we just took the rabbit. My pack was heavy, with two cameras, cushions, sleeping bag, food and so forth, while Calum carried a full rucksack. I was climbing a seven-foot fence and hoisting my pack over when it stuck momentarily on the barbed wire and a can of orange juice fell out. The sharp edge of the can hit me on the right eyebrow and blood poured out. I felt like a boxer losing in the first round through a cut. But I dabbed it, let blood mix with sweat and it congealed all right.

We left the rabbit on green sward far below where I could see it from the hide, then set the camera on a tree clamp on a thick forked stick jammed between the hide's outer wall and the cliff face. It was soon rock steady, the 300 mm lens resting in a moss and bilberry leaf bed. Calum checked that it was well hidden, then I focused the second camera on the rabbit as he walked out. I felt I was home at last, living with eagles again, and life seemed to take on new meaning.

The eaglet didn't rise from its prone position until 7.10 p.m. when it began to rend the bloody leg bones of a mature rabbit. Once it choked while trying to swallow a four-inch bone and had to bring it up again. Even in three days its feathers had grown noticeably, and its blackish-brown primaries were now some six inches long. Its tail was a comical fat wedge-shaped stump from which sprouted little black tufts of tail feathers tipped with white. When it finished feeding, its white crop below its white head bulged out, the biggest crop I had ever seen on an eaglet. It then had a doze, neck and head laid out over the nest twigs.

I had a long wait ahead, so I retired into the V-shaped fissure. I was half asleep when I heard a sudden crashing in the twilight around 11 p.m. and moved silently to the viewer. The mother had flown straight in through the dwarf trees, although they had grown larger than they were two years ago. The eaglet was making the squeaky twittering sounds I had heard before as she preened the few dark feathers emerging from its white back. Then I heard a deeper chittering too – coming from the eagle herself. That I had not heard before. She raised herself on her powerful feathered legs and the

152

chick crept underneath before its mother settled down on it again, her wide head facing me directly. After ten minutes I saw her glare out into the gloaming and with a noisy woofing of wing she took off again. I wondered if she had seen her mate flying to the perch post or roost tree with prey and wanted some for herself and the eaglet. Certainly she had brought nothing in. As she brushed through the small trees I realised once more that she had no fear of damaging her great wings on them.

I waited a while longer, but as she didn't return and the eaglet squeezed itself up against the cliff, I tried to get some sleep. The human mind tends to eliminate unpleasant memories and I'd forgotten just how uncomfortable and cold that rocky fissure could be. A few minor muscles, of leg, thigh, shoulder, arm or stomach, had to be tensed all the time to keep the bottom of the sleeping bag from sliding out of the hide, or just to ease pain in one part of the body or other caused by small rocky projections which a one-inch-thick strip of plastic foam did little to alleviate. As usual on eyrie watches I had vivid, often unpleasant dreams in brief periods of dozing.

June 10. I was woken sharply at 3.35 a.m. by a cuckoo that landed just above the hide, so close that the usual soft double note sounded like the start of a trombone solo. Then wrens took up the chorus with strident refrains, and a quarter hour later the chaffinches woke and chorussed away with their cheerful trippy songs. The eagle was not on the nest but the chick was standing up and preening its wings. At 6.50 a.m. the mother eagle swished past, sailing along in full but cloudy light, but she turned and came back towards the hide. Not once, as far as I could see, did she glance down at our rabbit which lay so prominently on the green sward far below. A clever old lady, she clearly distrusted its sudden appearance and the fact that it was dead, unlike last year's eagle at Eyrie 4. Each time the eaglet squeaked the usual '*keyow*' but she didn't come in. She swept past again at 9.50 but further out, as if just checking that the eaglet was all right. I heard the raucous '*kar*'s of crows higher above and saw the eagle turn and head upwards. Suddenly the crow voices sounded high pitched and I imagined the eagle seeing them away from the eyrie area.

There was a gliding rush of air at 10.20 a.m. right beside the hide and I just got to the viewer in time to see the mother eagle landing quietly on the near edge of the nest, away from the little trees, with something big in her talons. Then she turned and swept out again. The eaglet immediately began tugging at the prey – half a rabbit. I was surprised the mother didn't stay to feed it for it was not yet five weeks old. It coped well, tugging hard at the rabbit's ears and head to open up the neck while gripping the body hard with its talons.

From the rear I could see yellow patches on its white downy legs caused by abrasion from the nest twigs. It was a very strong eaglet for its age, making hefty stamps on the rabbit, twisting its head very fast from side to side as it tried to break a bone out from the tendons and pull off chunks of flesh. It was also a very chunky little eaglet with an almost round body, tipped by that silly little pin cushion of a tail. I was sure it was a male.

After backing to the nest edge and lifting his tail to send out a jet of excreta, he flapped his embryo wings, like sheets of thin waxy candles tipped with feathers, and reeled unsteadily round the nest, not forgetting to cling for dear life to the securely anchored branchlets. By 11.15 a.m. he had eaten enough and preened for half an hour, reaching way over his back and stroking the short dark tail feather tips through his beak. He quibbled at the edges of their waxy sheaths, snipping them off into powder which drifted away on the breeze, as if to hasten growth, then he tramped close up to the cliff, flopped down on his breast, and went to sleep.

At 2.05 p.m. one of the eagles flew by again, well out, just checking. I waited until I had put in twenty-four-and-a-half hours, decided neither eagle would be in for a while and, feeling cold from the sunless wind through the draughty hide, stiff in every limb, I packed my bag and the rucksack with the cameras and other gear and left. Just as I reached the foot of the cliff the mother eagle flew past, saw me but seemed unperturbed and vanished over the ridge with two lazy flaps. As she had ignored the rabbit I retrieved it for a stew. With the 40lb load balanced well by strapping the rucksack across my chest, I creaked away down the hill with aching knees.

June 13. Armed with a large wedge-shaped chunk of polyurethane I'd cut to jam into the fissure, to make it more level and comfortable, and a battery tape recorder to capture the eaglet's calls, I boated out, shopped, and met Calum at 3 p.m. It was a dull hazy day with blue-grey clouds threatening to the south west. We climbed the cliff, saw that the eaglet had another rabbit in the nest, and freshened the hide a little with greenery. On leaving, Calum had covered only two hundred yards when he gave our pre-arranged whistle which told me one of the parents was flying close – to which I did not reply. I hoped the old lady would come in *before* twilight this time.

I took a few shots of the eaglet preening and the increased dark feathers on his back. At dusk he was tugging away at the rabbit when a tinny clank made him stop and crouch down. It sounded like someone clanging mess tins together, a sound I would never forget from my army years. Was someone camping below the cliff? I daren't get out and look in case the eagle was about, nor did I want to give away the location of the eyrie or the hide. Instead, I leaned out over the void and in a low booming voice intoned 'Begone! Begone from here!'

There was a brief silence, another tinny clanking, then sounds of scuffing grass fading into the distance. After a while the eaglet got up, looked over the nest edge, apparently saw the coast was clear and resumed its meal. Whoever it was had probably decided that a place where voices boomed from dark empty cliffs was definitely not the place for an overnight camp.

At 9.10 p.m. I heard the swish of wings as the eagle landed but it took off again before I got to the viewer. Half an hour later the chick squeaked and in came an adult again but once more left immediately. Was there still someone down there? Now I heard ticking noises on the hide's roof – it had begun to rain. Quietly I stuffed a plastic sheet above the camera and where I was sitting on the chunk of polyurethane I had wedged into the crevice. I now found when I lay back on this that it was only a shade more comfortable for it thrust upwards into my lower spine, or hard into my hip bones if I lay crouched up on my side. Having forgotten my knife, I had only one remedy. I knelt down and bit chunks out of the hard foam wedge with my teeth until I had it more or less right.

In a brief patch of moonlight at 10.40 I heard a slight air movement, though the chick didn't cry out. I looked through a gap in the herbage in time to see the huge mother eagle circling and gliding just out from the eyrie. Her great wings glistened like frosted metal as she slipped through the air, the moon rays shimmering every twig and leaf of the trees below into shining light. She looked like a plane returning from a mission. Suddenly into my mind came the old Second World War song 'Silver Wings In the Moonlight' that Vera Lynn used to sing when I was a boy and watched the old prop planes in the Battle of Britain from a Sussex field. Now she turned and banked and came in very quietly from beside the hide like a great glider and landed on the nest in the open spot where she didn't have to brush the little trees. Immediately she started to brood the big eaglet which crept gratefully out of the rain and beneath her great uplifted wing as clouds once more blotted out the moon. What a fine

155

sight it was again to see her, the great cruiser of the skies suddenly grounded and being fussy and maternal about giving her chick comfort and protection.

How tempting to set up a flash unit to capture these wonderful moments, but I had always to care more for the birds' welfare than my own wants. My responsibility lay towards the eagle, not towards making a reputation. If in the finest part of conscience lies proof of the existence of what we call God, it is in the conscience we must dwell in peace.

The rain now intensified, the drops hissing down all over the eyrie and the hide, but the mother eagle slept, her head back under her wing, taking it all, as still and impervious as a dark rock. Huddled in the sleeping bag in the near freezing cold, the rain and wind evaporating the warmth from everything, I drew the thin plastic sheet over me, slowly so as not to make any crinkling noises, and dozed as best I could. I heard plops and plaps all night; rivulets of water ran into my hair and ears but most of me kept fairly dry.

June 14. I woke just before 4 a.m. when it was just light enough to see the eyrie. The bottom of the bag was wet through and my feet were icy blocks. I worked up to the viewer slowly – the eagle had already gone, after little more than four hours' sleep. How hard they have to work with a big chick to feed. How *could* anyone shoot or poison them? Although I had turned the camera down so I could see only half the birds, rain spray had fogged the glass and I had to withdraw slowly and wipe it clean. The chick was crouched low but its wings had enough feathers now to act as a tent and keep its sides tolerably warm. Eaglets have tough upbringings and have to adjust to harshness early. Two or three nights at this height in the Highlands, even in June, would kill off most humans without some protection, but this five-and-a-half week eaglet took it cold turkey for longer periods. By 5 a.m. it was up and shaking itself.

I heard curlews flying over the eyrie calling fast '*culee culee culee*'; cuckoos began at 4.15 and were followed by a single cock wren which perched in a small rowan by the nest and sang away by the eaglet as if trying to impress its huge audience of one. When the eaglet began cheeping at seeing a parent in the distance, I grabbed the tape recorder and captured this odd accidental duet. The eagle didn't come in.

At 9.45 a.m. the eaglet squeaked loudly. I got to the viewer fast but the chick was already eating from a small red deer foreleg which probably the male had dumped fast and left. I had heard nothing

156

above the wind rustling in the little trees round the hide and the sea's surgings below, for now a small gale had sprung up. I had missed the eagle coming in. Cold, wet, miserable, with the eaglet now supplied with food, I felt I was wasting my time staying any longer. But at 10.30 a.m. the chick called again, I leapt to the camera and got three shots of the mother who had floated in silently against the wind. She had no prey, turned and left again. A few minutes later I was still in position on the root when the eaglet squeaked briefly and I immediately pressed the remote control cable button for an 'insurance' shot before I got to the viewer. It was the smaller male bird, with the powerful bowed legs, and he had a dead stick in his beak. He looked about the nest, couldn't decide where to fit it, and flew off with it again.

Just after midday I heard an odd flurry of wings and peeped through the hide vegetation in time to see the female land on a mossy rock where the male was perched, coming so close he had to jump out of the way before flying off. I cursed, unable to move the fixed camera. Then up she went again with something in her talons. Seconds later, the eaglet '*keyow*'ing loudly, she landed with a half-eaten rabbit. This prey had not been exchanged in mid-air and she had clearly filched it from her mate, though he had probably meant her to have it, or else would have brought it in himself after his own meal. She landed so fast that she looked like a bronze arrow, but again she did not stay to feed the chick herself.

For two hours there was no action, the parents possibly having their siesta, so I used the time to cut a manuscript. Now the wind was so strong it kept bending the little trees to which the camera support was tied, so that the lens shifted its focus off the eyrie. Once a brown shadow went by, but by the time I got to the viewer, the eyrie was empty, the camera wasn't on it, and I wasted several remote control shots. How I wished it could always be like it was the first year – when I could lie down comfortably with my eye close to the lens all the time. Here, if I was not on the hard root seat, I had to stretch up three feet. But I stuck it out, and at 2.35 p.m. the eaglet gave a brief '*kewp*' and I shot the mother flying in. She had brought no prey, was just checking the state of the larder.

I now had over twenty-five shots of the adults, the most ever for a second visit to a hide, and I felt happier. But how I longed for some sleep, a good smoke of my pipe (which I had left behind to expel temptation) or a hot meal. Egg and tomato sandwiches were not much fodder against the damp, cold, perpetual discomfort of the cliff ledge. I had now found it best to stay in the bag all the time, and tie its opening cords over one shoulder like a bandolero, so that it stayed up high enough to keep me warm yet left both hands free. As I shifted as awkwardly as a seal on dry land I felt ridiculously like a mermaid!

As usual, the eaglet was a source of entertainment. He often lifted his big bandy legs high because if he trod on one end of a stick the other could rise up and trip his other leg as he walked. In the rain he shook himself like a dog, white head first, then the round football body, and ending with a unique and entirely separate twizzling shake of that absurd parson's nose of a tail. The effect was comical. When preening he definitely pulled at and stroked each feather out to its full length, the curves of his upper and lower mandibles almost exactly matching the feathers' own curved surfaces. He even pulled his own white down out, especially that still on the tips of the feathers. The down floated away to stick on the nest twigs, giving the whole nest after two weeks of this a shimmering white appearance. A sheep man looking up could believe it was lamb's wool he was seeing. It was all very delicate work for so powerful a beak, yet it was all done by instinct and there seemed to be no copying of the mother.

At 3.20 p.m. he cheeped again. I did not move to the viewer as the light was now strong and the eagle might have glimpsed something, so I watched as best I could through the front vegetation of the hide. As the cries reached a crescendo I pressed the motor drive button, and as the camera clicked away, up came the mother, landed, looked around, picked up an old piece of rabbit leg and took it away. I got seven good shots, two of her bursting through the trees. She had brought in half a grouse. The eaglet tugged and freed part of a wing which he vainly tried to swallow whole. His own wings, flight feathers now half grown, were heavy and kept slipping down his back. He shunted them back up again with irritated flicks and shuffles.

After eating for twenty minutes he flopped on to his breast for his third snooze of the day. At 5 p.m. I was just wrapping the foam pad in plastic when I heard two eaglet squeaks, then the bleating of a small lamb right below me. The shadow of the mother passed by. She brought in a young mallard which the eaglet immediately began to eat, ripping off chunks, down, feathers and all, at will. She had sailed right over the lamb as if it wasn't there, and when she left I saw again that she did not appear even to look down. It was almost as if some eagles have bred into their instincts that if they kill white

158

lambs retribution may follow. Certainly I knew now that in my region they preferred rabbit, grouse, deer carrion, ptarmigan, large wading birds, and even crows, to lamb meat, or else they feared an angry ewe.

After twenty-six hours in the hide, knowing she would not come in for a good while after delivering so much food, I climbed down with difficulty. It was a terrible walk out. The rain poured ceaselessly and after a quarter of a mile my boots and clothes were soaked. In the two packs I was now carrying the biggest load ever – tape recorder, cassette, two cameras, three lenses, torch, sixteen batteries, motor winder, control grip, films, my book manuscript, a mammal book, scissors, cord, fieldglass, wet sleeping bag and so on – a good fifty pounds. I was cold, stiff and my knees, especially the right one, hurt and cracked on the steep slopes where the uneven rocks had dug into my bones, hip bones too.

I finally stole up to the Land Rover and saw Moobli lying asleep, head between paws but at least on a foam bed. When I let him out he danced in welcome (he never barked without reason) but his iron tank system demanded no relief until he was well into his exercise run behind the truck. When I got out to let him back in, my bush hat blew off, and away he went to retrieve it from a muddy burn. What a good lad he was, I thought, giving him a loving hug when he returned with it. Without his sturdy, loyal companionship I would probably have given up the isolated life in the wilds by now. It was exactly thirteen years ago to the month that I had begun it.

After boating home, soaked to the skin in the torrential rain, I found even the insides of the cameras were wet. That night I had to take the last eagle film out of its cassette and, using the blankets as a 'dark room', dry it off with my body heat in bed.

I still faced a late checking of all the remaining eyries in the Lochaber area I had again been given. As I was far behind with my writing – my sole source of income – after the long family business trips to Spain I felt again I must have been touched to take it all on again this year. Well, this *would* be my last season for covering so much ground. When I sank between the sheets after a big supper I decided to go into the hide once more before facing the slogging climbs to check the other eyries. And how glad I was that I did.

11 · *The Wind, the Rain and the Cold*

Like flashes of orange flame, huge velvety northern eggar moths twinkled over the heather and tussock grasses on the hill, females dropping eggs at random, as Calum trekked me up to the eyrie again on June 18. It was a hot sunny hazy day and although we went slower than usual, perspiration still poured. After briefly freshening up the hide with greenery, I felt reluctant to spend another cold damp night in it after the heavy rain, chilled as ever because the cliff lay out of the sun for most of the day. Sweating on the climb-walk in, then spending hours in the cold tomb seemed a recipe for pneumonia. But just as my resolve seemed to dwindle I was to learn more this time than from any single visit to a hide so far. The eagles' world is a hard one and its secrets yield only to patience and effort, and slowly at that.

At first I thought the nest was empty and my heart sank when Calum left me alone at 4 p.m. for there was no movement in it. Then at 5.30 something dark moved in the bowl and the eaglet, his back almost covered in dark feathers, with the first brown ones sprouting on his white neck and chest, roused himself and stood up. He backed to the edge and let go a stream of white, then flapped his wings hard, the flight feathers grown enough to raise him up with each down beat. His dark tail feathers, held loosely like an old fan, were now some three inches long.

At 6.07 p.m. a slight air swish disturbed the stillness and the

In my fourth season – a five-week-old eaglet with bulging white crop.

The mother feeds her eaglet with infinite care.

In swept the male with a conifer spray.

The mother flew close to the nest to induce the eaglet to take its first flight.

After hard hunting in the rain the mother looks as scrawny as a vulture.

The chick trampolining on the nest to strengthen the wing muscles.

Nine-and-a-half weeks old, and ready to fly.

Moobli, my constant companion on eagle treks.

chick began to cry as I pressed the remote control trigger. When I reached the viewer, mother eagle was there with something pale in her talons. It looked like half a lamb, with dark flecks against the white. I waited until she turned to show her head and neck and took two shots, glad that she seemed to hear nothing. Then the camera jammed. The numbers dial wasn't working and I had miscounted by some eight shots for it was clicking emptily and I was afraid of tearing the film.

By the time I had put in a new one the mother eagle had gone again. For half an hour the eaglet just looked at the new prey as if not knowing what to do with it. But once he stamped his talons down and began to tug, I saw it was not a lamb but a headless unplucked ptarmigan. Now and then he hauled the feathers of a lightly speckled white wing upwards, or one of the bristly feet, and then I saw the red eye flash of the male ptarmigan's head, bouncing up and down in response to the tugs as if the dead bird was trying to peck back at the eaglet. He ate for half an hour, then lay down facing me, huge rounded wings out to the side, panting in the warmth with his beak open. After that he had a long sleep.

At 7.40 p.m. he stood up and ate again, tugging this time at the front leg of a red deer calf. Occasionally I saw the cloven hoof appear above the nest rim. After another rest, when he lay on his side with his ungainly yellow feet clenched like great fists, he stood up and tramped over to tug at the ptarmigan again. At 9.10 he squeaked from his lying position, but no eagle came in, and some minutes later he extended his long right wing out fully to the side, then his right leg too, expanding the talons out straight, stretching hard. But the talons did not stroke the wing. At 10 p.m. one of the adults went past and the eaglet climbed to his feet and called loudly for a minute, swivelling from right to left as if following the parent's flight. But neither eagle came in to brood him. On a warm dry night like this his mother had probably decided he did not need her shelter. I had a slightly less uncomfortable night, dozing in brief patches in my bag in the fissure.

June 19. The eaglet was not up at 4 a.m. as fingers of yellow suffused the grey and violet horizon, but half an hour later he staggered to his feet and began preening. Cuckoos had been calling since 3.42, followed by chaffinches just after dawn, one cock landing on the hide and deafening me with his cheery cadences. Down on the desolate marshes the occasional mournful '*coorli*' of a curlew rose through the early low mist. In the still, hazy air the biting midges infiltrated the hide but by 7 a.m., with the sun piercing the haze with soft light, their numbers lessened. For almost half an hour the eaglet rent the rest of the ptarmigan, then looked up and squeaked. Luckily I was in position. In swept the male eagle with a huge spray of fir and I got seven shots of him landing, with the eaglet bent in the obeisant solicitation posture, and of him looking about the nest with a wild distracted air, as if wondering what on earth he'd come in for anyway! Then he dropped the spray on my side of the eaglet, obscuring my view of it, and flew off again. The eaglet, disappointed, flopped down for a sleep.

At 8.45 a.m. the mother eagle swept by three times, as if showing her flight powers to the youngster for he barely squeaked and his head and eyes followed her flight closely. I was relaxing a few minutes later when I heard a brief '*wush*', saw a brown shadow float past, and got one shot of the mother landing with a young curlew, and another as she took off again. Surely with her chick just six weeks old she had not yet settled down to the 'dump and run' techniques that adults use when youngsters are well fledged. I still hadn't got a really fine shot of an eagle feeding a chick sideways, with both birds in full view. And that after four years' work.

Just then a male cuckoo landed on a tiny rowan sprouting from the cliff near the eaglet and surprised me with the power of the familiar double call which sounds so soft when heard from a distance on a summer day. He was so close it almost deafened me, breathy yet clicky, as if made by a large aluminium flute. I took a picture of the fascinated eaglet staring up at it.

The mother floated past again at 9.04, then turned and came in. This time, although she brought no new prey, she stayed. What a magical sight she now presented as I took time over my pictures, knowing I was near the end of another film. The sun danced the browns, fawns, russets and golds of her feathers into flaming lights. I was again impressed by the sheer majesty and quietness of her, the dignified aristocratic mien, the massive chest and shoulders and thick neck, arched at the back like a fighting bull's, the wide head and strong blue-black beak. The whole impression was one of nobility and serene power. She looked this way and that, each angle superb as I switched from auto to manual, varying exposures slightly in the tricky sunlight, mentally resolving that if these weren't the best pictures of all I would do a Highland dance on the camera.

The eaglet, which had been tearing and gulping down pieces of the curlew perfectly well on his own, had his wings open across the nest and with lowered beak was still squeaking, demanding that his mother feed him. And now she did, teaching him the real way to feed. She crept towards the curlew like a huge manacled cat and with a simple easy snip and tweak pulled a big lump off, lifted it up and twisting her head sideways delicately fed it to the eaglet. At last I had my sideways feeding shot with both birds' heads in fine profile. After that she spread her wings and sailed away. She had been on the nest a good five minutes yet I'd had to be sparing with my shots as I knew the film to be over halfway through, even though I could not see the dials without taking the camera down. Now I banged off two shots of the eaglet eating and then standing up with beak open, panting in the sun. With that the film ended.

On the new film I took shots of the eaglet mantling over the curlew, sitting on his hocks and stretching out one set of talons, so clean they looked artificial, in front of him; nibbling a toe with his beak, yawning, and with his wings spread out over the nest as if trying to keep them cool in the northerly wind which had sprung up. The eaglet fed himself again for twenty minutes from 10.20 a.m., then settled for a sleep.

I had just eased my cramped root-bruised haunches into the rock fissure when a loud '*wush wush*' alerted me to press the trigger. But when I got up to the viewer the eagle, probably the male, had gone again. He had, however, left another sprig of fir on the nest. Like the previous one, it had been left to the windward side and now, when I saw the eaglet tug the sprig closer, as if to tuck itself in, I had some new ideas about these leafy sprays.

When eagles begin visiting their eyries in late December and January, choosing which to use that season, they also bring in sticks to rebuild the nest. Later both sexes also bring in twigs with more foliage on them, usually fir, Scots pine, larch, even juniper, which also have a function in the rituals of courtship and strengthening the pair bond. Heather sprays plus moss clumps, crowberry, cranberry, bilberry and great wood-rush are also used to help line the nest for the eggs, but I had found that not all eagles line nests. Once the chicks have hatched and the new foliage is on the trees, eagles then bring in leafy sprays of rowan, willow, and less often hazel, beech and oak, but these are brought in mostly by the male in the later stages. These seem to be still pair bonding 'gifts', the sprays brought in after transferring prey to the female away from the nest, as the female does most, if not all, the feeding of the small chicks. Although a few accounts claim they do, I had never yet seen a male actually feed

163

chicks, but he certainly drops much food into the eyrie himself during the youngsters' later weeks.

These later sprays and twigs have a decorative effect too. I recalled that foxgloves had been brought into one eyrie, giving it a royal glow of purple, and when I found sweet scented bog myrtle on another eyrie it was almost as if it had been brought in as a deodoriser. Certainly these later sprays help to freshen up eyries where rotting prey remains are allowed to lie on the nest, for not all females take away these accumulations of bones and skin and even those that do don't remove everything. Such remains are then trodden down below the new sticks and leafy twigs.

After seeing this male drop two hefty sprays of fir needles on the windward side of the nest, and the eaglet tug the last one in more closely, it seemed just possible that they had been put there on purpose – to help screen the eaglet from the northerly wind. I recalled the old shed sheep fleece I had seen on Eyrie 18 – which also seemed to have been placed against the prevailing winds sweeping up the glen. Most of the sprays brought into last year's Eyrie 4 had also been placed on the windy side, I now remembered. One would not want to ascribe dogmatically such foresight and intelligence to a bird, but it seems a reasonable assumption.

At 10.50 p.m. I heard two woofing flaps of an eagle pulling up on the nest in the following wind but it had gone again by the time I had got to the viewer. When the eaglet fed next, I saw he was tugging a much browner bird's head. As he ripped I saw him swallow with ease the head of a male grouse, the bright red wattle, skull and beak. Then he tore the red stump of neck and flesh and feathers from back and chest. Satisfied, he deliberately wiped his beak several times on each side of the new fir spray. This seemed to be yet another use for such foliage. As if that wasn't enough, when he later lay down for a rest, he also used the spray to brush away flies and biting midges from his head and neck. This saved him having to stand up and scratch his head with one talon, as eaglets do in an amusingly dog-like manner. These were interesting discoveries.

I decided to wait longer to see what time the parents resumed feeding. Finally, overcome by thirst pangs as I had forgotten to bring a drink for myself, I left after twenty-five more hours in the hide. This time, as I often saw the mother eagle floating near the eyrie on the walk-outs, I clipped on the long 640 mm lens and carried it across my chest as I climbed down one-handed wearing both the packs.

I was glad I did, for just as I reached the bottom of the cliff, the mother came winging close by, as if showing the eaglet *this* is how you do it, this is how you *fly*. She saw me, didn't swerve at all, and I whipped the camera and its two-foot six-inch lens round like a shotgun in a rough shoot. Luckily I fixed upon her first try, focused with the pistol grip, and click, click, got two shots of her looking immense and dark against the blue of the sky, her great wings beating slowly but powerfully, eyes glaring from her wide wedge-shaped head. Again I felt an inner tremor at the close spectacle of evolution's natural angel of death. It was a chancy effort, far harder than shooting with a gun as one had to fix on her, get shutter speed, *f*-stop and focusing right in a mere two seconds. Fortunately, as the pictures proved to be the best close flight shots so far, I had most of the combinations right. She was in centre frame, and if the focus wasn't pin sharp, I didn't upbraid myself too strongly for she had been travelling at some sixty miles an hour. I had not expected to see her right then and was slightly off balance myself. So much so that I actually fell down after the second shot.

I took care over the tussocks on the way down as my right knee was hurting badly and the weak ankle was again giving ominous twinges. But warmed by the hard descent, I felt good by the time I reached the truck and gave Moobli his exercise run. Then I drove below Eyries 4 and 5. There seemed no-one about at John Ritchie's farm, so I parked and headed up the hill. En route I came across John, another crofter friend and Allan MacKay who kept his sheep round the eyrie I was now photographing. They were helping John to shear and mark sheep in an old stone tank. Cordial greetings were exchanged, and John said it was fine for me to go and check the eyries. He had not seen the eagles in the area that year. Shorn of the packs, I stormed up to the eyrie with Moobli, braved the sheer drop with wide-braced feet, and looked over. Eyrie 4, scene of all last year's observations, was black, empty and unused. And after another hike, Eyrie 5 showed no activity either. Before loading up the boat I summoned my tired limbs to gather dry cow pats for garden compost, and boated home feeling triumphant after the most productive eagle stint that year.

Two days later I boated out, posted off the manuscript of my new book and drove to see keeper Allan Peters, who did not know the situations at the eyries in his region. He had been busy with his 50,000 acres and training a new assistant, but he was interested in what I had found out. I drove and hiked up to Eyries 2 and 17, but both where unused, nor did I see either of the eagles. I now thought it likely the old grey mantled male had perished in what had been the harshest winter for sixteen years. After it and during the long wet spring that followed I had felt that only the healthiest eagles in their prime would breed successfully this year. That night I drove again to see Greg Hunter, who was covering his own area under Nature Conservancy Council licence.

He gave me the welcome news that the pair which had used Eyries 10 and 13 now had a healthy chick in a new sea cliff eyrie, and that pair 12 also had a chick, but this year in an unusual larch tree nest he had been observing. Again I envied his rabbit populations. A few healthy rabbit warrens in their home ranges are a great help to eagles, especially in the Western Highlands were hares are scarce, and greatly reduce any tendency to prey upon man's stock. (In America, too, where eagles are occasionally illegally shot by farmers, stomach analyses of 102 eagles showed that out of 115 food items, 43 were jackrabbits or cotton tails, 25 carrion, 20 upland game birds, 8 rodents and 8 sheep and goats. A study in Colorado and Wyoming found that at nine active nests, 77 per cent of the food was rabbits – who compete for sheep fodder – and rodents. Another study in north Colorado showed that 74.6 per cent of eagle prey was rabbits, 23.2 per cent prairie dogs, and 2.2 per cent rats and mice.)

Greg also revealed that Eyrie 15 was also unoccupied, so saving me a hike. In the dark, I then drove the long miles to overlook the winding glen of Eyries 6 and 7, arriving after 1 a.m.

I woke to see low wraiths of mists draped across the hills, the light dull and with misty drizzle being replaced by heavy falls of leaden rain. But with Moobli behind, happy to be on the Hill in any weather, I set off on the long return trek to the forbidding cliff. Somehow I negotiated the raging river, leaping on the slippery rocks without falling as Moobli barged half sideways through the torrent, and stumped deliberately up the last killer hill. With trousers soaked, I managed to climb up to the high brow shelf – the right-hand nest was unused while the other, which had contained only addled eggs for two seasons, had one browning leafy twig on it. There were no signs of new building or white eaglet excreta. Again I saw no eagles in the sky. I descended the hill and told Allan the facts.

By pre-arrangement I met young Calum at 2 p.m., but we decided not to go up to the Eyrie 16 hide after all. Another drenching shower had just passed over, I was soaked, and after the two new treks I didn't feel up to another night on the cliff ledge. The mist and rain would soak the lens anyway. We agreed to try again in four days' time. As I finally hiked up to the cottage, after hauling the boat out, both knees hurt and I had odd pains in my hips and lower back. I moved with a stoop like an arthritic old man. Wearing wet clothes all day from the morning trek hadn't helped. How I longed for a hot shower, but with no electricity I faced only a cold bath in the burn. Instead, I swabbed down with a basin of hot water and a flannel while standing on sheets of newspaper. I was no longer surprised that the average age at death of olden day crofters was 47. Who said hard work never killed anyone? Maybe whoever it was never did any.

Next day Moobli and I trekked up to 1,500 feet and checked Eyrie 1 on the way. The nest had disappeared and there was a rock on the ledge. I thought at first someone had ripped out the nest and thrown in the rock to prevent further building. But the fieldglass revealed too much nest debris round the base of the rock for it to have been thrown in. Sticks scattered over a large area of ground were a further clue – the last of the nest had been blown out by the winds since March, not uncommon among old nests. The nearest eyrie to me was now ruined.

For two days I rested, cutting winter hay for the deer and making eight-foot fence posts for the garden from a dead pine. I also trimmed all blackberry brambles, camouflaged my cameras with new paints and caught up with correspondence.

On June 27 I boated out with just a few fleecy clouds scudding across the sunny blue sky, but after Calum had walked me up to the hide, the west turned steely grey, darkened more and the first rain began to fall. I climbed up to the nest and took photos of the eaglet, now over seven-and-a-half weeks old. He hissed, raised his well-feathered wings in threat display and tried to drive me back with hard forward flaps. With head reared high, beak open and tongue upraised, he looked like a hooded cobra about to strike. Although I put my hand on the nest, he never tried to strike it with his talons. His back was all brown now, his tail feathers seven inches long but his chocolate brown wings were still blunt. His head was almost covered in lighter brown feathers, though there was still a patch of white at the back. His chest front was still white too and he had the usual white wing patches. We had seen neither eagle on the way up, and after Calum had checked that the lens was obscured and left, he gave no whistle. So he did not see one while walking out either.

A few minutes later the eaglet excreted, so he was still being fed, but his crop seemed empty and I had seen no prey in the nest. I hoped this meant his mother would be in with food before dark. The ledge debris was wet and soaked my knees as I sorted out the gear in the confined space. By 6.10 p.m. the light was so poor that, even at the 'bumped up' speed of 800 ASA and the aperture at maximum *f*5.6, I could only expose the film at 30th of a second, and the slight rainfall during our approach was increasing. I had to twist the lens down and right off the eyrie. Five minutes later the eaglet squeaked and I heard an eagle passing by but it didn't come in. At 9.30 I heard the mother swish past in the early dusk, the sound of her wings just discernible over the noise of the now-driving rain, but again she did not alight on the nest. Thirsty after the steep hike, I had soon drunk the can of orange juice. Now I found that the long life milk had gone sour, and in a slight fall during my climb to the nest I had somehow crushed the sandwiches into a soggy mash of egg, tomatoes, Marmite and banana.

There followed the worst of all my eagle nights. The rain penetrated everywhere. It fell with slaps and plops over the thin sheet of green plastic I tried to mould over the sleeping bag. Small runnels of water formed all over it, filled its plastic crevices and flooded down to soak the bag's bottom. I had forgotten the cushion and so had to cradle my head on the rocks with a pair of old socks to reduce the pain. Now and then, tiny holes in the crinkled plastic exuded rivers of icy water into my ear, down one eyebrow or into my hair. Rain dripped down from the soggy moss and heather of the hide's roof, hit the slanting rock by my head, then splashed sideways into my face. Even a brief doze was impossible.

June 28. By 4.30 a.m. the bag was soaked through. I was shivering and so cold that I was ready to pack up and go. I thought of humans lying abed in their homes far below – few would believe it could be so bitter at this height on what should have been a summer night.

At 5.40 a.m. I was briefly cheered by wrens being the first birds to sing in the rain, followed by a lone chaffinch cock, and the odd wind-note '*hô hô, ha ha ha*' of a cuckoo, the latest date I had ever heard this call. Two minutes later the eaglet squeaked and the mother eagle went by as if checking up, but she didn't come in. As always at this time of year, she was already out hunting after very little sleep. The eaglet had spent the night huddled under the overhang, right up against the granite face, trying to minimise the merciless wind, wet and cold. I had sworn last year that I would never work eagles again, yet I was still here, up this crazy cliff! Although I had kept the lens pointed down through the night it was all misted up, and at 6.10 the wind increased, making it more icy than ever.

By 7.30 a.m. I felt sure that neither she nor her mate could be out hunting in such driving rain. The eaglet was again crouched against the wall, either with head tucked back under a wing or else just staring disconsolately down at the nest twigs. He was the personification of dejection, occasionally shaking his head, his body and wings to get rid of the moisture. I slowly withdrew the camera and cleaned the lens, deciding to hold out until 9.30, then go.

An hour and twenty minutes later the eaglet squeaked, rousing me from a hunched nodding posture, but when the calls increased I creaked up to look through the lens as in came the mother, landing with a fast wet flapping noise of her wings, in her talons something tiny which, when the eaglet grabbed and swallowed it, I saw was nothing more than a single vole. The eaglet, still hungry, kept squeaking but she had nothing more for it. She walked across the nest slowly, looking down as if hoping to find food for herself, then both birds looked away to the north. The mother now looked as scrawny as a vulture with her head feathers sleeked down and soaked from the rain. She really was a sorry sight and I felt sad for her – how hard it must be to hunt in such conditions. I could now believe the stories of eagles trying to drive deer calves off mountain ledges. (Indeed, a few days later the old retired gamekeeper Ian McClintock told me he had once seen an eagle repeatedly flying at a calf to drive it off a ridge, and even buffeting it with its wings.) Desperate with hunger, an eagle, like any animal or man, would be driven to such measures.

I thought that, if we believe in a God who created the universe, then we must also believe God created nature's harsh system. And I thought too of man, the greatest predator of all, and of his attitudes, all too often, towards species such as eagles. We are all poor creatures in nature, but man is the dominant species. If we cannot forgive the so-called lesser being for occasional transgressions upon our stocks of yet other creatures we keep only to kill ourselves when we have often destroyed their lands and the natural balances, what hope do we have of forgiving each other, or of God forgiving us? It is the universal loving view of life, and perhaps only that, which raises us above the animals, and when we fail in this we demean our finest gift. We fail to fulfil our unique God-given inheritance. Yet even in such hard conditions these eagles had not taken a lamb, and there were still small ones about.

After the mother had left, I banged off two more shots of the wet

169

eaglet and came to the end of the film. But just as I was re-loading the camera he began squeaking loudly. Afraid of tell-tale lens movement if one of the eagles came in again, I made the change over hastily but furtively with my left hand while my right, braced against my right leg, which in turn was braced against the birch trunk, prevented me from falling off the ledge.

I took two shots of the squeaking eaglet, then two more as the male arrived with a twig of green heather in his beak. He must have come from shelter for he was not at all wet. He looked about, then flew away without leaving the twig. Four minutes later the eaglet cheeped and in flashed mother with a fledgling merganser which the eaglet gulped back in two swallows, first tugging off the head, then tossing back the body and little webbed feet. Ten minutes later in came the male, so fast I couldn't see if he had brought any prey. This time the sequence trigger didn't work, so I pushed the manual button with my left hand, re-loaded with tiny twists of left thumb on the winder, just in time for a glorious shot of him glaring straight towards me, great legs wide apart as he turned to leave, his wings open. I was looking forward to seeing *that* shot!

I soon discovered that the male had dumped prey, for now the eaglet tramped over the rough sticks and tugged at a brown bird with blackish webbed feet – a young cormorant. It seemed that in the rainy weather, the eagles had switched from hunting the high tops where they took ptarmigan or grouse, and from the lower hills where they took rabbits, to the shore marshes and coastal cliffs, so being able to catch the young merganser and cormorant. Either could have been snatched from the shallows or even from the sea's surface, but one could not know for sure without witnessing the catch.

It was further confirmation that these efficient avian hunters vary the field of operations according to weather. I realised then that last year's eagles had not been able to hunt the shore in mist and rain as much as this pair, for the coast near Eyrie 4 was more occupied by humans. It is doubtless this extraordinary adaptability that enabled the golden eagle to survive the direct persecution at the turn of the century and, later, the decimation of their ranks from ingesting pesticides from sheep carrion in the 1960s, whereas the sea eagle, mainly a fish eater, became extinct as a British breeding bird in the First World War largely through the direct persecution alone.

The eaglet had a harder task with the cormorant than most other prey, tugging at the breast and neck, exposing red flesh only at the third try. He managed to pull off a few small pieces, then went to the outer edge of the nest, though his crop was not full, and lay down for a rest. Once he looked up, comically following the progress of a small plane droning across the sky, as one would watch a fly crawling over a window pane. Twenty minutes later he had another go at the prey, swallowed a three inch bone with ease, some more meat, then indulged in vigorous wing-flapping exercises. After that he lay down for a snooze.

The eagles would not be in now for a long while and after thirty-one hours in the cold hide, equalling my longest stint of last year, I packed up and left. With both packs and bag soaked, everything heavier than ever, I tramped out, knees aching and cracking loudly after the slow, cold, tortuous, rock-crevice nightmare night. I felt beaten, tired, finished, that I could not learn much more about eagles at the nest, and that this was certainly my last season.

Maddeningly, within 300 yards the sun began to beam strongly and the rain clouds scudded away ahead of me. I took some more shots of the mother flying past, so used to me she made no change in her flying pattern. But I felt happy in spite of the tiredness as we boated home and Moobli ran along the shore. Once indoors I lit a big log fire and dried out everything.

Two days later Moobli and I set off on the hardest eagle trek to make a final check in the steep glen where his keen nose had helped me to find the eaglet in Eyrie 18 last year. We had covered four miles and were tramping over peat-hagged meadows at 2,000 feet when I had an astonishing experience. I stalked successfully and took four photos of a wild adult dog fox in full daylight – of it sitting down, walking away, looking back and then lying down to sleep in a cool peat bank! After the fine eagle shots in the last hide visit, it seemed like a final accolade to a nature photographer. What a fine film I must now have in the camera, I thought, estimating that shots 21 to 24 would be the fox. I thus had eleven more frames to expose on that film.

Eyrie 18 had a fairly new heather spray on the nest, along with a few newish thick sticks. There had been an attempt to build it up, possibly by the male alone, but there was no sign of any young. The dead rowan tree roosting perch, however, was being well used, with much excreta, huge four-and-a-half inch long pellets lying below it, with one long flight pinion and several broad brown and cream-streaked secondaries. Eyrie 19 was not only unused but most of the remaining twigs had been blown out too. I now realised it was not a good year for the region's eagles. We trekked on up to 2,300 feet westwards and searched the rockfaces on each side of the glen for new eyries – without luck. It was bitterly cold up on the tops in the north-west wind. We were caught in five showers and I changed my rain suit as many times. But coming back up out of the glen I was rewarded by finding unusually late starry saxifrage, moss campion, roseroot and globe flowers too. While all the sun-seeking flowers on the warmer southern slopes had died earlier, these flowers, with a later start on the cold northerly steeps, had outlasted them to bloom for longer in the summer sun.

When we finally reached home after the whole day moving on the Hill, we had covered over sixteen miles and 16,000 feet of ascents and descents, and my right knee was hurting and cracking away again. Moobli too was, to put it mildly, shattered. He flopped straight down in the kitchen with a loud groan. I had noticed him limping again slightly on his rear left leg over the last few miles.

As we drove south on July 2 to visit more eyries we met keeper Allan Peters who saved me a final hike to check Eyries 2 and 17. He had been getting roe deer out of that compartment and had seen that both eyries were still empty. That freed me to head off and check Eyries 21 and 22. A new gate had been erected across the track so that it was now a four-mile hike in – wasted because Eyrie 22 had, like 19, been almost blown out, and 21, apart from some browning rowan sprays, showed no signs of recent activity. It *could* have been robbed earlier, and I realised again how difficult it was for one man to check so many eyries throughout a season, especially in his 'spare time'. I tramped a further mile, found no new eyries, then all the way back to the truck in pouring rain. I drove to see young Calum, who agreed to put me into the hide early next day, then camped out by the side of the road.

July 3. '*Pop pop pop*', and Calum arrived on his trail bike at 6.20 a.m., grinning all over his face, for I was still abed. It took me five minutes to dress, wash, have a cuppa, and gulp down a hunk of bread and cheese. The midges were frightful – every cubic inch of air held its own vicious tenant. Moobli, who had leaped out of the truck window in the night to sleep on the grass, now regretted it; his eyes were swollen with many bites, and he constantly wiped his great paws across his face like a bear. I gave him a good run behind the truck before Calum and I made a long wet walk-in, the dew heavy on the long grasses.

The eaglet was now a young eagle with nearly all its rich dark

172

brown feathers, and just a small patch of white on the back of his head to match the white chest patch, tail band and wing markings. A few minutes after Calum had left I heard his double whistle – which meant that both eagles were flying near the eyrie. Reckoning I had two more shots on Eagles 6, the film which contained the best adult shots of the last visit and the four of the wild fox, I banged them off on the eaglet, expecting the lever to stick. But it was still winding on film. I took one more, another, and still the film was winding on. How could I have fitted thirty-nine shots on to a thirty-six shot film? A dreadful suspicion dawned that the camera was either only winding on half frames, or had slipped on some of the earlier shots – which would mean I had lost some of the best eagle photos. I just hoped there was another explanation as I removed the film and inserted a new one.

The eaglet was very hungry. His crop empty, and there seemed to be no prey remains on the nest. Twice he squeaked and glared upwards as he saw his mother pass by on her checking flights. But from 8.15 a.m. I heard her great wings going '*wush WUSH wush*' past the hide and eyrie at close quarters roughly every quarter of an hour. Each time the eaglet saw her coming he crouched down, and with a rising volume of squeaks, his eyes staring wistfully, he tried to solicit her into the nest by spreading and slowly beating his wings. It wasn't until I made a hole in the hide herbage and saw after each time she came close to the eyrie, she then swung out towards the opposite ridges and flew round again in an oblong path, that I realised what she was doing. She seemed to be showing the eaglet that *this* is how you fly, this is what *he* would have to do himself before long, if he wanted food.

There was silence after 9 a.m. and the disappointed eaglet relieved his hungry boredom by leaping about the nest, flapping hard but always grabbing at the sticks with his talons if a small gust of wind caught him. He could have flown easily for he now had almost his full 'sail' area yet he didn't know that and was as scared of the sheer drop as I was. But he instinctively knew the way to strengthen his wing muscles and treated the nest like a trampoline – bouncing up and down on it and, after getting another good grip, flapping powerfully against the clutch of his talons. Then he lay down for a twenty minute sleep. After that he stumbled up again and preened his feathers, rustling them up and stroking them through his beak, wisps of white down still coming from under the plumage to drift on to the eyrie sticks or the little trees around its ledge.

173

After reading for an hour in the rock fissure I was back in position by 11.20 and suddenly the eaglet began to squeak. I pushed the auto and sequence levers, and in came the mother but irritatingly from behind me, so I only got six shots of her rear view. She had brought some kind of game bird or wader with black unwebbed feet which I couldn't identify. Immediately the squeaking eaglet leaped on it with outstretched wings, tore it up and gulped most of it down in two minutes. At times he had crammed so much food into his throat he had to rear up and undulate his head and neck up and down with his beak wide open to ease its passage down his gullet. It wasn't greed but survival instinct after a long fast – cram all you can down while it's there.

When very young the eaglet prostrates itself, solicits, is submissive and querulous before getting fed. But in later weeks, when most of its feathers have grown, it advances to clutch prey, stands high, mantling its wings round it like a tent, with head and neck hackles raised, as if to stop any chance of the parent taking it back. Now, before she flew again, I saw this mother standing well back with a proud but conciliatory air.

At midday the male eagle came in silently and suddenly, dumped a young headless grouse and left. I took two more shots of the eaglet eating and ended the seventh eagles film. Having spent twelve more hours in the hide and taken 248 more pictures of eagles at the eyrie, I decided that would do for this season, and while the parents were having their usual noon siesta, I left.

On July 11, in blazing sunshine – as uncomfortable for hill trekking as rain – I set off with Moobli on a nine-mile hike round Eagle Rock Mountain. There was now no trace of any sticks at Eyrie 3 and the site was overgrown. At Eyrie 11 there were some wisps of old sheep wool on the remaining nest sticks and the hoof of a ewe which had clearly been brought in as carrion from a sheep found dead. Among the old sticks that had apparently been thrown out of the eyrie two years earlier I found a rusty old pair of sheep clippers. I could only speculate on how or why they came to be there and saw no signs of new nest building earlier in the year. A trek to the west side of the mountain next day revealed Eyrie 8 to be also untouched, with just a little reddish dust debris showing where a nest had been. There was no doubt now that it had been the worst year for eagle breeding in the years I had studied the area.

I had the sure feeling that the eaglet in Eyrie 16 would be flying any day now, but on July 13 I went up to the hide to check, arranging

174

with Calum to join me so that we could possibly remove the hide. I saw the mother eagle still making the 'tempting out' flights close by the nest but thought at first that the eaglet had gone for, from the foot of the cliff, the nest appeared to be empty. By now the nest sticks, the dwarf trees and the whole eyrie area were so covered in white eaglet down that someone inexperienced in eaglet biology could easily have believed it was wool from lambs.

As I climbed up I saw that the eaglet *was* still there, his fully feathered golden head moving in the nest well. Then he stood bolt upright, not trying to hide at all, and traded me look for look. What a huge imperious eagle he had become, even slightly bigger than his father with all the new-grown young plumage. There was no prey in the nest and I could not see any bulge in his crop. He kept holding his white-patched wings open, feeling the play of the wind, and once made two squeaks, peering into the distance as if he could see one of his parents flying.

I waited a while, and was just undoing the plastic sheet quietly from inside the roof of the hide when I heard a great whooshing of wings and, through a gap in the herbage, saw the eaglet fly away. He wobbled precariously for the first few seconds then, feeling the full powers of his wings and the guiding influence of his broad tail feathers, he adjusted to the wind currents with instinctive ease and flew with leisurely flaps to the far ridges north eastwards. Then he turned north west and after another 400 yards made a perfect landing on a rocky ridge above the heather. I felt sure then he had flown already, maybe more than once, but had returned to the eyrie to roost and be fed.

Calum and I had the hide down in minutes. After dispersing all the covering herbage and leaving the site looking natural, we carried my wrapped up 'torture chamber' down the hill. As we neared a high bluff the mother came right over it, merely forty feet up, a huge black shape against the sky, one pinion moulted from her right wing. While she appeared to be going slowly, she was travelling too fast for me to get the camera out of the pack. She soon located the eaglet, wheeling suddenly at the sight of it and descending as the ridge hid them from view. We decided to leave them to their rendezvous rather than try to stalk for pictures. Instead, I just raised my hand in silent salute. Poor season or not, the old lady had again proved herself a fine mother and, with her mate's help, had hunted well and provided ample food for her bairn. In a sense, too, she had been good to me, and I felt great relief that she had so soon found her flown chick and if all went reasonably well, he would help maintain the mature eagles in the West Highland skies.

When later I made out my report to the Nature Conservancy Council, I said that the long hard winter and wet spring had probably inhibited eagle breeding (also confirmed in talks with Dick Balharry and Roy Dennis, of the R.S.P.B.) and that I thought the old male from Eyries 2 and 17 was possibly dead. I had not seen him once in the entire year. I could only report two eagles that had definitely flown successfully and one of those had been from pair 12 on Greg Hunter's ground. Later, however, Greg told me he had also been able to report one chick flying successfully from an eyrie belonging to pair 10 which, being on his ground, I had not felt it correct to inquire about and include in my report. Even so, it *had* been a poor year for the eagles in all my inland areas after the harsh winter.

In August I had to head south for two weeks to sort out some complications in my father's affairs and do some biological research. It was when I put my seven eagle films into the CETA studios in London for their special development that I received a shock. The sixth film, on which I should have recorded the best photos of the season, had indeed gone awry. In my haste to put it into the camera with just my cold left hand after the worst wet night and without moving the lens because one of the eagles was flying in, I must have failed to fix it properly to the take-up spool. I had missed every single one of those good eagle shots on June 28, but miraculously, possibly after being shaken up on the trek, it had caught itself up and started going through the camera on my last shot of the wild fox sleeping in the peat bank. This photo, a very good one, was now the first on the film. That's how it sometimes goes in wildlife photography under harsh conditions. I had only myself to blame – I should have checked that the film spool was turning when I was operating the reload lever in the eyrie. I derived some comfort from having salvaged one of the fox shots. And I re-learned an old lesson.

I returned to the Highlands after an exhausting trip, with an injured owl and a sick male kestrel (given to me by the Putney R.S.P.C.A. Dispensary) which I was to nurse and release back into the wild. It seemed an anticlimax when my eagle report was acknowledged by the N.C.C. with a cyclo-styled form which said: 'We have noted our records.'

I saw no more eagles until Moobli and I were well into our autumn stag treks. On October 24 we had just successfully stalked and photographed the eighth stag with his harem of hinds when high over a peak to the north west sailed a large female eagle. I was sure it was Atalanta, and behind her came the much smaller male I had seen before. And bringing up the rear was a fine white-patched eaglet! We were too far away for the youngster to have come from Eyrie 16. Now I had the humiliating certainty that Atalanta had again successfully. bred on land near my home, and that there was an eyrie somewhere not too far away that I had yet to find.

12 · *Atalanta and Melanion's Twin Chicks*

As I landed the boat on a dull dark January day at the end of another tiring trip to Spain, I heard a yelping cry, stronger but like the mournful '*kloo-ee*' of a golden plover. I looked around and at first saw nothing, then I spotted the huge dark form of an eagle flying to the east just above the first 500-foot ridges. I had never heard the call before and it could only have come from the eagle, but the light was so poor that I could not see if it was the new eaglet or one of the adults. Eagles have been known, though rarely, to give odd yelping cries, high pitched like a terrier or a fox, and it is usually believed that they are giving vent to irritation or even anger. But there was something sad, almost suppliant, about this call, as if the bird were crying out from hunger.

How good it seemed, though, to be virtually welcomed home by an eagle. After several trips to carry my gear up to the cottage, I went to check the woods where I came across a dead deer calf and somehow found the strength to haul it up the hill.

I was outside next day, sledging in rocks to support the larch pole of my wind generator, when I saw Atalanta and her mate flying over Eyrie 1 from the east. They were already courting and the male treated me to a dazzling display, the kind that eagles make during courtship and to advertise their presence to other eagles in their home ranges. He flew off to the west, soared higher, leaned on the wind with closed wings and, like a giant trussed turkey, performed a steep nosedive for about 300 feet. Then he opened his wings, soared upwards, closed them again and made another spectacular dive, and like this yo-yoed across the sky for about two miles. The male eagle turned and sailed back towards Atalanta, was near her in a minute but turned off before reaching her to continue sailing in wide circles. How wonderful to see the great birds together again. I climbed up and found that they had already been at the carcass earlier, for it had been ripped open below the ribs in the eagle style.

Encouraging though the rare double sighting was, I had decided not to work with eagles again this year. There were many reasons; fuel costs for boat and Land Rover were now prohibitive. I wasn't getting any younger and the physical energy expended on all the long treks was enormous. I could no longer afford the sheer *time* it took when I was far behind in my writing, and my earnings were dwindling. Above all, I felt that after such a poor previous season all the eagles would be better off left to recoup totally alone. I now had many excellent eagle pictures and to want more seemed to me greedy and not justified.

On January 30 I was leaving on a supply trip when I saw Atalanta flying over Eyrie 1. She circled, turned south and headed right over the cottage. Was it possible that she and her mate were going to rebuild that nest? I decided again to leave them alone and not hike up to see.

Snow blizzards blanketed the ground during the next two days. With Moobli I found fox tracks in the front pasture and back-tracked them up the hill, hoping to surprise a fox out in the open for a photo. But the tracks ran out in snowless patches under the trees that lined the burn ravine. I had just stalked to within twenty-five yards of two hinds and a calf among the trees when we found a freshly dead old hind. She had died within forty yards of the calf carcass I had already hauled up on to the hillside. It was as if some benign deity was helping me to feed the eagles close to my home.

By now most of the treks were specifically for foxes and badger setts, for I wanted to improve my photos of these animals. We made a hard seven-mile trek eastward and back up the steep mountain above the long river valley and actually tracked a fox through the snow for over two miles and found its den. When we got home I realised it was the seventh anniversary of my first journey to see Wildernesse, and that I had unconsciously re-covered the route of the first exploratory trek I had ever made in the area. On February 10, tracking a fox uphill, I found that we were not far from Eyrie 1 and checked it with the fieldglass. The bare rock was still on the ledge, but far from there being any new sticks, the old nest debris round its base seemed more blown away than ever. Well, I was not working with eagles this year.

On February 21 Moobli and I were walking along the side of the north hill when a red deer hind suddenly got up from the heather and ran ahead of us, not seeking higher ground as a healthy deer would. I sent Moobli off with the command 'Don't hurt it!' – which he knew meant I wanted him to try to herd the deer back to me so that I could look at it. He pointed his huge muzzle down and ran after her as she turned downhill, a bad sign for only a sick deer which knows it can't run will do that. Suddenly she fell over in a wrap-tangle of legs. I got to her as she finished the somersault, then with one arm round her neck and the other hand on her rump I walked her down to the cottage. The watery rattlings in her throat as she breathed told me she had pneumonia. I managed to keep her alive for three days but finally she succumbed. When I skinned her I found encysted in her upper coat 143 warble fly larvae which had clearly added to her debility. She had milk too, which indicated she was probably the mother of the dead calf we had found earlier.

A sad incident, but there was no point in wasting the carcass. I removed the haunches for Moobli, then hauled the rest up the hill to join the others, now torn apart by foxes and other scavengers. As I sweated and heaved, cursing the tussocks that seemed to connive to block the heavy body's progress, I knew that the ageing process was not passing me by! And I left it on a flat place at about 300 feet.

As we reached the cottage again the clouds rolled by and the sun blazed down so strongly that I was reluctant to go indoors and finish the outline of my new book. I stuck newspaper over the window, worked hard, and in three hours had the draft beaten. Delighted, I went out to sunbathe awhile and saw the eaglet, which I thought had left the area, fly over the ridges above the new carcass. It did not appear to notice it and kept flying westwards.

An hour later, however, the eaglet flew back, checked its flight momentarily above the dead hind, then carried on to a peak to the north east, from where it would possibly watch to make sure that the coast was clear before coming down. Although I kept sporadic watch from the window, it didn't come down before dark. What was most interesting was that it was still on its parents' home range.

Next day I saw Atalanta and her mate flying to the west. Again the smaller male, bringing up the rear, performed his territorial and courtship display. He made frequent 'golden ball' dives, wings tucked in, pulling out each time in a glide, climbing again with just three or four flaps, then falling again. It was similar to but ten times more exaggerated and dramatic than the undulating courtship flight of woodpigeons. I felt sure that they would nest nearer me this year. It had been an exceptionally mild winter and once again the theory that eagles moved to the lower snowless ground on the edge of their range, or even over it, in harsh winters – when I never saw them – seemed correct.

Half an hour later I was investigating a 'giant's battleground' of tumbled rocks for fox dens and setts, when I saw the two eagles heading back to the east. I put the telephoto lens on the camera and managed one poor-light shot of Atalanta before they vanished over the peaks. I put the standard lens back on and had just photographed a badgers' sett when I looked up to see *three* eagles circling overhead. One of them was the white-patched eaglet, and it was giving out loud '*keyow*' chick cheeps.

Suddenly, before I could refit the telephoto lens, Atalanta and her mate wheeled abruptly away, and the eaglet set off on a long glide to the north east and vanished over the distant peaks. I felt that I might have witnessed the eaglet's farewell to its parents, that they had escorted it firmly rather than driven it away. Why else the sudden wheeling off? The possibility seemed confirmed over the following weeks for I never saw that eaglet again.

On February 26 I woke early to hear odd yelping calls delivered slowly – '*keeyoup*', then a pause and '*keeyoup*' again. I looked out of the window but saw nothing. I hurried into the rear room to see a black shadow on the hind carcass and, despite the poor light, I made out the form of an eagle. It tugged at the meat, swallowed a piece and hopped heavily to another part of the carcass, lifting its wing and showing just a few whitish feathers underneath. It was clearly not the eaglet whose patches were much larger and whiter. It was the male, Atalanta's new mate, and this again proved that he was a young bird. As I watched he flew from the carcass and, with a few ponderous flaps, looped upward and seemed to land in the trees above the burn's ravine.

I shoved on my bush hat and camouflage jacket and otherwise naked and barefoot sneaked out in the bitter frost, peeped cautiously round the corner of the woodshed and took a picture. To my surprise, a larger and darker eagle was also sitting in the trees – Atalanta! My heart thumped with excitement. As I saw the young male perched near the powerful female I suddenly thought of a good name for him. I would call him Melanion, after the mythical Greek youth who, after Meleager's death, accepted Atalanta's challenge that she would only marry a prince who could beat her in a foot race. Melanion won the race, and her hand, by throwing down golden apples which Atalanta paused to pick up. Yes, Melanion seemed an apt name. Not wanting to scare them away I resisted the temptation of another shot and went back indoors to leave them to it.

I ascertained that the eagles had gone, then in poor daylight spent a few hours building a perfect invisible hide among thick dead brown bracken some forty yards from the carcass. It seemed that the eagles were now much tamer towards me and knew that it was I who hauled up all the carcasses. I wouldn't work nesting eagles this year but this was too good a chance to miss.

At 6 p.m. I hiked up to where I thought the hide was and had a problem locating it again. But finally I crawled in with a sleeping bag to spend the night there, hoping to photograph the eagles around dawn. Just as on the previous occasion, snow fell through the night and the second sleeping bag, bought at the same time as the first, also slipped its zip. In the dark and narrow hide I could not see or move well enough to fix it. When I wasn't in a semi-frozen coma, I twisted cold side to warm side and back again through the night. All to no avail! After fifteen-and-a-half hours, with daylight (such as it was) well established, I gave up. Nothing at all had visited the snow-covered carcass.

Next day I was throwing sticks for Moobli to chase when I was surprised to see Melanion beating over the loch from the south. He appeared to ignore us, though I was standing by the porch, and landed in the top of a tall Scots pine on the highest edge of the west wood. Not wanting to scare him away, we retreated into the cottage and I hurried to watch him through the workshop window.

To my amazement, I saw him launch up from the pine, wheel in a short high circle, then zoom down at the tree, seize the end of a dead branch with his talons and, with powerful beats of his wings, snap it off! Then away he went over the ridges with the twig. Either he was helping Atalanta rebuild an eyrie or he was taking sticks to help her choose a site. In any case, he had come to *our* wood for some of his building timbers. I hoped that he would do so again so that I could photograph the event. It seemed a sizeable branch – about an inch thick – and again it reminded me of the physical power of the eagle.

Despite this new temptation to look for their eyrie, I stuck to my resolution not to work with nesting eagles this year – made easier by the fact that I was now successfully photographing badgers at a sett at dusk and having unusual experiences with them, whenever the mid-March snowfalls permitted.

I saw neither of the eagles again until boating out on a supply trip on March 25, when I spied Melanion flying above a wood two miles from the cottage. By then I had located just inside the top edge of that wood two fresh deer carcasses which were clearly being used by the birds. They had no need of more carcasses hauled up by me, which was just as well because I wasn't finding any near the cottage. I now felt almost certain that they would be nesting in my area.

That day I discovered that Roy Dennis of the R.S.P.B. had received a phone tip-off from a contact some twenty miles from me that suspected egg thieves had been seen near an eyrie, and Roy, two other R.S.P.B. officers, as well as police from as far away as Fort Augustus, were engaged in the chase. Greg Hunter was driving round checking that the suspects' car was not near any of the eyries we knew. Most of the eyries nearer me were too far from any road to be really endangered. All the same, on the way home I checked there were no unusual boats parked on either side of the loch. (Later I learned from Roy that four men had been caught and charged with stealing two clutches of eagles' eggs, but not from our area.)

On April 4 I had just exposed the last frame of a film on a hind and her calf in glorious sunlight on the ridges above when Melanion flapped and glided over my head from the east. Just my luck, for he was really low. Three hours later, while weeding the garden, I saw him flying near the ridges above the west wood. He had clearly seen me, and circled right over my head before going back the way he had come, just closing his wings slightly, leaning into the side wind, and travelling in that fast glide like some space machine. Again I realised the mastery of this unique flight quality. It is not merely due to the eagle's weight, for a swan or goose can't do it, but it did seem an odd action, to circle right over me and go away again – exactly as if I was being 'fetched' by an aerial dog! Or had he been after more 'timber' from the pine tree and, seeing me in the garden, had thought better of it?

I had no chance to witness a repeat performance because a few days later I had to head south on a vital and complicated work trip. On the way out I met keeper Allan Peters and told him I'd been photographing badgers in the dark. He said he was keen to do this himself and we agreed to work a big sett he knew about, on my return. While in London I took Moobli, who was still limping on his rear left leg, to a leading vet, worried that it might be hip displasia to which Alsatians are prone. Poor Moobli had to be anaesthetised so that he could be X-rayed on his back.

The news was not good. Moobli did not have hip displasia but there was an odd growth on the tibia bone where it joined the femur, almost certainly caused by arthritis. The joint could not close properly without trapping the tendon and, at times, causing him pain. It was not operable, the vet said, but he gave me some pills which he hoped would help dissolve the growth. Poor old Moobli. It seemed that the damp cold climate, life at our primitive home, the hard hill treks, had finally affected him. When I told the vet about my own knee pains, especially in my right knee which had cracked and hurt greatly during the past two years when carrying heavy packs on eagle treks down mountains, he said I almost certainly had arthritis too.

This unpleasant fact was confirmed a few nights later after an examination by the doctor son of a friend in London.

'Does it hurt when you are packing up or down mountains?' he asked me after depressing my kneecap with his thumbs and telling me to tense up and bring the cap into place again.

'Down, mostly,' I said with a yelp from the pain.

'That's right. You have osteo-arthritis for certain. But the actual knee joints are okay,' he said. After further examination he added cheerfully, 'If it gets any worse you can always have your knee caps off. They're not really necessary.'

'I'll stay as the good Lord made me,' I said. 'Unless it's life or death!'

The doctor said that no matter what training or diet I adopted the condition was incurable. Hmm.

It was early May before I was back in Scotland and Allan Peters and I finally boated down the loch to the big sett he knew. The badgers did not appear but Allan told me a sad story. On May 2 a local postman had been driving through a gate at the far end of the loch when he had heard a loud swishing noise. He looked round to see a huge brownish bird land heavily on the ground thirty yards away. After fastening the gate, he had gone over on foot and was within ten yards of the fallen eagle when its mate, which had landed beside it, took off. The eagle on the ground was dead. The postman had taken the great bird to the forestry office and it had been put into deep freeze. Roy Dennis had been called in and the bird was being

184

sent for analysis, but the report would take some time. The eagle had weighed eleven-and-a-half pounds and had a wing span of just under six feet, not large, which made me believe it was a male. Allan and I wondered if it had picked up poison put out illegally for foxes and crows, or had hit an overhead cable, which, knowing the eyesight of eagles, I did not think likely.

It wasn't until Allan had left that the possibility occurred to me that the dead eagle could be Melanion. If Atalanta was alone now, and had chicks to feed, she would also be looking for a new and third mate. Luckily the weather had been sunny for days which would help her to leave any chicks for longer periods while she searched for food. This seemed even more reason why I should stay out of the way. Next day I wrote some urgent letters, and on the boat trip to post them I kept a keen eye open for eagles but saw none. When I found a traffic-killed rabbit on the road, I picked it up, and later I was glad that I had.

The following morning I was surprised to see the huge dark form of Atalanta flapping and gliding towards me near the west wood. Then, as Melanion had done before my trip south, she circled right over our heads and set off back in a long glide in the same direction Melanion had taken. Once again I had the impression of a dog coming to fetch someone, but surely that was a ludicrous concept.

This extraordinary action, however, made me think more deeply about the whole problem. If indeed it *was* her mate that had died, and she had young chicks and had not yet found a replacement spouse, she would be having to brood them every night and, during bad weather, in the daytime too, as well as having to hunt for them on her own. A daunting task for one bird. I had to help provide her with food if I could. That I had already found a juicy fresh rabbit seemed more than a quirk of fate. And why *had* she flown over my head like that? Yes, I decided, I would definitely have to find out what the situation was.

Next morning, with the sun beaming through a hazy sky, I boated out with Moobli before setting off on a long hard trek to find – if there was one – her breeding eyrie. A drenching shower passed over as we landed below a steep slope. By the time we had climbed only 300 feet my trousers were soaked through from the clinging wet bracken. A fine start! The sun emerged again as I climbed towards the first ridges at 1,200 feet, and I found myself steaming with perspiration. After his long rest, Moobli was so happy to be back on the Hill that his foot hardly seemed to drag at all. I searched with the glass every rockface, knoll and protuberance in a mile-and-a-half of zig-zags from east to west, knowing that very occasionally eagles nest on the ground. Then, as I emerged from a gully, I saw the dark cross of Atalanta floating lazily along some far peaks. She was moving like the mother at Eyrie 16 had moved when checking her eyrie from above, and my pulse quickened.

I worked along a second range of peaks, with dark grey granite ledges below them. Often what looked from a distance like sheer rockfaces turned out to be just small escarpments with grassy ledges between. I headed west and climbed to some more peaks, zig-zagging between the ridges, searching their north sides too. After seven hard miles I began to feel disheartened. I decided that if I didn't find an eyrie today I would not look any more; I would just put out some meat above the cottage and, if Atalanta was in trouble, hope she would take it.

Far ahead I saw yet another range of higher hills and as I scanned a large dark buttress I saw a dot of pure white on what seemed to be a ledge. Could it be a downy young eaglet? To get there I had to descend seven hundred feet and make a new ascent to 1,600. Wearily I checked two more little cliffs, then set off down and up on the new long climb. I had about 500 feet more to go, almost sure the unmoving white dot was merely lichen, when I looked down the folding hills to my right. I saw a small rockface way below which had nothing on it but an oddly orange-tipped ledge which certainly contained no sticks of a nest. As I kept climbing towards the higher face I noticed that the orange ledge was longer than it first appeared, and through the glass I saw something white, like a feather, caught on herbage, the sort of feather an incubating eagle grows. Well, I'd better check it before going on. Knees hurting again, I descended the tussocky quarter mile to the ledge. There were a few white dashes on its edge, too small to be eagles', I thought; perhaps they were from young ravens. But the ledge seemed far too low for normally nesting ravens or eagles.

With difficulty I climbed an almost sheer bit, held on to the base of a loose rock wedged in heather and peeped over. The ledge was long, about five feet deep and was covered with wood-rush which had dried out in the days of hot sun. To my astonishment, my eyes suddenly beheld a ten-days-old downy eaglet, crouching down and tucking its flipper-like embryo wings tightly into its sides. Between heather tufts I also saw what looked like the end of an unhatched egg! There was no real nest, just a few scattered sticks over the wood-rush.

186

I climbed down rapidly and left the dead rabbit showing prominently on a huge flat mossy rock forty yards below the eyrie. As we left to head towards the loch shore Atalanta sailed leisurely overhead, showing no sign of anxiety at all, and I took several good photos of her. She had often seen me haul up dead deer; now I hoped she would take the rabbit and know that I had provided it too.

What seemed odd, with the unhatched egg there, was that she had not been on the eyrie when I had first approached it. Did she know it wouldn't hatch, that it was addled? Or had she left it in the warm hazy sun knowing it would not cool too fast while she was gone to find food for herself and the chick? Either way, it was still possible that dead eagle *could* have been her mate, for I had certainly not seen Melanion.

I looked back after about 300 yards – in time to see her sweep down to the rockface, which she must have circled, and land on the eyrie. This was the nearest any eagle had landed on its nest in sight of me. When we reached a heathery ridge about half a mile further on, I discovered a natural mossy armchair cut into a small but steep hillock, and over the chair like a sunshade spread a small rowan tree. When I sat down in it, the height of the side rock just reached my eyes and by laying my fieldglass on it I had a perfect if somewhat distant view of the eyrie. It would be a good place from which to watch without disturbing Atalanta at all. I saw her fly out, circle below the eyrie and land. After a few moments she rose again, flapping heavily with something in her talons and landed again on the ledge. She had taken my rabbit!

As we headed home I felt a tremendous surge of triumph. I had gone out alone to look for a possible but unknown eyrie in a great undulating land mass filled with likely sites and had found it in six hours. Eyrie 27! And Atalanta, who I was almost sure was having to cope alone, had accepted my gift of food. What a day, what an experience! Even so, I would stick to my resolution not to photograph from a hide this year.

Once, after a supply trip on which I found another rabbit, I hiked up to the rocky chair and watched for an hour, but again I saw only Atalanta fly from the ledge where she must have been brooding her chick. I hoped the sunny weather was helping her to cope all right, and left the rabbit in a prominent spot where she would soon see it. In late May I met Allan, who had sad news – he'd heard that the dead eagle found by the postman had in fact been shot. I tried to ring Roy Dennis for confirmation but he, in his busiest season of the year, was not at home. I later wrote to the scientific analysis units of the Department of Agriculture and Fisheries for Scotland asking if they would send me a copy of the report on the eagle when investigations were complete.

On my 52nd birthday I was trekking through some wooded cliffs two miles from home, trying to find the sett of the old badger that was visiting us at night, when I saw an eagle floating above the trees towards Atalanta's eyrie. It was not Atalanta but a smaller, younger and lighter bird, and I realised with relief that it was possibly her mate Melanion, who might not be dead after all.

Next day I hiked up to the rocky chair under the rowan and had only been watching for half an hour when I saw what seemed to be Melanion fly in from the east with something in his talons and swoop up on to the eyrie. I could not see clearly at that distance but could just make out the form of another eagle on the ledge. It appeared to be feeding from what he had brought in, or else was feeding the chick. I kept straining my eyes to see more clearly through the glass, when out from the recesses, where she had been partly hidden by the fringing heather, came Atalanta. Huge, dark and prehistoric in appearance, as she had been the day I first saw her over Wildernesse seven years earlier, she sailed easily away to the west. My relief and delight that she did still have her mate and at seeing the bringing of food and the change-over at the nest, was enormous. Again, I steeled myself to keep away, as much as I would now have liked to know if the egg had hatched out. (In any case, I had not applied for a licence.) At least she would need no supplementary feeding from me now.

In early June I saw Melanion flapping over the loch to Eagle Rock Mountain while I was boating out for supplies.

I was in the garden on June 9, photographing a rare clouded yellow butterfly, the first I had seen in my part of the Highlands, when I heard a common gull from the islet colony calling high up. It was mobbing Atalanta and it looked as tiny as a swallow against the immense eagle. Each time the gull dived in, Atalanta gave an irritated little flap of her wings, as if saying 'Okay. I've seen you. Now go!' I managed to take a few shots.

On the next supply trip I saw people coming back from a funeral service in the nearest burial ground. My tradesman pal Euan told me it had been for a farmer I had known who lived in a nearby village. As we talked I noticed he was smiling at something. When he asked if it was true, as I'd told Calum, that I wasn't working with eagles this year, I said it was, for I felt they should be left totally alone after the poor breeding season the year before.

'Well,' he said. 'You'll kick yourself now for an eyrie with two eaglets has been found along the loch a few miles from you. It would be your nearest ever.' He had heard this at the funeral but was not sure who had found it. *Twin* eaglets? Could they possibly be Atalanta's? Were they in danger? *Now* what should I do?

Hearing that a small wake to honour the memory of the deceased was being held at the home of my neighbouring farmer, I called in to pay my respects. My timid knock was answered by a cordial invitation to join the group, and he thrust a generous tumbler of whisky at me and indicated that I should sit at the head of the table. His wife even gave me some supper. The talk was stimulating as we all lauded the merits of our departed neighbour and discussed local matters. At some stage I said I'd heard that someone had found an eagle eyrie with twin chicks not far away.

My farmer neighbour laughed. It was *he* who had found it, by accident. He had been gathering sheep on the Hill when he happened to look up at a rockface. There, from a ledge, two large semi-fledged eaglets had looked down gravely at him.

'I've been waiting a chance to talk with you, Mike,' he said with a twinkle in his eye. 'I suggest a deal. I'll trade you the whereabouts of the eyrie for a new fox den! There's a fox out your way somewhere which has been at the lambs.'

Now, I didn't blame any sheep farmer for going after a fox that was killing his lambs but I didn't feel it would be right for me to trade the life of a wild animal in this way. There weren't any sheep near me anyway. I answered, truthfully, that I didn't know of any fox den that had any lamb remains round it. I recalled our talk last year when he had said that some farmers in the Highlands felt that, purely from the economic view, it would be better if all foxes and all eagles were eradicated. He was certainly keen on controlling foxes, and I wondered how he felt about eagles. But in the situation I felt it best not to ask directly. Instead I asked if the eaglets were all right.

'Aye, they're fine,' he said with mock grimness, then, guessing my thoughts, added: 'Don't worry. I left them alone – despite all the lamb remains in there.' I was taking a bit of a beating in this company. The lively talk continued while he kept filling our glasses. I said at one stage that I was still working on compensation for any lambs actually killed by eagles, told him how rare this was in our area, and said I would gladly try again if any of his live lambs were taken.

He thanked me for that but from previous experience on matters like government compensation for lost stock, always complicated and time consuming, he didn't think I would have much luck. He had once caught and kept many dead foxes in his deep freeze for a government survey on gut contents, and while he hadn't minded not being paid for all his time, he had felt miffed that he had not even been told the results. He again made the point that naturalists loved eagles but when they took lambs it was the farmer who bore the cost. I could see his point and I respected him as a hard worker who ran one of the best farms in the area. I resolved to take up the question of compensation again. By the time the party broke up and I was boating home in the near dark, I realised I still had not got the eyrie location from him.

Now I was plagued by doubts. *Was* it Atalanta's eyrie that had been discovered? Had the egg I had found in May hatched? Or had a second eyrie containing twin chicks been found? Euan had thought the eyrie was along the actual lochside ridges. Just how many folk knew of his twin-chick eyrie? Was it in danger?

By now I had spoken to Roy Dennis who confirmed that the dead eagle had indeed been shot. In his view the bird had definitely come from a territory much further away. Later, I received the lab report on the dead eagle from Dr A. D. Ruthven of the analysis unit in Edinburgh. It had been a young female, her oviduct active, and she had been shot through the side of the head with a 0.22 rifle. How she had managed to fly any distance so injured was a mystery. But as Roy had thought, she had come from a pair in a territory beyond Atalanta's. I wondered if she was from the immature pair I had seen flying in that region over four years before. It seemed highly possible.

I was worried that there was still a die-hard in the region who would shoot eagles. Roy had also said he was still busy checking suspects roaming the Highlands, now seeking live chicks of both peregrines and eagles. I had also had some brief correspondence with a man who was in the region wanting to film eagles at the nest for television, and he had seemed peeved that I hadn't rushed out for a suggested rendezvous many miles away for 'a talk about eagles' when no official proposition had been made. I weighed all these facts carefully and decided I ought to look for a possible new eyrie and also check Atalanta's. It seemed as if I were being dragooned into working on eagles again this year, that I ought to put up a hide near Atalanta's nest, just to keep an eye on it. I telephoned Dick Balharry, set all the facts before him, took his advice and duly applied to the N.C.C. for the necessary licence.

After days of heavy drizzle I boated out with Moobli and made a long hard search of all the lochside ridges, but I found no new eyrie. I had a task re-locating Atalanta's among the far ridges, for now I was coming at it from a different angle, the many folds in the hills all looked different. Then we came across some wide spaced tracks that appeared to have been made by a caterpillar-tracked vehicle. We followed them for a mile where they flattened out the long tussock grasses and I was surprised to find they passed some 250 yards below the rockface that contained the eyrie. I looked up – the ledge seemed deserted. Hell!

Then, as I climbed up the steep slope, I thought I caught a glimpse of something brown and yellow move behind the heather on the ledge. I had to find out for sure, so I climbed right up. I held on to the loose rock wedged in the herbage, feet trembling on tiny projections, and peeped over. Immediately, like great chocolate brown bats, two eaglets rose from below the cliff face and batted their two-thirds grown wings at me. They hissed. One was almost full-fledged but the other, some four or five days younger, had more white down and its head was still nearly all white. Clearly the 'unhatched egg' I had seen had been just part of the shell from which the second eaglet had already hatched when I first found the nest. The chick must have been hidden from my view behind some heather further along the ledge. The older eaglet now turned its back, tramped over the ledge, tipped its head down into the heather like an ostrich and shoved its brown feathered tail up in the air. The younger chick seemed less scared, lowered its wings and stayed where it was, regarding me with an anxious but quizzical gaze.

My heart pounded at this unusual sight – twin eaglets, the elder nearly eight weeks old, successfully co-existing in the same nest. I wondered if it was the greater timidity of the larger chick – for eagles are as individualistic as people – that had allowed the smaller to survive. It would be fascinating to watch how they got along. Certainly both had grown fast, indicating Atalanta and her mate were efficient providers. There was only a piece of rabbit on the nest and just before I climbed down again I saw among the few sticks on the ledge were a rowan spray, an oak spray and – only the second time I'd ever seen it – a spray of beech leaves too.

I hastened over the rough steep ground and found an ideal spot for a hide thirty-five yards away and level with the eyrie. By sitting on the grassy slope behind some L-shaped rocks conveniently covered with long heather I found I had a perfect view of it. It would be good to work from a ground hide again instead of dangerous cliff ledges. I was just measuring up for the shape of it when both Atalanta and Melanion came soaring over the ridge above the eyrie. Only 200 yards up, they clearly saw me raise my camera and Moobli lying nearby, but neither showed the slightest anxiety, just soaring in lazy circles. And twice Melanion swooped and dived near his larger mate as I clicked away, though he held no prey and she did not turn to extend her talons. I had no way of knowing if they really identified me as the individual who had hauled up carcasses through the past winters, but there seemed an oddly peaceful, almost 'friendly' atmosphere in the air as they sailed onwards. I felt happier as we boated home, for if anyone had been to visit the eyrie they had at least left the eaglets alone.

Hide erection was impossible next day because of teeming rain, but when it eased up the following morning, I used the time to boat out and stock up on new camera film and general supplies to last a long time. I also obtained a new dead rabbit. On the way home I called to see the neighbouring farmer, who was out working, but I reiterated to his wife that I would try for compensation for any lambs actually killed by the eagles. As she saw my serious face, she laughed, but in a kindly way.

'He *would* have told you where the eyrie was, but in the mood that night, he was just pulling your leg,' she said. 'You've no need to worry, Mike. He won't hurt the eaglets.'

I felt relieved, though I had secretly felt he was a better man than to have done so. All the same, I was still worried about the shot eagle not so many miles away. Every time a boat passed down the loch I wondered if it contained a man with a gun and kept my glass on it to see if anyone landed in line with the eyrie.

Two days of westerly gales and torrential rain followed. During a slight lull I was altering the hide's shape when I heard one of the islet common gulls making loud '*keeya*'s overhead. I looked up to see it winging frantically towards the west wood and was then amazed to see the huge shape of Atalanta sitting in the same pine tree from which Melanion had taken his 'building timbers' earlier! I dashed indoors for the camera and the rabbit and when I got out again she was winging round above the cottage. She looked black and half soaked with the rain. 'Poor old lady,' I thought. She and her mate, with two great hungry eaglets to feed, might be finding it harder to

192

In my fifth season – a rare sight. Atalanta has raised twin eaglets.

Atalanta – like some ancient gryphon from another world.

She landed, blocking the chicks from view, and revealed a god–like face on her right wing.

Melanion came sweeping in, a headless ptarmigan in his talons.

He seemed to hang in the sky as the chicks cried for food.

Melanion watches approvingly as Diana mantles over the prey he has brought in.

Atalanta carried out unwanted decaying scraps of grouse.

Diana calls as Melanion leaves to hunt again.

At last, Atalanta's eaglets are ready to fly. Diana exercises her wings, watched by Apollo.

hunt. I held out the rabbit, then threw it into the front pasture and retreated into the cottage. She saw it all right, circled round twice, but then two more gulls came winging over from the islet and the three of them began to harry her with near swoops and loud calls. She went into a fast glide across the loch towards Eagle Rock Mountain, easily outdistancing her tormentors in seconds. At that moment I could almost have discharged a barrel at the gulls myself, though they were only instinctively trying to protect their own chicks. But for them, I felt sure that Atalanta would have come down for my rabbit. How odd that with hunting harder in the driving rain she had again come to the cottage area, as in winter. If a deliberate act, it seemed a great compliment, and that they *knew* I was friendly, and remembered I had hauled up the dead deer.

Next day the rain was even worse. After hauling my boats out of reach of the rising loch, I made the inside of the hide waterproof by stitching on grey mailbags, which I also painted to resemble lichened rocks. The rain stopped next morning so I left the hide drying and hiked up with Moobli with other materials, a supply of long life milk and the refrigerated rabbit in case the eaglets needed food.

From a quarter of a mile I saw Atalanta sailing over the rockface and waited until she had gone again before I hastened up. As I dug out rocks, realising that because of the steep slope I would have to make do with a sitting rather than a lying-down hide, I saw both chicks watching me with great interest. Their crops were half full, so they were not starving, and I could see the remains of a crow and what looked like a curlew on the nest. I decided to keep the rabbit for another day. I prepared the hide's base, dug a sitting place, carried in rooted heather taken from where the eagles would not notice, and replanted it in strategic places to obscure the final hide. I was working fast but carefully when something happened which made me feel that perhaps with this particular pair such infinite pains were not necessary.

'*Keyow keeyow*' I heard the eaglets squeaking in voices of slightly different timbre. I saw them standing with outstretched necks and beaks and then, to my utter astonishment, in swept Atalanta with what looked like a young grouse in her talons. She landed on the ledge, stepped to one side as the larger eaglet mantled over the prey, watched it feed a few moments, then leisurely turned and left again. I just stood there, rooted to the spot. Without a single wing beat she sailed south before turning to drift down the glen to the east. Although we were only thirty-five yards away and I had been moving as I worked, she had apparently ignored us, as if she *did* know we were harmless, and had brought food to her bairns. Either that or she had not seen us, which seemed unlikely. I had never known anything like it happen before.

As we tramped out again, Moobli travelling well, as if he had become adjusted to the weakness in his rear left leg, my own knee seemed to have been miraculously cured. I felt curiously elated, oblivious to the rain showers. I had a strong feeling that I was possibly in for some of the most profound experiences I'd ever had with eagles – 'my' eagles, I thought, before inwardly acknowledging the stupidity of such a concept.

13 · The Most Profound Experience

Midsummer day, June 24, opened with two brief showers and then the grey clouds scudded away. Before the sun had climbed high enough to clear the east wood trees, it burned against my cheeks. This was the day. I would go before it became too hot. For the second time in his life, I shut Moobli in the cottage with food and water and set off on the long hard slog to the eyrie with full pack and carrying the heavier hide under my arm. Up between the steep tussocks, through bogs and clinging bracken that obscured jagged rocks, clambering in and out of burns with some places so steep I had to use one hand to climb, I slowly weaved my 50lb load up to the rockface.

I paused to rest now and then, and to scan the sky with the fieldglass, but neither eagle seemed to be in the area. Dumping my load at the hide site and removing the rabbit which I had chopped in halves, I hurried below the nest ledge, where both eaglets were standing bolt upright. I knew when I threw the rabbit halves in that it was going to be an unusual day. On the first toss the rabbit's head, chest and forelegs brushed the slanting cliff wall and landed quietly in front of the smaller chick. On the next the haunches just cleared the edge of the ledge and came gently to rest beside the larger chick which was standing three feet away. They couldn't have gone in more accurately if they had been sent along wires.

Making the hide was so easy it was as if I had an invisible helper. I

195

wove its outside meshes with heather, grasses and bracken and in just over an hour it was so perfect I myself could not distinguish it from the terrain. Just after I had slid pack, camera and lenses inside, both Atalanta and Melanion came over low and made two lazy aerial circles. Foolish though it may seem, I felt almost as if they were saying welcome. I now *knew* in my heart that these eagles knew me well, *did* identify me as the source of some of their winter carrion, and that, if I was not exactly a friend, I was at least harmless. I was now working with the instinct that comes to one who spends years alone with the creatures of the wild, for if you live among them with a humble mind and a quiet physical presence, you will gain their confidence and learn their ways. When they flew over a ridge to the north west I slid quietly into the hide.

I had no sooner set up the camera and was looking through the lens a few minutes later when Atalanta swept in without warning. Neither of the eaglets saw her coming. I recalled the year when I had spent four nights out on cliff ledges without an eagle coming into the eyrie and now here was an adult landing within ten minutes of my entering a hide alone. She was a huge and dark old lady, and the normal golden mane behind her wide, aged, almost reptilian head was a rich dark copper, and there were pitchy streaks in the dark but rich browns of the rest of her plumage.

She looked at my two rabbit chunks with an expression that said 'Where the hell did *they* come from?' After watching the big chick, which was already rending the haunches, she picked up the head and chest section and dropped it gently before the smaller, which then stamped on it, mantled its wings and also began to eat. Atalanta never once glanced in my direction, nor appeared to hear the heavy click of the camera shutter. She stood for a few moments behind and dwarfing the chicks, then satisfied the chicks had good food, she left again. I followed her with slightly moving camera and got a shot of her dropping low with her great wings wide open.

I watched keenly for evidence to support the legend that in twin chick nests the larger will harry, peck and generally victimise its smaller sibling – though it is known that once both have survived together for three weeks or so this sort of bullying ceases and the bigger accepts the presence of the smaller bird. This certainly seemed the situation at this nest. As the small eaglet turned sideways and tugged at the rabbit, the bigger, its crop now full of my offering, stood placidly beside it and watched it eating with a peaceful but interested air.

After a few minutes the smaller chick flapped its wings a few times, then stared at something else on the nest a couple of feet nearer to me. Then it tramped over, stamped down with both sets of talons and began to rend a headless hen grouse that Atalanta must have brought in. As she had landed with her back to me I had not seen it in her talons. Again the big eaglet just looked on peaceably as the other hauled up the wing feathers and a furry foot with its beak. Then the larger chick flopped down on its chest and had a snooze. The other finished feeding, stood on the nest edge and yawned with wide opened beak, then also flopped down behind a sprig of heather.

Half an hour later the big chick got up, flapped its wings and stalked over to the grouse left by its sibling and began to tuck in again. Their principle seemed to be stuff it down *now*; there may not be any more for a long while! The smaller eaglet also got up and watched the other eating, again without any sign of rancour. Then both birds stood close together. I had the distinct impression that they liked one another. I felt sure then that the large eaglet was a female and the other a male, and that had helped them get along together. Maybe it is only when both chicks are male or both female that they fight and the stronger out-competes and dominates the other until it perishes through not receiving enough food. This, however, would contradict the popular theory that when twin chicks hatch out they are nearly always of opposite sexes.

I suspected that the big chick was only two to three days the elder. She displayed more goldy-brown mane on her head and neck, while the smaller eaglet still had white on his forehead, throat and a little up the back of his neck. Once, when the big one had just sat down, her brother made a slight peck at her beak – she just opened her own beak wide in response. The fact that the eyrie ledge was some ten feet long and curved in a slight crescent shape may also have had something to do with the younger's survival. They could be and sleep apart, and even stay completely out of sight of one another. The close co-operation between the parents could also have had an effect, for they kept in closer touch than any other parents I had known. I nearly always saw them together on my approaches. I had also seen Melanion actually bringing food to her when Atalanta had been brooding the chicks. Young he may be, but probably a very good male, handing over plenty of food.

Through the afternoon the eaglets entertained me royally as I sat on a foam cushion in the earth seat I had excavated and looked side-ways through the lens. Once, when both were lying down with their wing 'elbows' bulging out to the side, a dragonfly looped past. Instantly both heads shot up and rolled almost upside down as if about to wring their own necks as they followed its flight. Half an hour later the big chick hauled a meaty bone from the rabbit haunches and tried to swallow it. The smaller looked on as she lifted head and neck high in the air while trying to gulp it down, as if to say 'You'll not make it with *that* one!' But she did. They watched each other preening, tramping about, and even squirting over the nest edge. The smaller eaglet seemed to like the sun more than his sister for he sat on the rim for a long time, back to the wind, which kept whipping his 'kilt' up, exposing the still white rump and belly under the dark tail feathers. He must have kept cooler that way. His beak was open now as he panted fast like a dog. I tried to count the movements of his sides. He seemed to be breathing at about 110 times to the minute. This heat did not penetrate the hide, however. I also took a good shot of him standing with crop distended.

As I watched him basking in the sun while his bigger sister lay in the shade of the cliff, I suddenly thought of good names for them. The sun-loving male could be Apollo, god of the sun, and as was also true in the Greek myths, his sister could be Diana, goddess of the chase, who drove the moon chariot.

After her rest, Diana performed wing-flapping exercises, making almost circular beats so that the tips of her lower flight feathers, the 'ailerons', swept up by her chest at the end of every flap. She was feeling how they performed against the wind and but for clutching the ledge herbage hard, each downbeat would have taken her into the air. She sat down breast first, cocking her tail up first as usual, so as not to risk damaging her tail feathers. Then she crawled across the nest into the shade on her haunches, using the locomotion method of a very young chick that cannot yet walk.

Later, I took shots of her standing up, twisting her tail to the side to preen it with her beak, while smaller Apollo, lying down, seemed to be looking up her skirts. Suddenly Diana stopped, let her tail down and glared at her brother as if to say 'What are you staring at?' At about 8 p.m. both eaglets glared up into the sky from lying positions, Apollo squeaking first with shrill '*keyow*'s, then Diana with her slightly deeper shorter '*kyow*' calls. Both birds stood up, heads extended, making a loud duet, '*Keyow, kyow, keyow; kyow*'ring loudly from the amplifying face of the cliff behind them. What an exciting crescendo of music it made in that wild remote glen, for it told me a parent was coming in.

Suddenly there was Atalanta in the lens, floating like a ghost, down, down, down; all that bulk and weight yet travelling slowly and airily until, with uplifted wings, like a great glider, she landed on the eyrie, blocking both screaming chicks from my view. She folded her wings, picked up the skinny remains of the grouse as if to check the eaglets had eaten all they could of it, turned and dropped it on the nest rim. When young Apollo came creeping to her with his head down, soliciting, she pecked gently at his still full crop with her beak. Then Diana came from behind a clump of heather and blocked Apollo off. The mother looked at her too, and from one to the other, her whole mien one of enormous maternal pride at having reared two such fine chicks, thoroughly enjoying their calls and solicitations. She turned to something she had brought in, which again I had been unable to see as she had come in from behind me. It was a young ptarmigan. In the fine weather she, or Melanion, had been hunting the high tops. She tweaked off a feathery snippet from the breast, stepped round importuning Diana and fed it to the wing-fluttering Apollo. Then, with another brief look round, she picked up the grouse remains in her beak and took off.

A magical day, and the best first visit to a hide ever in my experience. And to think that originally I had decided not to work eagles this year! The eagles had not only accepted the hide but also seemed to have forgotten it. Not once had Atalanta looked towards me and she had been totally relaxed on each visit.

I dared not leave for a while, although it was now cold in the hide and the shadows of hills were long in the dying sun. The eaglets were still cheeping occasionally. I waited until they ceased and had again settled down, each so full with busty crops that neither had tackled the ptarmigan, and slid carefully out of the hide.

Now the excitement was over I felt the pain in my haunch from spending twelve hours in much the same position, the damp in my legs from the heather, the coldness of my feet. I was so glad of the exercise on the long descent that I barely noticed the aches in my knees. I boated home to receive a warm whining reception from Moobli, threw sticks until he was tired, forced myself to make suppers for us both, knocked back a few celebratory drams, and crashed happily into bed. Reality, life, had begun again.

June 26. After cutting two hazel bracers to spring out the roof of the hide a little more, I set off early with two cameras in the pack. From a long way off I could see Diana on the edge of the nest and as I passed by into the hide she watched without alarm. Something white and shimmering in the heather of the ledge made me think a dead lamb had been brought in but, once the lens was set up, I saw it was just white eaglet down. Again I realised how easy it would be for someone without binoculars and experience to make this same mistake.

I decided to work with the motor drive today in the hope of good flight shots of an eagle coming in. I was just loading a film into the other camera when I thought I heard a human shout. I listened . . . Hmm, must have been mistaken. Just then big Diana began to squeak – and in came the male Melanion, beautifully from the side, a young rabbit thrust in front of him, held by only one set of talons. '*Snig snig snig snig*' sang the camera's motor drive sweetly in my ear as with one downbeat, an upbeat and one more downbeat, he landed softer than a ballet dancer on the eyrie, his feathered shanks stretched so far below him that they looked like Cossack boots. Now I saw how much smaller and more compact he was than Atalanta. He had a brassy look to his golden mantle as he stood and solemnly watched Diana mantle her wings and start to tug at the rabbit. He had such a natty, dutiful, well intentioned air about him that I almost felt I should have called him something suburban, like Woodley.

He looked at Diana's heaving back and neck, then at her feet, at her back and then down to her feet again, as if making sure she was holding the prey correctly and could manage all right. He made no attempt to feed either eaglet. Then he walked across the nest and glided off downwards. Diana watched and '*kyow*'ed as if to call him back. Now she tramped away from the rabbit and Apollo, who had emerged from behind some heather, took his turn to feed from it. Then both lay down to bask in the sun, facing opposite ways.

This time I distinctly heard a human shout, then another. I knew the sound well, having been on a few gatherings myself. The farmer and a helper or two were herding sheep off the hills, about as hard a task as lugging hides and full packs up the steep rough slopes, and the shouts were to work the collies and stop any sheep doubling back. Would he or any of them visit the eyrie, or even stumble over the hide? A few minutes passed before I heard the heavy clump of boots coming nearer, pass by on the slope below and finally recede into silence. My presence and the hide remained undetected. Neither had anyone attempted to climb up to the eyrie or look into it. What a good man he was really – he had indeed been pulling my leg. I resolved again to take up the compensation question, though as yet I had seen no lambs brought into this nest.

About an hour later Apollo began to call, soon joined in chorus by Diana. The sounds reached a crescendo, I poised the lens seven yards from the eyrie and using a fast shutter speed in the strong sunlight I snicked off five good shots as Melanion came soaring in with a headless ptarmigan. He seemed to be travelling even more slowly than before, as if through invisible oil, and I knew, if I had guessed the exposures right, that I was securing my finest ever flight shots. In one he seemed to be literally hanging in the sky, both wings up showing some youthfully creamy feathers, the grapnel talons of his right foot holding the ptarmigan and his great yellow left foot extended for the landing, as both chicks hunched down and cried through open beaks, their eyes glaring with hungry anticipation. Again he made no attempt to feed them, and Apollo looked quite disappointed. As his father left again he clamped his feet on to the ptarmigan and tucked in.

A few minutes later both eaglets called again. Now the huge dark mother, evidently seeing Melanion land, came in with her talons empty. She looked at the ptarmigan, ate a morsel herself, then tweaked off several pieces and fed them to Diana who, annoyingly, kept her back to me. Then my film ran out. I changed it feverishly, unable to change cameras in case the movement scared her. When I looked back, Atalanta was still there. How vast she seemed, her eyes looking dark red below the jutting ridges of her wide head; such power was invested in her broad chest and back that she looked like some gryphon from another world. She was so serene and stately that neat 'fancy-panted' Melanion seemed a mere consort to Her Majesty. Yet he worked hard, dutifully and well. He clearly was much younger than she and I wondered if he could be even a third mate, for he looked almost adolescent in comparison, and so anxious to please!

Atalanta watched the eaglets feeding and preening and tramped up and down the nest inspecting the prey remains as I took shot after shot. She picked up the oldest grouse remnants and bones in her massive beak and as she left, unlike Melanion, she jumped slightly upwards. My first two shots clipped a bit off her wings but the next had her dead centre.

At about 2 p.m. Apollo began trampolining about the nest, working his wings with clumsy sweeps, bouncing up and down awkwardly and clutching the ledge herbage hard with each set of talons as he stepped along. Diana lay out of sight, having a snooze. After squatting on his haunches to pick his talons clean with his

201

beak, Apollo also lay down, stretched one wing right over the nest and hauled it back, almost appeared to sigh, then put his head out straight and slept too.

I was reading a book at about 4 p.m. when Apollo was again the first to sound action stations – and I was just in time to snatch one shot of Melanion as he came rocketing in with a young curlew in *each set* of thrust out talons! He appeared to let go of one, then he tramped three feet towards me and dropped the other. This way each eaglet had one and there was no need for them to quarrel. If this was a deliberate act it denoted great intelligence, for it helped to ensure that there were no fights between the chicks. He stepped back and with an air of immense pride watched his son and daughter ripping into the new feasts. Suddenly Diana lost her grip on the curlew and staggered back with a fast wing flap. The tip of her wing struck her father and he blinked in surprise, for he had almost been knocked off the ledge and took a wing-flapping step backwards himself.

He walked across the ledge, flapping his wings hard and also holding himself down with his talons – as if telling the eaglets they ought to do *more* hard wing-flapping exercises, and this was the way to do it, for soon they would have to fly. Then he took off, wings bending like supple sprung steel. Never had I known such success in so short a time.

I spent a painful night on the thin foam cushion but the book helped to take my mind off the twinges and aches. Mother Atalanta came in at dusk, spent the night in the eyrie without brooding either eaglet but was gone when I looked through the lens at first light. There was no action for a long while, and after twenty-six hours in the hide I went home. All I wanted now was to get all four eagles in the eyrie together.

June 28. Determined to press my 'good luck' spell, I tramped wearily back to the hide in fine cloudy weather. It was a Saturday, but as I left a helicopter arrived and began scattering clouds of phosphate of potash over some forestry compartments across the loch. The noise, reflected back from the high hills, seemed fearful and I hoped that it wouldn't trouble the eagles several ridges inland. Whether it did or not I don't know, but neither eagle came in at all, and when I looked into the nest I saw they had no need to anyway – there were partly eaten carcasses of grouse, ptarmigan, mallard and curlew lying there. The eaglets had enough food. Neither did they need any brooding, whatever the weather, at this stage.

I took pictures of Diana flumping up and down about the nest with heavy wing beats, lurching towards the edge, then grabbing hard while still waving her 'arms' to stop herself going over. Often Apollo watched her efforts. Then she went to lie behind some heather.

Later she came back and began to tug at the duck. It was only when she raised her wings and I saw more white that I realised I was watching Apollo. He too had now grown most of his golden head and neck feathers and also looked fully a young eagle. At least the helicopter racket did not appear to upset the eaglets. As twilight fell Diana emerged, walked over to the far side of the nest where Apollo was already asleep and lay down right beside him, as if wanting his close company. I had another tortuous night but I kept warm in the nor-north-west breeze for I had brought my best sleeping bag.

June 29. Up at first light, the eaglets began preening their upper breast feathers with acute snake-like bending of their necks. Occasionally Apollo gave peevish cheeps, looking towards the high mountain where his parents caught ptarmigan. Well, it was Sunday and the helicopter would not be working – I was bound to get one of the eagles before siesta time. I took a few shots at sunrise, then decided I ought to put in a new film. No sooner had I removed the first than the eaglets squeaked, Atalanta swept in with nothing, had a brief look round and before I could snap shut and wind on, she had gone again. Muttered curses.

Both eaglets fed pickily from the previous prey and did more wing flap exercises, taking ponderous jumps about the nest, feeling how their bodies moved according to the direction of the beat. Once Diana leaped right over her brother. I was sure she could have flown and would before he did. What would happen then? Would the parents go off with her and forget about Apollo, or would one look after her while the other continued to feed him? I had never worked with grown twin chicks before and was interested in finding out.

To my horror, the grinding chopping noise of the helicoper began again at about 9.30 a.m. – Sunday or not. Occasionally the eaglets peered into the distance and cheeped – maybe they mistook its distant flying form for one of their parents. Doggedly I sat on, my book taking my mind off some of the pains in hips, back, knees and ankles, for no matter what position I adopted in the confined space, I always had to brace myself against the steepness of the slope. Eventually I decided the eagles were 'spooked' because of the helicopter, and when the eaglets were peacefully asleep, I left.

I was loaded down with gear as I intended now to make only

one or two daytime visits to the hide, to check that the eaglets flew safely. The hard descent seemed longer than ever. I had pulled a back muscle somehow and my knees not only hurt but cracked loudly. I was so whacked when I got home that I could hardly pull the heavy boat from the water. I had spent thirty-seven hours in that painful place, breaking my own record by six hours, yet had not taken a single picture of an adult eagle. But my delight at the earlier success remained.

On July 2 I was trekking up by a shorter, steeper route with just my camera in a rucksack when, from about half a mile away, I saw the great blackish brown form of Atalanta lazily floating westwards high above the eyrie.

Suddenly she twisted, plummeted down, went into a fast glide for a good quarter of a mile, then swooped down with a rush beside a large rock on the far hill. Through the fieldglass I saw her wings flapping hard, as if trying to buffet something with them, and she was jumping up and down as if trying to overpower some animal. I tried to get the camera from the pack but as I didn't want to miss what was happening, I only did it with half an eye. Whatever she was after was reddish brown and certainly no rabbit – either a fox or a small deer calf. It seemed an odd struggle, annoyingly obscured by the rock, but the animal seemed to be snapping at her and she to be jumping back slightly. Then she leaped downwards again and sort of bounced back into the air, beating her wings hard. Now I had the camera out, heard the click of the shutter go off as I tripped it accidentally and found I had come to the end of a film. Through the glass, I saw her gain height, then soar quite easily with what looked like a young fox in her talons, though there was no brush dangling, and land on the eyrie. I couldn't see what she did there but she stayed only a few seconds before taking off again and soaring to the east. I waited until she was out of sight then hurried up to the hide, freshened it briefly and slid inside.

Whatever she had caught was not actually in sight, but I saw that Diana was about ready to fly. She kept looking at the ground below the ledge, steadying her legs as if about to jump, half opening her wings, then looking at her brother as if about to say goodbye! They often looked straight at each other now, holding the mutual gaze for several seconds, almost in a kindly way, which was quite touching.

Diana's ruddy-golden mane was complete and Apollo's had only a few white flecks in it, but his wings were shorter. Both eaglets fed sporadically from whatever their mother had brought in but it

204

remained irritatingly out of sight. They showed some boredom now, preening occasionally, lying down and staring into the sky, giving infrequent cheeps as if trying to call their parents in.

I knew this period well – when the adults know the young are almost ready to fly and so visit far less. Night brooding is over, and long spells of boredom, a little judicious semi-starvation, plus the tempting fly pasts by mother or father, are what in the end induce eaglets to take the plunge into the wide world. At 7 p.m., after eleven more hours without either eagle coming in, I left. I climbed up to the ledge and peeped over. There on the nest was a quarter eaten hefty fox cub, its tail not fully grown and still in the spindly stage, together with the forelegs of a lamb. I took some photos of the cub to show and give to the farmer. How many lambs will a fox kill in its life? It's like asking how loud is a trumpet. He had once told me he estimated a fox family killed eight lambs per season on average in our area, but no-one could be sure. Well, here was a fox that would never kill any. And public relations work on behalf of the eagles was the main motivation of my working with them after all.

Then I had an idea. I was not too tired so I tramped to look at some cairns amid big jumbled rocks in the vicinity. There, below the rock beside which I had seen Atalanta kill the big cub, I found a fox den with three more lamb legs scattered around it. I felt then that Atalanta had been attracted by the sight of the white woolled carrion and had taken some for the eaglets. Coming back that way this morning, she had seen the cub out in the open by chance and had killed it. If true, she had not killed any lamb to get the forelegs. What was interesting was how she had clearly spied the fox when soaring, had deliberately lost height fast, then gone into a rapid glide behind the rock – to thump down on the fox and fight to kill it when it could not have seen her coming.

That an eagle of Atalanta's size and strength could kill a reasonably sized fox without much trouble I could well believe. I recalled reading about a falconer called William Humphreys who in the 1940s actually trained golden eagles to hunt foxes by using a stuffed fox as a lure. One of his eagles had killed eighty foxes and its method was to thump hard into the fox like a rocket with its talons, then grip it by the mask with one foot while the other was fixed into its back, so that it could not bite. Dick Balharry had also seen an eagle kill a big fox cub that season, taking almost twenty minutes before bearing it away with ease. He had had several experiences of eagles taking foxes. And of course eagle-fox fights, and foxes as prey items at eyries, are not uncommon in eagle literature of the past.

I got back to see Moobli, staid old trooper that he was, calmly looking at me through the study window. But he did look fed up! Well, it was the last boring spell for him. I would now only go into the hide for one more short period, to try and witness another first flight of an eaglet. If not, I would have to go yet again to make sure they had flown safely and take down the hide. Moobli could come with me then.

Next day we were on the hill above the cottage when I heard the high pitched '*crrruck crruuk*' calls of an excited raven. The nearest pair had hatched three young and were now teaching them to fly and find food on the north-west ridges. I looked up – there, about half a mile high, were Melanion and Atalanta soaring to the west, and the calls were coming from a tiny speck of a raven swooping like a midge around them. They went into a fast glide, soon lost it, then turned to circle low over our heads. I raised my hand in friendly greeting. Immediately both eagles turned and zoomed off in the direction of their eyrie.

After two days of drizzle I set off for the last short visit, carrying two sheep hearts from the butcher in case the eaglets needed food. My trousers were soaked by the long wet bracken and when I reached the hide the eyrie appeared to be empty, a misty deserted air about the place. Had they flown already, as early as July 5? Or been taken? I had to take a closer look as it was no good entering the hide if they had gone. I had just reached the foot of the cliff, still seeing no sign of the parents, when Diana launched herself from a rock twenty yards below, flew south for fifty yards then turned with the wind, circled back to the north east and vanished behind the ridges!

I had walked past just above her but without seeing her at all, though she could have been obscured by the bracken surrounding the rock. I noticed her flight was not at all wobbly, so she may even have flown before but had come back to the eyrie to be fed. I climbed up to the ledge to see if younger Apollo was still there, possibly lying down in the heather clumps. There on the nest was a *second* half eaten fox cub, which appeared to have been slightly plucked. These eagles were 'useful' to the farmer! There were also a young duck's foot and the lower half of a grouse in the eyrie. But of Apollo there was no sign. Had he somehow come to grief?

As I walked back to the hide there was a noisy woofing sound – and Apollo took off from a rock on the ground thirty yards north west of the eyrie. I had missed seeing him too! I felt I must be going blind. His flight was wobbly, his white barred tail switching from side to side as he took the same route as his sister, riding round with the wind and also vanishing behind the same crest but further up it. This, July 5, was the earliest I had known eaglets to fly, but both were well advanced and the long fine spring had helped hunting, both parents co-operating well. The fact that there was plenty of meat left on the fox and on the half grouse proved the eaglets were well fed when they had taken their first tentative flights. The whole eyrie was now wet and slippery with downy feathers, decayed rush and vegetation, soaked with sour smelly animal juices, bones and bits of decayed flesh. Maybe the young eaglets had finally had enough of it after the two days of heavy rain, and with all the other factors inducing a first flight, had felt it would be fresher on the rocks below the eyrie where mum and dad could still find them easily anyway.

That was that. I quickly took down the hide, distributed its herbage under rocks and among other growth so that the site was as natural as before, rolled it up, and after gulping down an egg sandwich, was on the weary slog home. The wet canvas made the hide heavier then usual. I was a good mile away and just turning a bend to lose sight of the eyrie when I spied the speck of Atalanta heading over from the west. As eaglets soon spy parent birds against the sky and call out to them, I felt sure they would be found soon enough.

Next day when I woke to lowering clouds and threatening rain I no longer felt sure and trekked out again, with a delighted Moobli this time, to try and ascertain that the eaglets and their parents *were* together. Before we cleared the ridges south of the eyrie I saw Atalanta quartering the ground a quarter of a mile east of it, and she was flying as low as a harrier, as if looking for one of the eaglets. Then I spotted Diana sitting on a high ridge, where she would have landed after her flight from the rock in the bracken the day before. Had she sat there all night?

I didn't want to interfere with Atalanta's search, if that was what it was, so we moved to the rocky armchair and kept watch. Soon I saw her go to the ground amid a patch of bracken, and through the glass I saw Apollo sitting there. Atalanta was standing proudly beside him but she did not appear to have any food or to feed him. At least I knew both eaglets *had* been located and that all should be well. I didn't try to stalk nearer for pictures but reluctantly slid back and hiked home with Moobli. Maybe I had been foolish to worry – eagles can see each other at great distances. I'd long proved that.

Over the next two days, however, when there were heavy

showers, my doubts returned. The most dangerous times for eaglets are during their first days of flight and then their first winter. On July 9 I put some meat into my pack and trekked out yet again for a final check. If I found a hungry eaglet I would do my best to feed it.

From almost a mile away I saw a large dark bump on a high conical heather-covered rock three hundred yards past the eyrie that had never been there before. My glass told me it was an eagle, and I thought it probably one of the eaglets that had returned to the nest area and was waiting to be fed. To keep out of sight yet get nearer, I dodged back and climbed some steep parts so that the eyrie face hid our approach. But with his bad leg Moobli could not climb one almost sheer outcrop, so headed west and swung back towards me higher up before I saw what he was doing. The eagle on the rock must have seen him for suddenly it flew eastwards over the ridge just above us. It was Melanion. I had just taken a shot of him when Atalanta came heading over too, so close I could see her eyes and great talons held bunched up against her body. I got two shots of her as well. Then I heard an eaglet squeaking from the ridge above us, not from the eyrie which was still 150 yards to our left. I guessed what had happened. It was Atalanta who had been sitting on the heathery rock. Melanion had been near the eaglet, had spied us coming up though I hadn't seen him. Atalanta had seen Moobli, then both had headed away to the east, taking a good look at us on the way.

It was wonderful to know that both parents were keeping close to one eaglet anyway. I decided to head across and check the eyrie ledge itself. To my surprise Apollo was back on it, standing high and bold as brass. He kept preening himself while I took some shots. He had flown back up to the nest, and his crop was full. I felt even more cheerful and thought it likely that Atalanta had been sitting on the high rock in full view of the eyrie, trying to tempt Apollo to fly again and join the family on flying and, later, hunting lessons.

I climbed up to see if the conical rock was a perching post or place where eagles carry prey to dismember and pluck it before taking it to the eyrie. On the way Moobli's scenting helped me to find a dead white-faced tup lamb that weighed about 16lbs. There was a bloody wound in its throat and the lower ribs had been penetrated; the heart and lungs were missing. I was disappointed, for it seemed possible the eagles had killed this lamb, though the throat wounds indicated that it might also have been killed by a fox from the den not so far away. Certainly the eagles, probably Atalanta, who I'd seen on the high rock, had been feasting on the lamb for much wool had been plucked and scattered about.

Apart from the two lamb forefeet I had found earlier in the eyrie, which could have been picked up as carrion, this was the only evidence I had from my observations that these eagles might have killed a lamb. The third I could believe had been actually killed by eagles in all my studies. If I laid the death of one lamb at these eagles' door I felt it was as much as one could fairly do. Surely no farmer could complain about that when they had also killed two foxes. There must be a sense of proportion, especially when scientific research has shown that 13 per cent to 17 per cent of lambs usually die in their first weeks from natural causes and accidents in harsh areas such as this.

The top of the rock had indeed been used to dismember prey for in the heather and crowberry leaves I found grouse and rabbit bones, and a deep impression nearby indicating that it was also used as a roosting spot. We hiked over to check the fox den but it hadn't been used for some days – not surprising that the vixen moved after losing two fox cubs to the eagles. A discreet moonlight flit had apparently taken place.

I now headed back to the eyrie, meaning to check it for new prey remains. I was well past the hide site, still level with the eyrie, and saw that Apollo was now lying down in the sunlight. I decided not to worry him after all.

Suddenly there was a tremendous *woosh*ing behind me, something touched the hair on the top of my head, and I saw the mighty black and brown mottled form of Atalanta drop low before me and sweep straight over the head of Apollo in the eyrie, as if telling him to get down or get out! She missed my scalp by about half a inch but had she been bent on attack she could have broken my neck, for I hadn't heard her coming and was totally unprepared. What a frightening yet thrilling moment! At any rate, Apollo seemed to take his cue, for a few seconds later he launched himself from the eyrie and with a few noisy flaps soared away towards the same ridge as on his first flight and vanished from my view. I climbed up to the nest, found no new prey. The second fox carcass had also been removed and all that was left were three toothed jawbones which I removed for my collections.

I now knew that Apollo was in close contact with his parents but I also wanted to be sure it *was* Diana I had heard squeaking from the ridge above us earlier, and that I had not imagined it. I climbed away above the eyrie, headed north west, then worked round in a circle to the east, examining every knoll on the way. Not until I had trekked right round and was a quarter of a mile east of the eyrie did I find an eaglet. It was standing on the ridge, half covered by long grasses. I sneaked closer on my belly, took a picture of Apollo without scaring him away, then cut down a small gully towards the south west. We were just passing below a high grassy shelf when something made me look up. There, mere yards from us, was Diana! I was far too close for a photo with the long lens. Aware that Moobli was staring at the huge bird with amazement, I just looked away again as if not interested and carried on slowly. She watched us go by with such calm sang froid that it seemed we were just old familiar objects. Once I was far enough away to get her into focus on the 640 mm lens, I quietly turned, took a picture, then left her sitting there.

A short distance nearer the eyrie I found two roosting spots close to one another on a grassy shelf of the steep slope, where many white downy feathers had become entwined with the grasses. It seemed to be the place where the eaglets were spending the nights for there were also several huge pellets – one measuring five-and-a-half inches – and small prey bones there. I dropped a piece of meat near each one as a final gift.

Now that neither eaglet was in the eyrie I went back to it again to see if I could find a better hide site for a future year where I could work closer and see the entire ledge. There was not. But on a high shelf above the eyrie I found the remains of an adult raven, just wing feathers, backbone and some ribs left. It seemed one of the noisy mobbing birds which so often harassed the eagles when they flew above the cottage had finally received its come-uppance, and had ended up as a meal for its temerity.

As we headed down again for home, both eaglets regarding us from their same vantage points on the high ridges, Atalanta, with Melanion not far behind, came soaring back from the east. There was nothing more I could do now. All the eagles were safely together and I would not go up there again with food. It was now entirely up to nature to take its course.

A great wave of tiredness came over me, as if my limbs and body knew the work was done. But I didn't mind, for I also knew I had seldom felt happier in my life. So ended a season in which I had not intended to work with eagles again, but which had turned out to be the most intriguing and wonderful of all.

14 · *Flying Free*

Summer now passed and merged into autumn. As if to show the eagle days were not the climax of the year, other wildlife experiences became more intensively successful than ever before. I nursed a new injured tawny owl, a lovely female kestrel with a broken wing, and released them both successfully back to the wild. An old badger turned up wounded one night and placidly lived in the kitchen with us for three weeks, eating half as much as Moobli, until her wounds healed. Then off she trundled again into the wild woods. (The full story is told in my book, *Out of the Wild*.) But always the highlight of any day was a glimpse of one or more of my eagle family.

Boating for supplies on July 24 I saw one of the eaglets land on a high ridge above the lochside. The hill sheep were being gathered and as a billowing white wave headed towards the ridge, it took off casually and soared back to join Atalanta who was circling above the eyrie cliff. Next day Melanion flew above the cottage towards the eyrie, half closing his wings as I took a shot, so that he looked as thin as a swallow.

Dick Balharry and Roy Dennis, who visited Wildernesse, discussed with me the thorny question of government compensation to farmers for any rare cases of stock-killing by eagles. Both men agreed with the letter I'd had from the Nature Conservancy Council and again stressed that any such scheme would be open to wide abuse. Years ago when the R.S.P.B. tried paying 'reverse bounty' fees to those who had successful eaglets on their lands, some applied for eaglets that didn't exist, others left them alone until the fee was

211

paid and then killed them. There were so many uncheckable requests, and it proved so costly, that the scheme was dropped. It was also felt to be quite wrong to pay people merely for not breaking the law.

Roy disclosed that in Norway, where eagle populations were slightly in excess of Scotland's, the eagle was totally protected in 1968 after years of persecution. But a compensation scheme for reindeer farmers was also introduced. It had been found that, while the graph for eagle breeding success had risen slightly, payments to the farmers who claimed eagles took young calves had shot up steeply! Even with the paid force of special Reindeer Police, it was impossible to check every claim. Livestock owners, therefore, just filled in a form and all the local policeman could do was countersign it, saying he knew the farmer to be an honest and trustworthy man.

A scheme to compensate farmers in the Highlands for the few lambs actually killed, as apart from those taken already dead, would demand proof that the eagles did the killing. But how? One farmer may only have to drive near an eyrie and walk half a mile to collect proof. Another may have to hike six hard miles up into the hills. If you let the latter off proof, a man who had to walk two miles would also demand to be let off. If one farmer did not receive compensation but his neighbour did, resentment could be caused. It would need a small army of checking officials all over Scotland. Farmers may accept a few pounds the first year, but as the word about the scheme got round, they would probably want the full price, up to £30. 'Aye, 'twas the lamb I was saving for breeding, my fine wee ram!' It would be administratively and economically impossible.

Farmers and crofters receive several grants and subsidies from British taxpayers' money as it is, especially hill sheep subsidies in this case. Take away the subsidies and there would not be a sheep left in the Highlands within a very few years. A good thing, some conservationists would say, but the fact is that sheep carrion in winter is a mainstay of eagles in the western Highlands. If a rare instance occurs where eagles are killing stock, the aggrieved owner can notify Scottish Natural Heritage (which took over from the N.C.C. in 1992), the R.S.P.B. or the Scottish Office in Edinburgh, for some action to be taken. So far, however, not a single licence has been issued for the taking or killing of an eagle for such alleged offences. If farmers or crofters are paid for the few cases of eagles taking live lambs, then the gardener deserves to be paid for voles eating his pea shoots, the fruitgrower for bullfinches pulling off buds, your wife for blackcurrants taken by birds, and so on.

Farmers in Britain receive in improvement grants alone roughly fifty times more money than the government doles out to its official conservation body. After months of talking about, and much correspondence on, the compensation issue, I realised that it was useless, and probably wrong, to pursue it further. The answer lies not in compensation for rare cases of stock taken but in education and the evolvement of a more universal sense and responsible attitude by land occupiers towards wildlife. First, we must identify and conserve areas where rare species are already breeding. Then those who actually own, occupy and work the land could be helped by management agreements or grants to become its real guardians.

Roy Dennis told me, 'We are all part of the whole natural scene and accidents happen, and for us to expect everything to go just right all the time is rather greedy. "Nothing must touch our stock" is the thinking. But there are storms, late snows, floods, and the losses in such natural disasters are huge in comparison with a few lambs taken by eagles. It's like fishermen who go on about a pair of mergansers or goosanders, or fish farmers about otters, seals, herons and ospreys taking fish. Then you have a huge flood, or sudden disease, and more young fish and eggs are washed out or die than by a pair of goosanders in a thousand years. You wake up one morning after a storm, all is battered down and you can do nothing. But you see an eagle fly over your flocks and you curse it. No, it's not right.'

More than 30 golden eagles have been recorded by the R.S.P.B. as having been poisoned in Scotland since 1979. These deaths result from baits put out illegally to kill off predators that prey on game stocks – yet because of the difficulty of finding such poisoned baits, or the dead birds, this figure merely represents the tip of the iceberg of what is actually being poisoned. Also in the same period, a further 14 eagles are known to have been shot, and 7 eyries destroyed. At last the judicial system has realised the seriousness of these threats – as well as from egg and chick-stealing gangs – and anyone found guilty of killing an eagle, or taking its eggs or young, can today be fined up to £5,000 and/or be sent to jail.

One more point here – many land occupiers, farmers and crofters derive income from the tourists who treble the Highland population in late spring and summer, by providing bed and breakfast accommodation, by hiring out caravans and even, sometimes, their own homes. Tourism brings more than half a billion pounds a year to Scotland. But how many would come if they knew that they could never see any of the magnificent wildlife which makes Scotland one

213

of the finest nature reservoirs in Europe? From this angle alone wildlife is a vast and, yes, tangible resource, apart from its immense aesthetic value. And the great golden eagle is a peak 'indicator' species, because a land fit for wildlife, especially eagles whose needs are critical as they are at the top of the food web, is a land truly fit for people.

When Roy Dennis visited me, I gave him a map of all the eyries I knew of so far. He was especially delighted at the success of the twin chick eyrie I had been watching, and naturally I hoped the eagles would appear 'on stage' while he was at Wildernesse. It was not until we were boating out next day, however, that we saw some of the family. As we chugged down the loch both Atalanta and Melanion appeared in the sky, circling over their eyrie face, and between them was one of the eaglets though they were too far away for me to identify which chick it was.

After hauling out the boat, I was picking a supper cabbage in the garden when I heard an eaglet squeaking. I looked up to see the bigger eaglet Diana flying over the ridges towards the west, while close behind her flew Atalanta. Diana rolled oddly in the strong south winds and it was clear she had not yet attained anything like the flight mastery of her mother. Now Atalanta suddenly turned north, circled once, then set off in a fast glide to the east, leaving Diana to carry on westward alone. It was as if the huge young eagle had been told to get back to the eyrie where she would be fed later. But where was young Apollo? I wondered now if *he* was all right.

On August 22 I was in the boat three miles up the loch when I saw three figures in red anoraks standing on the south shore looking my way with binoculars. Then one of them looked up and pointed. There, flying low over my boat, was Atalanta! I looked back and saw Melanion circling lazily over the loch just in front of my cottage. I gave a loud '*Keeyoo*' whistle, the kind I had sometimes made if I had seen either of the eagles when hauling up carcasses, and pointed towards Melanion with a dramatic gesture. As though obeying me, Atalanta immediately turned and power glided towards her mate. Then, away they went, circling close together. I wondered what the three watchers made of that, though of course it was mere coincidence.

Now I began to worry again. I had not seen Apollo at all since July 9, and six days earlier Diana had seemed to be flying oddly. Were they *both* all right? Next day I hiked up to the eyrie with Moobli and searched around. While I saw no eagles, on the long return journey at least I didn't find any dead eaglet either.

214

Three days later I had just started writing this book when I heard the raucous calls of hooded crows. Wondering if they were mobbing an eaglet, I hiked up with Moobli and had just crossed the burn at a gap between the trees when I saw a crow diving and swooping near an eagle perched on a high ridge. But for the crow, the eagle would have been hard to spot against the background of the dark hills behind it. It took off, flapping weakly and gliding as much as it could and landed awkwardly on a rock only 200 yards further to the east.

Wanting to identify it, I climbed a little higher, whereupon it flew again, still rather weak, and headed westwards. Just before it vanished over a crest I saw the white barred tail and the bigger wing patches – it was Apollo. I hoped he had not been abandoned. Later I took a piece of meat up to the high heathery shelf. Next morning it had gone and while a buzzard, crow or raven could have taken it, I knew at least that a fox would not take meat with man scent on it at this time of year. I just hoped it had been eaten by its intended recipient.

While Apollo and Diana were having what were normal problems for eaglets coping with survival in the wild in their first flying weeks, I had at least discovered that the other eagles in the area had done quite well. The pair from Eyrie 16 had again raised an eaglet successfully but in a new eyrie, so had pair 14. Pair 12 had been rearing an eaglet, again in a tree nest as last year, but Greg Hunter found it had vanished in June, too early for it to have flown. However, the pair which had used Eyries 10 and 13 in the first year also reared an eaglet to flying stage. Although I had not checked all the other eyries this season, this meant that, with my two chicks, at least five more had flown successfully in the region this year, perhaps helped by the long fine spring after the harsh winter and the wet spring of the previous year.

It was on October 26, as we were hiking along the rough boggy loch shore a mile from home, that the climactic experience came which brings this book to a close. Just as the sun beamed through a gap in the grey clouds, I looked up to see two eaglets heading westwards above the nearest crests – Atalanta, closely followed by Melanion. As I watched, he looped and dived down on her and she turned almost upside down as if to acknowledge his late courtship instincts, so confirming the close bond Atalanta and Melanion, and before him Meleager, had always maintained.

Suddenly, higher up, I saw two more eagles heading over towards the couple from the east. They were the eaglets! Diana and Apollo, their slightly different sizes now obvious, were now flying well, and their white under wing patches gleamed metallically, blazing like flames, in the afternoon sunshine. Now the four great birds soared round each other and re-crossed each other's paths, vanishing now and then behind misty wisps of cloud, only to emerge once more to prove to my wondering eyes that I was not seeing a mirage. Then, to my amazement, two *more* eagles, an adult male and female, came heading over from the north. For a few moments, there were *six* eagles in the sky, all sailing and circling amicably around each other.

I had only known this multiple flying of eagles in autumn twice before. I stared entranced with thudding heart. I was more certain now of the lessening of territorial instinct after the nesting season. Eagles, the most magnificent birds of prey in the world, seem quite tolerant of each other in autumn and winter. This makes sense for species' survival if there is more winter carrion in one area than another. And had I not seen other eagles at these times flying over the home range of Atalanta, Meleager and her new mate Melanion, yet never witnessed one instance of their being molested or driven off?

As I watched them now, vanishing from my view one by one over the peaks, I knew that even if I devoted the rest of my life to studying just them alone, I would never solve all the mysteries surrounding these great birds. I felt it a matter of great shame that R.S.P.B. studies have shown that about a third of nests fail due to human interference of some kind, that eagles still suffer from extensive shooting and poisoning in the eastern grouse moors, and from persecution by a few shepherds in the west, and that Scotland's golden eagles are believed to be in slow decline because of these factors. Surely, in a more conservation conscious world, it is time that all such witless persecution was ended.

As I turned once more for home I felt that today's extraordinary sighting was the real working climax. After some 1,500 miles of hard foot treks in the mountains, 520 hours in cramped, cold and sometimes dangerous cliff ledge hides, I felt that in a small way I had succeeded in the quest that had begun eight years before when I had first seen mighty Atalanta circle the spruce tree at Wildernesse.

*

When Roy Dennis visited Wildernesse, he told me that the R.S.P.B. had three eyries marked on the map of the area. He was delighted when I gave him my map with the 27 eyries that I, Greg Hunter,

Allan Peters and our helpers had located over 300 square miles, and he spent an hour copying them down. The following year, when the N.C.C. and R.S.P.B. initiated a long-term government survey of the golden eagle in Britain, the map, together with the years of information that Greg and I had provided under our monitoring licences, eased the task of the research team. The final honour came when the scientist in charge of the field work chose my region as his own main study area, and I was hauled out of 'eagle retirement' to help with the less accessible eyries, and Greg continued to monitor his. That story, a direct sequel to this, is told in my book *On Wing and Wild Water*.

Eagle Appendix

1 Range and Distribution

The golden eagle (Aquila chrysaetos) ranges right across the world's Northern Hemisphere and is the most widespread eagle on earth. It occurs in Spain, with substantial populations of some 600 pairs, northern Italy, the Balkans, and the main mountainous ranges of Europe, including parts of Germany, Czechoslovakia, Hungary, Roumania and eastwards across northern Iran, Afghanistan, Turkey, through Tibet, northern China and Mongolia to Japan. But it is absent from south Asia, India, Burma, Thailand and Vietnam. In the north it ranges from Britain (nearly all in Scotland), Norway (with 310 to 420 pairs), parts of Sweden, Lappland, Finland, then eastwards across Russia in a broad belt but missing the Arctic far north regions, to Kamchatka. Small populations also exist in the mountains of north Africa, mainly the Atlas range.

In North America (A. c. canadensis), believed to be a slightly smaller and darker sub-species than in Europe, it is found from northern Alaska southwards through the Rockies and Sierra Nevada mountains including California, Colorado and Texas, into Mexico. Its main breeding range is in the area west of the 99th meridian. In Canada it ranges from the Yukon and the Rockies, and eastwards from British Columbia, skirting north of the Great Lakes into Quebec, Labrador and then into parts of north-eastern America. It also occurs sparingly in western North Carolina and eastern Tennessee.

In Britain the golden eagle was found in many parts of England and Wales as recently as 130 years ago, with records of one shot at Woburn Abbey, Bedfordshire, in 1820; one seen but unsuccessfully shot at near Matlock, Derbyshire, in 1843; one captured at Somerford Park, Cheshire,

218

in 1845; one shot near Hungerford, Berkshire, in 1847; one killed in March 1864 at Thornton Hall near Pickering; one shot at Osberton, Nottingham-shire, in 1857; a dead one picked up on Stiffkey Marsh in December 1868; and one shot near Shrewsbury, Shropshire, in December 1884. But by the early 1800s the golden eagle had become extinct as a *breeding* species in Eng-land. In Wales it appears to have survived as a breeder until the late 1800s, one was found on Snowdon in 1880, but there are none breeding in Wales today.

In Ireland the golden eagle ceased to breed after 1912. By then the only British populations were centred on Scotland, estimated at well below 200 pairs, and they had been and still were suffering great persecution by game keepers, sheep farmers, grouse sportsmen, and egg collectors. They vanished from southern Scotland altogether and by World War I were largely confined to the Highlands. The war provided an accidental amnesty to help them recover slightly, as did World War II and the stronger Protection of Birds Act 1954 when they were made a First Schedule bird, protected by special penalties. Slowly they recolonised south-west Scotland and today some half a dozen pairs are nesting south of the Highland Line.

Golden eagles are found today throughout all the Highlands from the Mull of Kintyre north to Caithness, through the main mountain ranges but not along the broad belt of low agricultural land from the Firth of Forth to the Dornoch Firth. They are also found on the larger islands of the Inner and Outer Hebrides, and in the early 1970s a pair began nesting in Orkney for the first time since 1844.

A single pair returned to nest on the Antrim coast of Northern Ireland from 1953 to 1960, though they were believed to do much of their hunting across the sea in Scotland, then disappeared. By the late 1960s there were signs of a slow recolonisation of the hill areas of north-west England.

For many years it was believed that there were only some 270 to 280 pairs in Britain, plus 50 to 60 immatures and unattached young adults which form loose pools on the periphery of home ranges, from which adults find replacements for lost mates – or which form breeding pairs among each other when mature and find an unoccupied home range of their own. However, in 1982/83 after the government's fullest survey ever, in which I was privileged to take part, no less than 598 home ranges were identified in Britain – 2 in England and the rest in Scotland, mainly the Highlands. 511 of these ranges were occupied, 424 by pairs and 87 by single eagles. In 1982 alone, some 260 pairs laid eggs but only 182 of these raised young to fledgling stage (210 young in all). But 1982 was a good year, of mostly fine weather, for breeding eagles.

Ten years later, in 1992, the government conducted another survey on similar lines to the first. I was told in February 1994 that the data was 'still being processed', though why it should take four times as long as it did to gain the results of the first survey is anyone's guess. Certainly most 'eagle men' I spoke to confirmed that it had been one of the worst breeding seasons in 15 years. However, Roy Dennis was kind enough to inform me that while there had been increases of eagle numbers in Perthshire, matched by decreases in the central Highlands, the final figure will show little change from the 1982 total of 424 pairs.

The various regional Raptor Study Groups, which made a major contribution to the survey, have published some of their figures, and the results are interesting. Out of 344 sites checked, 86 pairs fledged a total of 99 to 101 young. The bad weather certainly affected some regions. Although 64 out of 79 pairs in Argyll laid eggs, only 17 got as far as fledging young (19). North-east Scotland is traditionally a productive breeding area, but in a poor season only 12 pairs laid eggs and only 7 raised young. In the Central area 7 of the 12 checked home ranges were occupied, 5 pairs laid eggs but only 3 chicks were fledged. In the Western Isles, of 24 pairs that laid eggs only 11 reared young (13). The figures for the whole Highland area (east and west) is hard to evaluate for the number of sites occupied by pairs is not revealed. However, in 126 of the sites checked a total of 44 young were fledged, so the area fared better than most of the others. Overall, in my view, it is a far from cheerful picture.

A pair reached the Lake District in the late 1960s, laid eggs in 1969 but failed to hatch them. They reared one eaglet in 1970 and since then have bred a total of 17 to flying stage. In 1975 a second pair were found to be breeding in the Lake District and in the seven years of their existence, until the female died in 1982, they raised only three chicks (Dave Walker told me that the male hung on for another three years, did not find a replacement mate, and eventually disappeared). It is estimated that young eagles suffer up to 70 per cent mortality before they reach breeding age, so probably a dozen of these young perished. One sure discovery was that the 1986 eaglet was found dead under power lines a full 75km from the nesting valley.

2   Prey Brought in to West Highland Eyries
(Observed over five years)

Rabbit	Fox, adult	Rabbit
Hooded crow (2)	Water vole (7)	Woodmouse
Raven	(Observed by R. Balharry)	Red deer carrion
Rabbit	Crow.	Crow
Crow	———————————————	Water vole
Short tailed vole	Lamb carrion	Red grouse
Rabbit	Rabbit	Hooded crow
Crow	Rabbit	Rabbit
Red deer carrion	Kestrel nestling	Red deer calf carrion
Black headed gull nestling	Crow nestling	Rabbit

Curlew, young	Cormorant, young	
	Red grouse	Rabbit
Lamb	Ptarmigan	Rabbit
Crow	Red deer calf carrion	Hooded crow
Rabbit	Lamb carrion	Curlew
Red grouse	Hooded crow	Red grouse, young
Lamb carrion	Herring gull	Red grouse
Rabbit	Rabbit	Ptarmigan, young
Rabbit, young	Rabbit	Rabbit, young
Rabbit, young	Rabbit	Ptarmigan
Golden plover	Red deer carrion	Curlew, young (2)
Rabbit, young	Rabbit	Red grouse
Ptarmigan	Red grouse	Ptarmigan
Rabbit	Mallard, young	Mallard
Rabbit	Ptarmigan	Curlew
Hooded crow	Red deer calf carrion	Fox cub
Curlew, young	Curlew, young	Lamb carrion
Red grouse	Red grouse	Fox cub
Woodpigeon	Short tailed vole	Mallard, young
Ptarmigan, young	Merganser, young	Red grouse
Rabbit	Cormorant, young	Lamb (near eyrie)
Short tailed voles (2)	Wader, unidentified	Red grouse
Red grouse	Red grouse, young	Rabbit
	Sheep carrion	Raven

3   Heights of West Highland Eyries (In order of lowest to highest)

200 FEET	950 FEET	
300	1,000	Average Height: $962\frac{2}{3}$ feet.
700	1,000	But this figure is distorted by the two
700	1,000	unusually low eyries at 200 and 300 feet.
750	1,050	Take these away and the average height
750	1,100	of the remaining eyries, a more accurate
800	1,100	reflection, is: $1,013\frac{1}{2}$ feet.
800	1,150	
830	1,150	
900	1,200	
900	1,200	
900	1,200	
900	1,300	
900	1,600	
950	1,600	

4   Direction Eyries Face (In order from North clockwise)

N	S	It is interesting that there are 14 with
N	S	southerly aspects, as against 13 with
N	S	northerly aspects, with 1 facing
N	S	due east and 2 facing due west.
N	SSW	
NE	SSW	
NE	SW	
NE	SW	
NE	SW	
NE	WSW	
E	W	
SE	W	
S	NW	
S	NNW	
S	NNW	

5   Greenery Used to Freshen Eyries

Heather   *Moss*   *Hazel*
Great wood-rush   *Grass tufts*   *Oak*
Rowan   *Ash*   *Beech*
Bog myrtle (Sweet gale)   *Bilberry*   *Scots pine.*
Fir   *Crowberry*
Foxglove   *Bear berry*

Bibliography

Books

BROWN, LESLIE H., and AMADON, DEAN, *Eagles, Hawks and Falcons of the World* (Country Life Books, Hamlyn, 1968)

BROWN, LESLIE H., *British Birds of Prey* (London: Collins, 1976)

CRUMLEY, JIM, *Among Mountains* (Edinburgh, Mainstream, 1993)

DARLING, F. FRASER, and BOYD, J. MORTON, *The Highlands and Islands* (London: Collins, 1964)

GORDON, SETON, *Days With the Golden Eagle* (London: Williams and Norgate, 1927)

GORDON, SETON, *The Golden Eagle* (London: Collins, 1955, and Melven Press, Perth, 1980)

MacNALLY, LEA, *The Ways of an Eagle* (London: Collins and Harvill Press, 1977)

NEWTON, IAN, *Population Ecology of Raptors* (Poyser, 1979)

TOMKIES, MIKE, *On Wing and Wild Water* (London: Jonathan Cape, 1987)

TOMKIES, MIKE, *Last Wild Years* (London: Jonathan Cape, 1992)

Papers and Journals

BROWN, LESLIE H., and WATSON, ADAM, 'The Golden Eagle in Relation to its Food Supply' (*Ibis* 106, pp. 78–100)

DENNIS, R. H., ELLIS, P. M., BROAD, R. A., and LANGSLOW, D. R., 'The Status of the Golden Eagle in Britain' (*British Birds* 77, pp. 592–607)

EVERETT, MICHAEL, *The Golden Eagle* (Edinburgh: William Blackwood, 1977)

HOUSTON, DAVID, 'The Effect of Hooded Crows on Hill Sheep Farming in Argyll, Scotland' (*Journal of Applied Ecology* 14, pp. 17–29, 1977)

Bibliography

JENKINS, D., WATSON, A., and MILLER, G. R., 'Predation and Red Grouse Populations' (*Journal of Applied Ecology* 1, pp. 183–95, 1964)

LOCKIE, J. D., and STEPHEN, D., 'Eagles, Lambs and Land Management on Lewis' (*Journal of Animal Ecology* 28, pp. 43–50, 1959)

LOCKIE, J. D., 'The Breeding Density of the Golden Eagle and Fox in Relation to Food Supply in Wester Ross, Scotland' (*Scottish Naturalist* 71, pp. 67–77, 1964)

LOCKIE, J. D., RATCLIFFE, D. A., and BALHARRY, R., 'Breeding Success and Organo-Chlorine Residues in Golden Eagles in West Scotland' (*Journal of Applied Ecology* 6, pp. 381–9, 1969)

NEWTON, IAN, 'Birds of Prey in Scotland: some Conservation Problems' (*Scottish Birds* 7, pp. 5–23, 1972–73)

SANDEMAN, P. W., 'The Breeding Success of Golden Eagles in the Southern Grampians' (*Scottish Naturalist* 69, pp. 148–52, 1957)

WALKER, DAVID G., *The Lakeland Eagles* (Published by author, 1991)

WATSON, ADAM, 'The Breeding Success of Golden Eagles in the North East Highlands' (*Scottish Naturalist* 69, pp. 153–69)

WATSON, JEFF, LANGSLOW, D. R., and RAE, S. R., *The Impact of Land-Use on Golden Eagles in the Scottish Highlands* (Nature Conservancy Council, 1985)